KATHERINE JACKSON FRENCH

KATHERINE JACKSON FRENCH

KENTUCKY'S FORGOTTEN BALLAD COLLECTOR

Elizabeth DiSavino

Copyright © 2020 by The University Press of Kentucky

Scholarly publisher for the Commonwealth,
serving Bellarmine University, Berea College, Centre
College of Kentucky, Eastern Kentucky University,
The Filson Historical Society, Georgetown College,
Kentucky Historical Society, Kentucky State University,
Morehead State University, Murray State University,
Northern Kentucky University, Transylvania University,
University of Kentucky, University of Louisville,
and Western Kentucky University.
All rights reserved.

Editorial and Sales Offices: The University Press of Kentucky
663 South Limestone Street, Lexington, Kentucky 40508-4008
www.kentuckypress.com

Unless otherwise noted, photographs are courtesy of the Berea College
Special Collections and Archives.

Library of Congress Cataloging-in-Publication Data
Names: DiSavino, Elizabeth, author.
Title: Katherine Jackson French : Kentucky's forgotten ballad collector /
    Elizabeth DiSavino.
Other titles: English-Scottish ballads from the hills of Kentucky.
Description: Lexington : The University Press of Kentucky, 2020. | Includes
    bibliographical references and index.
Identifiers: LCCN 2020004315 | ISBN 9780813178523 (hardcover) | ISBN
    9780813178547 (pdf) | ISBN 9780813178554 (epub)
Subjects: LCSH: French, Katherine Jackson, 1875–1958. |
    Ethnomusicologists—United States—Biography. | Women musicians—United
    States—Biography. | Musicians—United States—Biography. | Ballads,
    English—Kentucky—History and criticism. | Folk songs,
    English—Kentucky—History and criticism. | Women—Southern
    States—Social life and customs—20th century. | Ballads,
    English—Kentucky. | Folk songs, English—Kentucky.
Classification: LCC ML423.F76 D57 2020 | DDC 782.42162/130769—dc23
LC record available at https://lccn.loc.gov/2020004315

This book is printed on acid-free paper meeting
the requirements of the American National Standard
for Permanence in Paper for Printed Library Materials.

Manufactured in the United States of America.

 Member of the Association
of University Presses

For my mother and father

In Scarlett Town, where I was born
There was a fair maid dwelling
And every youth cried, "Well away!"
Her name was Barbara Allen.

        British/Scottish/Appalachian ballad

Contents

Introduction 1

PART 1. "THIS SPEAKING SOUL"

1. "The Spirit and Sap of the Stock" 7
2. Young Lady from London 14
3. Act Two 26

PART 2. "THE STURDINESS AND TRUTH OF SONG"

4. "A Fortnight of Balladry" 59
5. Berea Beloved 73
6. A Comparison of the Ballads of Katherine Jackson and Olive Dame Campbell/Cecil Sharp 112

PART 3. "ENGLISH-SCOTTISH BALLADS FROM THE HILLS OF KENTUCKY"

7. Introduction by Elizabeth DiSavino 139
8. Introduction by Katherine Jackson French 141
9. "English-Scottish Ballads from the Hills of Kentucky" 145
Appendix A. A Note on the Ballads 205
Appendix B. Informants for the Ballads of Katherine Jackson 209
Appendix C. Time Line of the Ballad Wars 210
Notes 217
Bibliography 245
Index 257

Introduction

Every study begins with a question and ends with many others.

When A. J. Bodnar and I began a fellowship project at Berea College in 2012, the name of Katherine Jackson French was unknown to us. We entered the vast vault of the Berea College Special Collections and Archives at Hutchins Library and entrusted ourselves to the tender mercies of the archivists Harry Rice and Shannon Wilson.

It was Harry who first told us about Katherine Jackson French. I was intrigued. She was a woman who had attempted to publish a large collection of ballads (over sixty by some accounts) seven years before Olive Dame Campbell and Cecil Sharp's landmark *English Folk Songs from the Southern Appalachians* (1917).[1] She was one of the first women from Kentucky to earn a PhD, the second woman to earn one from Columbia University, and the first from south of the Mason-Dixon Line to do so. Paradoxically, she was a southern woman who studied and taught in the North but kept returning home.

The more I learned about her, the more questions arose. Why had this girl from London, Kentucky, gone north and east for her education? As one of eight children, why had she—a girl—been singled out for higher education at the end of the nineteenth century? What influences did she encounter in her youth that led her to this calling? How did her family, friends, and neighbors react to her northern relocation (to New York City, of all places)? What led her to collect folk songs? Why did she continue to return to her hometown? Why did she finally settle in Shreveport, Louisiana? Why, though she lived out her life there and later died in South Carolina, is she buried in London? What did she have to say on topics other than folk songs? In short, just who *was* Katherine Jackson French?

Of all the questions that arose, the most vexing was, why did Berea College offer to help publish Jackson's folk-song collection in 1910 and then not see it done? And, if the collection had been published, would her depiction of early Appalachian balladry have painted a different picture than the one in Campbell and Sharp's genre-establishing *English Folk Songs from the Southern Appalachians*? How might that crucial first impression of Appalachian balladry in particular and Appalachian folk music in general been different if Jackson had published first? As a professor of music education and music at Berea, I felt a personal responsibility to examine these issues and to see her story told.

The story of Katherine Jackson French is, like many stories, more complex than it initially appears. She was a woman who perpetually had a foot in two worlds. Born a scant ten years after the end of the Civil War, Jackson represented a bridge between eras and regions, between the rural South and northern academe, between academe and rural folk music, between the nineteenth and the twentieth centuries, between what women's limitations were according to the mores of her time and what she knew they should not be. Her education and travels constitute an impressive vita but did not diminish her love of home. She was a proper southern wife and mother, but she also held a doctorate and was an author and a professor. Her attempt to publish her collection of Kentucky ballads through Berea was a signal failure in a lifetime of professional achievements. Had she succeeded, hers would have been the first large and scholarly collection of southern Appalachian balladry ever published.[2]

All these things led to a fascination with Katherine Jackson French on my part, resulting in my determination to uncover and tell her story and see her collection of ballads finally published with the support of Berea College. The college—in the persons of Dean Chad Berry and Chris Green, the director of the Loyal Jones Appalachian Center—agreed, and that collection is now finally appearing here.

The songs included in the last chapter of this biography mark the completion of a project begun by Katherine Jackson in 1909. It has taken over a hundred years for her manuscript to see print, and it has been my honor to oversee that task. Indeed, I felt it imperative that it be a Berean who finally saw to it that Berea's promise was fulfilled and Jackson's story told.

And, thus, here is her work, and here is her story. It is a tale that has never before been told in its entirety. This unremembered life and this unremembered work deserve appropriate notoriety, both for the sake of equity and for what we can learn from them.

There are many people to thank. Thank you first to Anne Dean Dotson, Ashley Runyon, and the University Press of Kentucky for their interest in this project. Thank you to four rounds of careful readers for the Press who insisted that Jackson's story be told cleanly but with enough context to position this tale within the times, issues, and places that are its setting. At Berea College I want to thank Chad Berry for his permission to publish the ballads and for his support of this project; Chris Green, who steered me toward examination of the role of George Lyman Kittredge during the early Ballad Wars, supported funding of the separate commemorative publication of the ballads, and spent many tedious hours proofreading the same; Loyal Jones for his interest, collegiality, inspiration, and example; my wonderful colleagues in the music program, including my department chairs Dr. Stephen Bolster, Dr. Kathy Bullock, and Dr. Javier Clavere; and Professor Mark Calkins, whose interest in Jackson's "Barbara Allen" nudged me back into her collection. Also thanks to my partners in traditional music mischief at Berea College Al White, Dr. Kathy Bullock, Dr. E. J. Stokes, and Tripp Bratton; Deborah Thompson for her insights into women and other hidden voices in Appalachian music; Division Heads Dr. Rick Meadows, Dr. Carol de Rosset, and Billy Wooten for their encouragement and support; and the Hutchins Library Sound Archives Fellowship Program along with its special, anonymously funded trust and its facilitators, Terri Thompson, Rachel Roberts Lakes, Mark Calkins (again), and Ethan Hamblin.

I would be remiss not to sing the praises of the staff of the Berea College Special Collections and Archives at Hutchins Library and thank them for their diligence and help: the sound archivist Harry Rice, who can magically lay his hand on any text, recording, or artifact, no matter how obscure; the archivist Sharyn Mitchell and her keen eye for periodical articles pertaining to the subject at hand; Shannon Wilson, formerly of the Berea College Archives, for his excellent history of Berea College; and Rachel Vagts for heading one of the best collections of southern Appalachian materials in the world. Thanks also to Susan Henthorn for information regarding women holding doctorates in Kentucky.

Also, I owe a huge thank you to Mary Katherine (Kay) Tolbert Buckland for her generosity with time and material; Ron Pen, formerly of the University of Kentucky, for his support and wonderfully detailed suggestions; Chris Brown, an archivist with Centenary College, for miraculously digging up not one but three former students and colleagues of Dr. French's; Shirley Kelley and the Shreveport Woman's Department Club for their interest, information, and enthusiasm; Betty Smith for her deep knowledge and love of balladry and her willingness to share it; Emily K. Gattozzi, curator of the Ohio Wesleyan University Historical Collection at the L. A. Beeghly Library; Jocelyn K. Wilk, associate university archivist at Butler Library, Columbia University; Michael Frost at the Sterling Memorial Library Manuscripts and Archives, Yale University; the Filson Historical Society; the good-hearted folks at the Laurel County Historical Society who kept offering me lunch; of course Arpi, who was (as always) my companion during the first round of research that led to this book and offered his unending love and support; and, last, Berea College itself for finally enabling the publication of this story and collection.

PART 1

"THIS SPEAKING SOUL"

The keeping alive of such verse shows a wholesome and sane effort to meet a needed demand, and is the result of a distinct poetic gift, applied to all subjects and all sorts of spirits and made most effective when some passionate mind is aroused. . . . This speaking soul is an effective possession, increasing [the mountain balladeers'] love for liberty, their endurance, their restraint, and manliness, all expressive of the spirit and sap of the stock.

Katherine Jackson French

1

"The Spirit and Sap of the Stock"

In 1610, in Jamestown, Virginia, a group of eleven men met and swore a compact to each other. They were adventurers and planters, willing to gamble their futures in a new world, and willing to entrust those futures to each other. They had no guarantee that they were not simply throwing their lives away. They swore anyway. One of those men was John Jackson, an ancestor of Katherine Jackson French's.[1]

Or so avers Katherine Jackson French's version of family history, which includes a family tree that traces back to Charlemagne. A different family history, written by Jarvis Jackson in 1882, paints John Jackson, the original immigrant, in a less than flattering light. This John ran out on his apprenticeship, deserting his master, and abrogating his contract. He indentured himself to a ship's captain, came to America, and married a woman named Jarvis (or Gervaise) while they were both still servants. "That constitutes the start of the Jackson family of America," concludes Jarvis in a matter-of-fact manner. Uncontested, however, is the fact that one John Jackson was born in 1762. Twenty years later, this John Jackson married Mary Hancock, whose father, Stephen, was the nephew of John Hancock, a signer of the Declaration of Independence. John was awarded land in Madison County in payment for serving in the Revolutionary War under Baron von Steuben. He and Mary were married in Richmond, Kentucky, and theirs was the first bond of marriage written in Madison County. The newlyweds bought ten thousand acres of land in Laurel County, Kentucky, and settled in the northern part of what was to become London. John, Mary, and their son Jarvis thus became known as the founders of London. John and Mary had eight children; the youngest son, Stephen, was born in 1810. Little is known of Stephen except that his wife was named Minerva and that his son, William Harvey Jackson, was

London, Kentucky, 1870s. Courtesy of Laurel County Historical Society.

born on March 7, 1830. William was Katherine's Jackson's father; at the age of twenty-seven, he married Maria Louisa McKee, who was a cousin of Sam Houston's.[2]

This genealogy, warts and all, is necessary to understand a basic aspect of Katherine Jackson's family. They understood themselves to be a first family and not merely a first family of London but one of the first families of America.[3]

Katherine Jackson's father had a life like many small-town Kentucky boys in the nineteenth century. He worked at various occupations in London into his early twenties. When he was twenty-three, he helped drive a herd of cattle from Keokuk, Iowa, to California, assisting Captain Will Garrard. He returned to London after that and, at the age of twenty-seven, married Maria Louisa McKee.[4]

By 1870 William Jackson had established a store in London. He developed the square where his store was located, and it became the town's business center and a hub of activity. He rented out space to the London post office, a dry goods store, and a barber shop. In short, anyone who went to London for any kind of business transaction went to a space owned by Jackson.[5]

Katherine Jackson, age four. Courtesy of Kay Tolbert Buckland.

Jackson was a successful man with a growing family (which would eventually include eight children) and a growing business in a growing town. It was into this environment that Minerva Katherine Jackson entered the world on January 18, 1875.[6] She was born in the family cabin at Raccoon Springs, near Lily, a humble location for the beginning of a remarkable life.[7]

Early Years

Minerva Katherine Jackson was the Jacksons' sixth child. Presumably named for William's mother, the young Minerva Katherine, or Kittie as she was called by friends and family, attended the Laurel public school and Laurel Seminary.[8]

Laurel Seminary was the first institution of its kind in southeastern Kentucky. It opened in 1858. Students came from Laurel County and beyond. The curriculum included courses in algebra, arithmetic, English literature, English grammar, Latin, deportment, and history. Many Laurel Seminary graduates were trained to become teachers. After the Civil War, the school "helped people come back from the degradation into which the evil influences consequent upon war had lowered them."[9]

There is little information on Jackson's childhood other than her school attendance and the fact that her brother Jarvis died in 1884 when Jackson was nine. The only surviving photograph shows a serious-looking little girl of four staring intently into the camera with a furrowed brow. From local accounts of her father, however, we can glean certain details about the town in which Jackson spent her formative years.[10]

William Jackson's business ventures were well attested in the public record during the time of Katherine's childhood. "Jackson and McKee have ice-cold soda water at their Brick Drug Store," trumpeted one large ad in the local London paper, the *Mountain Echo*. Mr. Jackson was an aggressive marketer, which no doubt contributed to his financial success and local fame. Every resident of London knew his name. The Brick Drug Store was the center of all things commercial in London. A picture taken of the building in 1888, when Jackson was thirteen, shows a large, solid structure hovering over dirt streets and dominating the immediate area, an impressive building for a small town. William was doing well, and this enabled Katherine to have a financially secure childhood.[11]

Some of the activities that took place on the town square were musical. The London Brass Band, headed by "Professor Chiesman," played there periodically as early as 1877. "The brass band is here and the boys knock us out of our boots every night. O, gracious! Somebody hold us!" cried the *Mountain Echo* in July of that year.[12] In 1890, a bandstand was erected on the public square specifically for that group. In 1893, the floor over Jackson's store became the London Opera House Office. Space over the drugstore became the headquarters of the London Cornet Band.[13]

It appears that William Jackson (and perhaps his wife, Maria) had an interest in music and that Katherine would have grown up in an environment in which music had a hefty presence, a circumstance that came to figure prominently later in her life. Music seemed to run in the Jackson family. Katherine's sister Mamie went on to attend the Cincinnati Conservatory of Music and then return to London to teach music at Laurel Seminary.[14] As Erica Rumbley notes: "As the nineteenth century progressed into the twentieth, music became the most popular of the ornamental studies and gradually became accepted as a respectable career path for cultivated ladies of the middle and upper classes. Most well-bred ladies during this era received musical instruction."[15] It seems likely that, if Mamie was afforded the opportunity to study piano, as many daughters of upper-middle-class families did, Katherine was too. The adult Jackson owned collections of piano music and vocal scores; she also knew how to handle music dictation and notation. In addition, she occasionally noted in her diary that she "played" for guests, though she did not indicate which instrument, and that she played the organ in church. It is likely that, in addition to growing up surrounded by music, she had some music training during her childhood, as did most young women raised in similar circumstances.[16]

Expanding Horizons

William's success as a merchant enabled the family to send Katherine to Science Hill Female Academy in Shelbyville, from which she graduated in 1893 having followed the diploma course. It is here that we begin to get hints about the mind-set of her parents, and it is here that the arc of her education first begins to rise.[17]

Most southern preparatory schools in the 1890s existed to mold girls into what Joan Marie Johnson characterizes as the "traditional southern lady ideal: domesticity, purity, submissiveness, piety . . . charm, dependence, grace, manners": "Southern educators believed that the southern lady ideal . . . could be taught. . . . The ideal is the formation of women for womanly ends."[18] Education was permissible, in other words, but only to induct women into what Barbara Welter calls "the cult of True Womanhood," in which a proper woman exhibits "traits of piety, domesticity, and purity." The ideal of education in this case is indoctrination, not enlightenment, and an unyielding and systematic implementation of gender roles.[19]

Science Hill was different. To girls thirsting for knowledge, the academy was a kind of miracle. Founded to educate girls in the wilderness in 1825 by the resolute Julia Ann Hieronymous Tevis, with the help of her Methodist minister husband, John, it had indeed initially focused on "education as moral force for women as future wives and mothers."[20] Not so different from the typical southern girls' preparatory school of its time, it took as its original mission "to make an elegant, cultivated, refined woman for society, and fit for the higher duties of home life."[21] Yet, from the very start, it offered classes not only in ladylike refinement but also in reading, writing, arithmetic, grammar, history, rhetoric, and astronomy.

Morality, according to Tevis, must be informed by an educated mind, and, thus, science was an important part of the academy's curriculum. The fact that science was being taught to girls was so unusual that the school was called Science Hill. Tevis also adopted as the school's motto: "Woman's mind is limitless. Help it to grow." She inculcated in her young students the belief that the world was theirs to explore. With a firm and deferential faith in the divine, she taught that there were no limits, that *can't* was an excuse rather than a reality. This was the attitude of Science Hill from the time of its inception to its demise under the Poynter sisters 114 years later. Everything was possible—even for girls. [22]

During the tenure of Dr. Wiley Taul Poynter as principal, beginning in 1879, Science Hill's mission changed from preparing women to be educated, good wives to preparing them to be scholars. Poynter saw a changing world and wanted a more prominent place for women in it. Married to an educated woman (his wife, Clara, was the "female principal" and became principal after his death), he saw Science Hill as a place to prepare young southern women for more powerful roles in society. Under the Poynters, the curriculum, especially in the sciences, was expanded. The Poynters insisted that the regular course work be as rigorous as that at any boys' school, and, thus, Dr. Poynter immodestly claimed: "A diploma conferred by Science Hill means something."[23]

The school grew. The building was expanded. Poynter even got Science Hill included in the lyceum circuit, which meant a steady stream of visiting speakers in a chautauqua-like atmosphere. Science Hill became "one of the preeminent girls' preparatory Institutions in America," and Shelbyville became a cultural center that eventually featured an opera house at Seventh and Main.[24]

By the time Katherine Jackson arrived at Science Hill in 1891, the place was a palace. "A large covered court nearly one hundred feet long and thirty feet wide, with a gallery around it, affords all the conveniences of exercise at any time, and especially in bad weather," boasted the 1890–1891 catalog. The gym included unladylike things like weights, clubs, and dumbbells. All eleven teachers were women, and all those teachers were graduates of northern universities and conservatories, including Smith, the University of Michigan, the New England Conservatory, and Wellesley.[25]

Jackson attended Science Hill for only her last two years of high school. It is uncertain whether that was due to her parents' reticence to send her, the cost of the school ($252 without music lessons, the option the Jacksons took for their daughter), or the fact that she was not ready earlier. It speaks well

Katherine Jackson and Friends, Science Hill Female Academy. Photograph by A. J. Bodnar. Courtesy of Kay Tolbert Buckland.

of Jackson's early education that she could dive into the difficult Science Hill curriculum at that late point and still excel. Setting a pattern for achievement, she was chosen to speak at commencement in 1892.[26]

It took a special kind of young woman to attend Science Hill, a progressive, even radical school that hosted a steady stream of speakers from whom flowed a fountain of mind-opening ideas and prepared its students for a life, not just of the parlor and the nursery, but of the mind. It took an even more special set of parents to recognize the rightness of this opportunity for their daughter. William and Maria changed Katherine's life by sending her to Science Hill. There is no doubt of this. There is no record of William and Maria's conversations regarding Katherine's education. In the end, however, while it was William's money that sent Jackson to Science Hill, it was Maria to whom Jackson dedicated her doctoral dissertation in 1905.

2

Young Lady from London

Katherine Jackson and her sister Mamie Jackson Catching were hired as teachers at a mission school in Laredo, Texas, from 1895 to 1896.[1] "We are all very sorry to see Miss Kittie leave," mourned the *Mountain Echo*, "as she is one of the most pleasant and amiable of London's young ladies and will be greatly missed by all."[2] At that time, a college degree was not needed to teach public school. Jackson took advantage of that, relocating to Texas, and acquiring a year's worth of experience as a teacher. While home in London in March and June 1895, she prepared for college with tutors. This preparation proved effective; her academic record card indicates that she passed out of all her freshmen and sophomore courses when she entered Ohio Wesleyan University in 1897.[3]

It was not the norm for women to attend college in the 1890s, but it should be noted that at that time few men attended college either. In 1890, college attendance nationwide was 3 percent of the US population overall, and 20 percent of college attendees (0.6 percent of the overall population) were women.[4] As there was little in the way of serious advanced study available to women at southern colleges, many southern women turned to northern schools for their education. The historian Rebecca Montgomery argues: "The lack of colleges in the South was an attempt to keep women in traditional roles. Instead, it propelled the brightest and best of Southern women into the seedbed of Women's Rights and Progressive Movements."[5] This is, correct in effect, correct, but the causes are more complex.

By 1900, 2.8 percent of southern women attended college. While actually a much higher percentage than the overall figure for women nationwide, this is still quite a low. There were a number of reasons for this. For one thing, the pool of southern students from financially secure backgrounds was somewhat limited. According to Peter Temin, after the Civil War the American

South faced three insurmountable financial problems: a reduced demand for cotton, the loss of slave labor, and the physical destruction left by the war. The cost of college tuition was out of reach for many families in the postbellum years. Further, while women's colleges did exist in the South (Decatur Female Seminary, e.g., was founded in 1889), the curricula of most such schools tended toward grooming students for the traditional role of genteel woman and wife rather than for professional or academic life. This may have been a continuation of conservative southern cultural momentum or perhaps nostalgia for a social order that had come crashing down with the end of the war.[6]

For that minority desiring a serious education, few colleges in the South offered bachelor's degrees in rigorous academic programs to women. The only remaining choice for those seeking such degrees was to go north. Katherine Jackson made that choice.[7]

The best of the southern preparatory schools for women (including Science Hill) had special relationships with and groomed their students for the Seven Sisters: Vassar, Wellesley, Smith, Mount Holyoke, Bryn Mawr, Radcliffe, and Barnard Colleges.[8] Jackson, however, chose to attend Ohio Wesleyan University, passing its stringent entrance requirements in all subjects, including English, Greek, Roman and medieval history, mathematics, antiquities, natural sciences, and Latin.[9]

While not one of the Seven Sisters, Ohio Wesleyan was one of the earliest institutions of higher education in the country to educate women. Coeducation itself was in Jackson's time a fairly recent innovation. As a result, the hostility of male undergraduates toward coeds was fairly widespread across the country. Roger Geiger notes that on many campuses women were resented, ostracized, and ridiculed, and Pamela Roby holds that this hostility was spurred in part by the fact that women with college degrees were marrying and having children at a lower rate than their noneducated counterparts, fueling racist hysteria about the engulfment of the white race by immigrants from Italy and Ireland and people of other undesirable ethnicities. This hysteria was soon to fuel anti-immigration laws, racially motivated violence, and a one-sided reinterpretation of the mountain people of Appalachia that played into one of the major endeavors of Jackson's life.[10]

Jackson attended Ohio Wesleyan only from 1897 to 1898, according to her student record card. She graduated in one year and nine months.[11] Nevertheless, a great deal is revealed about her from her time at the university. For one thing, she rejected the idea of a limited collegiate role for women. Instead of taking just the "ladies'" literary track course of study, she completed that track plus extra course work and earned a bachelor's, completing the more rigorous "classical" course of study. She was not the only woman to do so. One-third of the graduates pursuing the classical track were women. Jackson even went beyond what was required for that track, taking three semesters of music courses that did not count toward either degree. This indicates a high personal motivation to better her music skills and knowledge, which were to come in handy within the next decade or so.[12]

Second, there is evidence that she thought outside the box. In March 1898, the senior women issued *The Senior Girl's Edition of The Transcript*, for which Jackson served as business manager. It was not customary for women to work on college newspapers at that time (though at Ohio Wesleyan a few served in minor roles). This exclusion may have served to inculcate in the Ohio Wesleyan women a desire to seek outside validation. In a rebellious gesture, and in the kind of decision that might have come from an organization's business manager, the editors sent a copy of *The Senior Girl's Edition* to the apparently more open-minded DePauw University *Palladium*. Their bold move was rewarded. A critique from the *Palladium* reads: "It is ably edited and typographically perfect."[13]

Third, Jackson was a leader. Organizations with which she was involved suggest the kind of limitless energy she brought to organizing and executing her endeavors. The year that she was named vice president of Ohio Wesleyan's YWCA group, the university paper reported that the group had grown "in interest and influence as well as numbers" since the previous year and praised its "high standards of organization."[14] Other issues of the school paper mention personal qualities that would help her achieve her ambitious aims: vigor, energy, interest, influence, organization, and an enterprising nature.

Fourth, Jackson achieved success and recognition quickly. Though she had been at Ohio Wesleyan for not even two years, she was called on to take part in the dedication of the Slocum Library in the spring of 1898. She presented the key to the library to the junior class on behalf of the senior class and made a presentation speech. The *College Transcript* notes the twenty-two-year-old's ability to conduct research, write, deliver a speech, move an audience, and even touch on a momentous event with appropriate humor. It states: "[Jackson] completely captured her audience, showing vast research and an observing eye. The rendering was characterized throughout by great smoothness. She told of our appreciation of the slow-come library, to [*sic*] late to aid us in our finished knowledge. 'On the top round of our glory we look back and consider '99 to be next worthy and most needy of the prize.'"[15]

Fifth, Jackson's intelligence is evidenced by her academic record. The classical track was demanding. Compared to the "ladies'" literary track, it required more hours in difficult core subjects (like languages, sciences, sociology, and philosophy) and more difficult course work within each subject. Jackson did extremely well. Not only did she, as we have seen, pass out of her freshman and sophomore years, but her grades were invariably high.[16]

Sixth, her work in and experiences with English and music would serve her to great advantage ten years later when Jackson assumed the mantle of ballad collector. As part of her course of study, she had three semesters of English philology and five semesters of music classes (and was credited with two semesters before her arrival, indicating a prior level of advanced competence). In addition, Monnett House, where she lived, had a banjo club. Banjo clubs were a passing fad on college campuses at the time, but the presence of one at Monnett House is of particular interest given Jackson's later encounter with the instrument in the backcountry.[17]

Seventh, Jackson threw herself fully into any activity with which she was associated. Much of her extracurricular effort during the spring of 1898 focused on Class Day. In March, she had been appointed one of three students (and the only woman) to serve on a committee to organize a series of events during commencement week. To be trusted with so prominent an activity within only one and a half years speaks to her drive and determination and to the impression she must have made on her professors.[18]

Eighth, she had a sense of humor, which was on display when she spoke at the Class Day ceremony. "Miss Jackson told how the girls sneaked out of Monett and went to the dedication of the Slocum Library," reported the *Transcript* with tongue firmly in cheek, "and the only regret is that it cost the faculty $20,000."[19]

Finally, while from the upper crust of London, Kentucky, Jackson was not particularly well-off compared to her peers, and she seemingly had a reputation for caring little about social mores and material wealth. A jesting and ironic prophecy in the *College Transcript* at the time of her graduation reads: "And so as we go out into the world in later years we shall expect to hear . . . Katherine Jackson became suddenly rich, and has given herself up to a fashionable life."[20]

In April 1898, Jackson's mother came to visit. Jackson's father was taken ill around this time and had only eight months left to live, so this may have been the visit when Maria came to tell her daughter the awful news. It does not seem to have slowed Jackson down. She continued to take part in normal college activities. She took tea with friends. She played tennis. She went on an excursion to a "picknick" at "Magneetic Springs" with a male friend and a group of students. Whether because of or in spite of her father's illness, she appeared determined to soak in every moment of college life that she could.[21]

It is not known whether Jackson's parents made the trip to her graduation ceremony, though, owing to William's declining health, it is not likely they did. Her sister Adelaide did travel to Ohio and was there to see Katherine Jackson receive her bachelor of arts degree in June 1898.

Jackson taught in Alabama the fall of 1898 and then spent some of the winter at home and the rest with her sister Addie in Georgia. Both Addie and Katherine came home in late December of that year to be with their dying father. William H. Jackson, who had meant so much to the town of London, died of stomach cancer on January 2, 1899. In an undated article, "JCM" avows: "The writer has never seen one endure such suffering with so much patience and resignation as Brother Jackson." JCM also discloses: "By close attention to his own business [he] amassed a considerable competence." He characterized Jackson's life as "blameless" and asserts: "[Jackson] called his wife and children about him and bade them an affectionate farewell, reminding them of the joyous reunion in store for them." He refers to "the largest crowd seen at a funeral for many years" and recounts that Jackson, an active Freemason, was buried by the chapter that he helped found.[22]

After their father's passing, Katherine and Adelaide Jackson returned to Bailey Station, Georgia. Katherine then went back to teaching in Alabama, but later that year she commenced her studies for a master's degree at Ohio Wesleyan University.[23]

The university had no residence requirement for a master's degree, and Jackson apparently lived at home while working on hers. In fact, of the eighteen graduate students that year, only three were in residence.[24] It usually took at least a year to complete the degree, "depending on the amount and quality of the work done [rather] than upon the time spent in residence."[25]

Still living in London, Jackson continued to engage in social events popular among young women of her time and class. In July, she attended the In-

The Jackson Family: Siblings Lou Jackson Eberlein, John Jackson, Mayme Jackson Catching, Moriah Louise McKee Jackson (mother), Adelaide Jackson, Annie Jackson Pollard, Robert Jackson, Katherine Jackson. Courtesy of Kay Tolbert Buckland.

ternational Epworth League in Indianapolis, and, finding time for recreation, she went on a foxhunt in December.[26]

No grades or work are accessible from Jackson's master's studies at Ohio Wesleyan, but, in 1900, four out of thirteen master's degrees were awarded to women. And one of those women was Katherine Jackson.[27] She completed her work in one year and attended the commencement ceremony in June 1900, although she had been present on campus so infrequently that the school paper listed her as "one of the visiting alumni."[28] She received her degree either at that ceremony or later that year.[29]

True North

After obtaining her master's degree, Jackson was offered a full scholarship at Yale University in 1900–1901 but elected instead to teach English and history at Belhaven College in Jackson, Mississippi, which she did from 1900 to 1902.[30] She then made the highly unorthodox decision to pursue a doctorate and, in the fall of 1902, headed north to New York City.[31]

Jackson attended Columbia University from 1902 to 1905 as a student in the "School of Philosophy, part of the Graduate School of Arts and Sciences," a little more than fifteen years after the first doctorate was earned by a woman at the college. The preface to her dissertation records that she studied in "the departments of English and Comparative Literature." While attending Columbia, she lived on West 123rd Street, just down the hill from the campus and across from the newly designed Morningside Park. She listed London as her permanent address, indicating that she still considered Kentucky home.[32]

One can only imagine what it must have been like for the young woman from Kentucky to find herself in the middle of bustling New York City in 1902 and at a large university like Columbia. First of all, the fact that she was a southern woman attending college made her part of a minority demographic. As we have seen, in 1900, less than 3 percent of southern women attended college. In general, women constituted a minority of the student population at virtually all colleges. For example, at Bryn Mawr in 1910, only 5–8 percent of the students were women; women made up an even smaller percentage of the student body at Holyoke.[33]

Jackson would also have been considered to be a southerner. And, apparently, she self-identified as such, as evidenced by her application for a Southern Fellowship in 1904. Though Kentucky officially fought for the Union (in reality, it was split and spent the war in civil turmoil) and was thought of as part of the West rather than the South until after the Civil War, by the 1890s it had been clearly recast in the minds of nonsouthern Americans as a slaveholding, southern state. Also, as mentioned, Jackson belonged to a family that prided itself on being descended from the first Virginia settlers. Joan Marie Johnson contends that southerners worked to retain their identities while attending northern schools. Surrounded by people with different views and values, and perceiving a need to defend their heritage, they often formed clubs based on their common background. This was especially true for students from border states. It is not clear whether Jackson attempted to shed her roots while in New York or whether she looked to hang on to them. Later in life, she kept close to her hometown of London, returning yearly, and continued to embrace the Kentucky part of her identify. While there is no evidence that she was a member of any sort of southern club, it is possible that she might have been involved in some such formal or informal organization, given her social skills, class, background, and propensity both to join and to lead.[34]

There is another issue to consider as well. At family gatherings, there is often an unwanted relative, a guest who is ugly and rude and obscene and vile. His presence is dreaded, his absence longed for, and, when he is gone, we prefer not to think about him. In the American family, that guest is race.

The question of race must have been ever present at Columbia during Jackson's time there, just as it was everywhere and still is. Laws suppressing the rights of African Americans were rising with alarming rapidity in the South. Precursors to the second incarnation of the Ku Klux Klan were stirring. Two to three African Americans were lynched every week in the South during this time period in horrible and hideous ways and in carnival atmospheres.[35] The faux science of eugenics was in its heyday in academic circles, with scientists putting their racist theories into practice through the forced castration of African Americans, immigrants, and "undesirable" poor whites.[36] Millions of southern African Americans (and poor whites) were trapped in the poverty of the sharecropper's life. When we consider that the students at Columbia were largely the grandsons of Union soldiers, we must assume that questions about race and slavery were faced by southerners at the university on a daily basis.

Many southerners still fostered deep prejudice against African Americans.[37] The ever-progressive Columbia University admitted black students in small numbers by Jackson's time, so friction or at least strained relationships were inevitable.[38] In addition, Jackson lived just north of Columbia in Harlem, which was predominantly white at the time, but African Americans were starting to move in in large numbers. Jackson undoubtedly had neighbors in New York who looked a lot like her servants back home. While in her dissertation she praised antislavery writers, there is no record of how she felt about her African American neighbors and fellow students in New York. Living in Harlem must have involved some adjustment on her part, to say the least. She had grown up in an atmosphere in which bigotry against African Americans was accepted. Racist violence had occurred regularly in London during her childhood. The local newspaper reported on and condemned some of these acts but treated others (like a nighttime visit from the Ku Klux Klan to a black woman) as though they were funny.[39]

In addition, there were few female graduate students at Columbia at the time—and so far only one woman had earned a doctorate—so the social cohort available to her would have been limited.[40] She was acquainted with women at Barnard College, however, including some in administration. A recommendation letter from the dean of Barnard states that she was "prominent and influential in the graduate student body" and that she "was a woman of executive power."[41] There is no record that Jackson sought companionship outside the college.

Jackson pressed ahead diligently with her doctoral studies. One of her professors, W. P. Trent, had suggested that colonial literature in Pennsylvania was, at the time, a largely unexamined topic, so she chose this subject for her doctoral dissertation.[42]

At 163 pages, her dissertation is the most extensive single piece of writing we have by Jackson. From it, we learn quite a few things, not only about her subject, but also about her own personality: confident, swift spoken, intelligent, curious, divergent thinking, capable of sharp humor, focused, tolerant but firm in her faith, and persistent. She praises Francis Daniel Pastorius for his 1688 opposition to slavery and admires early Philadelphia for the "variety of peoples and liberality of doctrine"; it is a place "where a man might belong to any or no sect, and yet be regarded as a good citizen." Speaking of the poet James Ralph, she remarks dryly: "Ralph was one of the race of editors whose morals are not to be dwelled upon." She writes admiringly of Benjamin Franklin, calling him "far-sighted, sensible and fearless," and discusses his beliefs without condemnation and with outright respect. Conversely, she labels Paine's *The Age of Reason* "an attack upon revealed religion, filled with coarse and vituperative illustrations and written in a wholly irreverent spirit, which gained the author exceeding unpopularity in England and America."[43]

The dissertation gives a good sample of Jackson's writing style. It displays long sentences that are spun out in an almost sermon-like and poetic manner. Jackson is quite conscious of the rhythm and sound of her words. Her writing is high-toned and passionate. She approaches her subject with authority and certainty. This is a style that she displayed throughout her academic career.

Finally, the scope of the work itself provides a final clue to Jackson's powers of perseverance. This was a prodigious undertaking. She has nine pages of sources listed in her bibliography, roughly totaling two hundred sources. Her primary sources came from many different locations, including New York, New Hampshire, Pennsylvania, Rhode Island, Massachusetts, Ohio, and New Jersey. In 1905, travel to archives required a significant investment of time and money. Such an effort exemplified great determination, focus, energy, and resourcefulness on Jackson's part.

Dr. Katherine Jackson French. Courtesy of Kay Tolbert Buckland.

Jackson completed her dissertation in 1905. Though her name was listed in the June 1906 commencement program, she was awarded her degree (with an English major and a comparative literature minor) on February 13, 1906.[44]

Consider the enormity of this statement: Katherine Jackson was awarded her PhD from Columbia University in 1906. In 1900, three years before Jackson commenced work on her degree, only 204 women in all of the United States held doctorates, 6 percent of a total of 4,000 overall. Moreover, Jackson was, according to her obituary, the first woman from south of the Mason-Dixon Line to earn a doctorate from Columbia University, only the second to do so in the history of the college, and one of the first Kentucky women to earn such a degree from any "standard university." For this achievement alone, she should be accorded a degree of respectful notoriety. When we add her role as one of the first major ballad collectors in the United States, a century's worth of disinterest in her becomes all the more puzzling.[45]

There are possible reasons for the lack of contemporary attention in her home state. For one thing, in 1906, an academically accomplished woman would not necessarily have been deemed admirable by the press or the general public. Then, there is the matter of the southerner (or westerner) "gone north" (or "east") for her education, again, something that might not have been perceived in a positive way. After the Civil War, resentment of the North grew in Kentucky, which was torn in two by the conflict to begin with; it is unclear whether Jackson's accomplishments were accepted or resented by the people of London. To complicate matters, after receiving her doctorate, Jackson taught for one year at Bryn Mawr and three at Mount Holyoke, thus completing the Science Hill/Seven Sisters connection, not as a student, but as something more exalted—a faculty member, a full-fledged part of the perpetuation of great northern institutions. During that time, she studied briefly at Yale, the ultimate symbol of elite northern academe. This leads to the question of "getting above her raising," another possible source of friction. Finally, she had been formerly known in London as a nice young woman of good breeding, one who had often been praised for displaying socially acceptable feminine virtues in what passed for the local paper's society column. A doctorate from an Ivy League college probably did not fit that comfortable and socially acceptable feminine image. Whatever the reason, Jackson's academic accomplishments did not garner praise, in her hometown or elsewhere. In fact, she received more attention in London four years earlier when she attended the Grand Hop wearing pink chiffon and diamonds.[46]

Ballad Seeds

Jackson's ballad-collecting interest began in her New York years. In addition to her studies in English while at Columbia, Katherine took courses in Spanish literature, which included Spanish and Moorish balladry. In her notes, she writes that the ballad "is a dead form . . . can't expect it to yield literary influence."[47] She was also quite taken with El Cid, noting that more ballads had been written about him than any other Spanish figure, some going back as far as 1612. Her interest in balladry was thus already budding when, in 1905, a group of her friends told her they had heard a lecture about uncollected ballads in the hills of Kentucky given by two "instructors" from Berea College in Berea, Kentucky. Jackson was familiar with Berea. In fact, when she was seven, her family took her there for a visit, during which she caught a cold severe enough to bear mention in the local paper. Perhaps it was that the lecturers were from Berea, or perhaps it was simply the unexpected encounter with a bit of home while so far away, but the subject of Kentucky mountain music caught her attention then and there, in the middle of New York City.

"They talked of the many ballads in the mountains of Kentucky, which no one had collected. A nursemaid had taught us Barbara Ellen but no other. I determined to investigate at my first free moment," she later wrote. In this way, she was moved to undertake a grand expedition, adventuring into the hills of eastern Kentucky when she returned home few years later.[48]

After she earned her doctorate, Jackson returned to London in June 1905 and gave a party for her friends in August. She returned home again briefly in July 1907 while she was teaching up north. She also engaged in some postgraduate work at Yale University from 1907 to 1908.[49]

In 1909, Jackson obtained a leave from her position at Bryn Mawr to work on a textbook on Old English. She used some of that time to return home to tend her ailing mother. Maria must have recovered because, in the fall, Jackson's journeys into the mountains surrounding London to collect the ballads of Kentucky began. These trips, the resulting collection, the five-year quest to publish it, and the question of Jackson's "stolen thunder" will be examined in part 2.[50]

3

Act Two

After collecting ballads in 1909, Jackson stayed in Kentucky and worked on getting them published through Berea College. But her world began to change on her marriage to William Franklin French in 1911. Gray eyed and auburn haired, "Frank" French was a dashing, handsome man. He had held the rather glamorous job of mountain mail carrier as a young man, was a graduate of Washington and Lee University and Kentucky Central College, and was a thirty-second-degree Mason. He was in London to do some legal work in 1899, shortly after William Harvey Jackson's death. It is possible that he worked on executing the terms of Papa Jackson's will and that he may have seen Katherine Jackson during this time. In fact, the two had known each other since 1893; one photograph shows them on a picnic at Cumberland Falls, and another depicts them in a buggy together, shortly after Jackson's graduation from Science Hill. It was not until September 11, 1911, that they tied the knot, however.[1]

After the wedding, Katherine French was still busy with her ballad collection. In 1914, she did some teaching at the Sue Bennett Memorial School, as she had when she had returned to London in 1899–1900, and she became dean there in 1915 for one year. The story of her recruitment is an unusual one. Apparently, her predecessor, a man named Lewis, was "a holy terror." He favored physical discipline, sometimes punching children in the face. He punished one child so severely that the father took him out of school and built a separate school building in his own yard so that his son never had to look on Lewis again. Lewis was so detested that, at one point, two young men left a cow in the administration building, the resultant effluvia apparently intended as a comment on his reign. Problems with him got so bad that the town fathers informed Belle Bennett, the school's head, that, if Lewis did not go, she would lose the school.[2]

William Franklin French. Courtesy of Kay Tolbert Buckland.

At this point, Bennett had had enough and asked French to become dean. Dr. French had a young child by then (Katherine, born in 1913) and replied as any new mother might: "Now Miss B. I got a baby to take care of." Bennett's curt reply: "A nigger can do that."[3]

It may be historical presentism to find such matter-of-fact use of the word *nigger* to be jarring, but that use provides an ironic window into the dichotomous mind of someone who considered herself a champion of black people. Belle Bennett was involved throughout her life with organizations that benefited African Americans. She started "Bethlehem Houses" (community houses for African Americans), organized a "Colored Chautauqua," taught Bible school to black children, and urged various women's organizations to take up responsibility for what she called "this great race of people." Yet the word fell from her lips as easily as a leaf from a tree. The term was acceptable among whites in the South in reference to black people and was still used freely in speech and print, though white women of Bennett and French's class may have viewed it as too common to employ in polite company. But it is not just the use of the word. Bennett's pronouncement that a black woman could tend her baby so that French could do other, more important things highlights the constraints within which African Americans lived then and would live for the next half century, in part because people like Bennett continued to reinforce them unthinkingly. Bennett's well-meaning but Kiplingesque view of white people's responsibility toward black people is comfortably housed in an unspoken and assumed superiority of race and class. That view is unmasked by the use of the word *nigger,* by the assumption that the coarse and demeaning term would be accepted, by the unthinking invocation of a demeaning black societal role, and by the urging of French to capitalize on it. Bennett knew that French would not judge her poorly. And French did not. In fact, she continued to admire her greatly. And she took the job.[4]

In this rather inglorious and ugly way, French became dean of the Sue Bennett School. She served only a year but quickly became enamored of the school and its Methodist-inspired mission. She later wrote a history of the Sue Bennett School and Brevard College in the booklet *The Story of the Years in Mountain Work,* in which she extolled the virtues of Sue Bennett the woman, her sister Belle (the caretaker of the school), and the role of Divine Providence in the founding and keeping of the school. The Jackson family had such a good continuing relationship with the school, in fact, that the school piano later wound up in the living room of Katherine's oldest sister, Lou Eberlein.[5]

In 1916, French addressed the Council of Missionary Workers of the Women of the Methodist Church in Georgia. The visit is cited in a newspaper article that also references her ballad work and concludes that she is thus "well-qualified to speak of the life, manners and possibilities of the Appalachian mountain people."[6] That same year, William Franklin French unearthed a promising opportunity: to become the head of a new car company called Bour-Davis. This necessitated a move, first to Detroit, then to Shreveport, Louisiana. French, the dutiful wife, hung up the academic robes and went with her husband. In truth, she might have resigned anyway as she had given up on her ballad project with Berea and was pregnant again. She was also older—forty-one, a risky age for a second motherhood at that time. While in Detroit, she miscarried, losing her second child, a son. The miscarriage rendered her incapable of bearing more children.[7]

The move to Shreveport in 1917 marked the start of the most professionally satisfying period of French's life. The Frenches settled into a house on Jordan Street. They found old music manuscripts in the attic, which they kept;

apparently French intended to keep up with her own music making. After a short period for settling in, she engaged in what was to be her longest-lasting project: the formation of the Shreveport Woman's Department Club.[8]

The Woman's Department Club of Shreveport

As previously noted, many southern women graduated from northern colleges and after returning home forged new roles for women there. Women's clubs were a vital avenue for this endeavor in the late nineteenth century and the early twentieth. They were ways in which women could gather in a socially acceptable environment, share meaningful and educational experiences, and engage in efforts addressing social issues like slavery, suffrage, and temperance. While women could not yet vote, their visibility and moral influence had an impact on men's decisions. Thus, they walked the tightrope between acceptable female roles and social activism.

White women had been banding together for various causes since the American Revolution, when thirty-seven upper-class women, led by Esther Deberdt Reed, formed the Philadelphia Ladies' Association to raise money for the revolutionary army. Their subscription efforts included seeking donations from not only from wealthy women but also from middle- and lower-class women, intentionally bridging the class divide by including women below their class standing in their fundraising efforts. Their door-to-door solicitations were tolerated because they were acting in support of their husbands' endeavors. In fact, they raised over $300,000 (in Continental currency) from fourteen hundred donors.[9]

The women's club movement proper began in about 1830 in the North. Free black women were among the first to organize, concerning themselves with "mutual aid and self-organization." White female societies and relief societies also formed during those years to address problems the government did not seem inclined to address, including issues concerning widows, orphans (including black orphans), and the mentally ill. Women were permitted to take part in such efforts because the matters they were working with were seen as ones of nurture, extensions of the life of the home.[10]

During the Civil War, women organized on both sides to help with nursing and rehabilitation of the injured. These efforts were not just accepted but welcomed, and the temporary autonomy that they provided women was tolerated. It is after the war that some of the efforts of organized women became controversial. For one thing, the infantilization of women, particularly in the South, gave white men an excuse to engage in acts of horrific violence against black men in retaliation for supposed acts of sexual depravity against innocent and helpless white women. For another, in the late nineteenth century and the early twentieth, women's organizations began to engage with social issues. Women's clubs were not seen as threatening until they began questioning matters like slavery and suffrage. As long as they built schools, medical dispensaries, and shelters for the homeless, they were considered to be operating within acceptable limits. Even temperance was seen as an acceptable issue, for it was framed in terms of the home, that is, the suffering caused by alcoholic husbands. However, as Anne Firor Scott points out, once these clubs supported prison reform, sex education, minimum wage laws, and suffrage, opprobrium came down on their heads, and they were accused of trying to revolutionize the social system, subverting the relations of women and men, and threatening the sacred institution of marriage.[11]

Women's clubs in the South had a later start but followed roughly the same trajectory as their northern counterparts. Barbara Smith Corrales notes that it took at least a generation for them to catch on in the South: "The role of women's organizations was initially less significant in patriarchal southern communities that severely restricted public expression by women, but, over time, southern women's clubs effectively loosened social restraints, permitting a broader application of the feminine gender's 'natural traits' (nursing, nurturing, and moral guidance). Women utilized this new freedom to promote reforms, eventually including woman suffrage."[12]

However, not all women's clubs, North or South, promoted progressive policies and goals. In the South, the United Daughters of the Confederacy, founded in 1894, used Lost Cause mythology and sentiment to promote a kinder, gentler story about the antebellum South. Chapters erected statues, established Confederate veterans' homes, and, most importantly, in the early twentieth century used pressure from their twenty thousand members to urge textbook companies to put a pro-Confederate spin on "the War between the States." This pleasant fiction promoted an emphasis on the states' rights angle and painted a picture of kindly, elegant, dashing masters who loved their slaves and treated them well. It was an image that was to persist throughout the South for at least half a century and echoes still.[13]

Few women had a wider and longer-lasting impact on the organization and operation of any women's club than Katherine Jackson French. Her work with the Shreveport Woman's Department Club endures to this day; the club is still in existence and sponsors lectures, concerts, and gatherings.

Founded in 1919, the Shreveport Woman's Department Club was an organization that initially focused, for the most part, not on politics, but on educating the city's female residents. French and the other founders envisioned the club as a place where women could go to learn, to study, and to better themselves. This meant providing what was essentially a college-level curriculum in a variety of subjects for only the price of membership dues, or a "nominal sum."[14]

The Woman's Department Club grew out of the oldest literary club in Shreveport, the Hypatia Club. The offshoot group called a special meeting in November 1919, presided over by J. D. Wilkinson, the president of Hypatia. Plans were made for a women's group "whose aim and objective would be to provide a center of thought and action, thereby focusing the strength and artistic growth of Shreveport and vicinity."[15] Dr. S. B. Hicks was elected president. Katherine Jackson French doubled as vice president and "Permanent Chairman of the Board." The group resolved to seek a permanent location and establish a free reading room and library, with the goal of being open all day. Lectures, art exhibits, and music classes were to be offered. After the resolution establishing the club was passed, French and two other women rose to speak of other women's department clubs they had been involved with or knew about. A committee adjourned briefly and came back with working bylaws. Once the bylaws were approved, eighty-eight women joined the newly formed club on the spot. French then rose to announce that she would deliver the first lecture, on behalf of the literary department one month hence, that it and all her lectures would be free of charge and open to the public, that the class would progress as fast as it wished, and that anyone could attend her lectures without preparation so that women who were too busy to do homework (and perhaps those who could not read well) could be accommodated.[16]

That first lecture by French, "The History of Drama," was held a month later, in January 1920. The 125 women in attendance were too many to fit into Mrs. Cecilia Ellerbe's living room, so the group chose the Council Chamber at City Hall as its regular meeting place. Meetings continued to be held there for five years. During that time, the group carefully raised money through bazaars, teas, and donations and hired an architect to build a permanent home.[17]

It is not clear whether the membership of the Woman's Department Club of

Shreveport consisted of only the city's upper crust, but certainly its founders and administrators were from that circle, which accounts for its fund-raising success. The membership fee was $15.00 per year, which had the purchasing power of about $220 in today's terms.[18] Nonmembers paid "a nominal sum" to attend events, a fairly egalitarian practice that seemed to invite not only the wealthy but also the middle class to attend. It is extremely likely that the club was white only; I have found no pictures or any other evidence to contradict that conclusion, which is a logical one given the mores of the place and time. By the late nineteenth century, women's clubs nationwide were made up mostly of upper-class white women who were not burdened with the menial tasks of homemaking.[19] When she cofounded the club, French fit that mold; she had a servant at home, no career as of yet, and little to occupy her other than her activities at the Methodist church. Her name and the names of the other founders frequently appeared in local newspapers as hosting teas and dinners. She was included in the top tier of Shreveport society, though she and her husband were, apparently, never really wealthy. Her pedigree and education probably account for a good deal of that, her faithful activities with the Methodist church for more, and her well-developed social skills for the rest. As women's clubs tiptoed societal lines of gender, French bridged lines of class with apparent ease.

One cannot read the notes from the early meetings without noticing the steady presence and guiding hand of French. When a chair quits, which happened four times in the first year, she moved that a committee be formed to find a replacement. She recruited the first guest speaker for the club, Judge Ben Lindsay. She gave instructions on how to behave during the Metropolitan Opera star Geraldine Farrar's recital ("absolute silence"). It was her suggestion to get a lawyer to apply for a state charter, and she made many suggestions to amend the group's bylaws. Every time the group encountered a problem, whenever something needed to be done or addressed, French was there to do it. She emerges from this mass of club minutiae as a capable, dedicated, insightful, practical, knowledgeable, and tireless woman.[20]

The gorgeous Georgian mansion that became the permanent home of the Woman's Department Club was finished in 1925. The first lecture given in the new hall was French's closing lecture of the 1924–1925 season. As seats had not yet been installed, audience members perched themselves on boxes that the construction workers had left behind. This worked out well, as the

Woman's Department Club, Shreveport, interior. Photograph by Elizabeth DiSavino.

discomfort prompted each member to pledge "the price of one opera chair" for the new auditorium.[21]

French stayed on as board chair until 1928 and continued teaching English literature every Friday for free long after that. She taught in her regalia, linking her students' fledgling efforts with her own impressive academic achievements, and focused on her area of expertise: English and classical literature. Her lesson plans were detailed. She did not talk down to her students but expected them to keep up. A typical year of lectures covered the miracle plays, the morality plays, the early comedies, the early tragedies, Elizabethan drama, and Jacobean drama.[22] But French's goals were not only to educate the minds of the women of Shreveport but also to enlighten their spirits:

> This course of lectures is presented this year, not so much to increase your knowledge in the abstract sense and develop dramatists, as to heighten your desire for more learning, until it becomes a yearning, an obsession for deeper truths, more lasting beauty, and more eternal good . . . to promote a great spiritual bond for all humanity. . . . This larger outlook that comes from books and work, brings with it a freedom, an emancipation from what is small and petty, with a contempt for wealth as wealth, and a contempt for power as power, and a contempt for society as society, and gives one instead interests and influences which should soften the hard places and make life brighter for many in reach. . . . Men may grow mighty of heart and mighty of mind, magnanimous, which is to be great in life, to have made progress in living. It is not to have more trappings, more public honours, more fortune, more footmen. He only is advancing in life whose heart is softer, whose blood is warmer, whose brain is quicker, whose soul is more personal, whose spirit is entering into living peace. This sheds an inward light and can vouchsafe an inward lustre that shall survive the undaunted quest, until the mind becomes a thousand times more beautiful than the earth on which its possessor lives. This looking for beauty, with an open mind and open heart, will bring a greatness of thought, and consciously and unconsciously crowd back the evil, the unrest, the bitter, the hate, and show infinite values and final accumulation of all good. Let us determine to study more constantly every aspect of real knowledge, fill our minds only with things of permanent value, hoping some day to grasp deeper knowledge, to realize more exquisite beauty, more genuine good, and after all is said, that is Truth and that is Eternal.[23]

By 1920, the club had taken stands on several social issues, including a minimum wage for women, an eight-hour day for female industrial workers, and the stance that "part of a prisoner's wages should be paid to his family." These were relatively progressive positions for a southern women's club to take. The fact that French held great influence in the Woman's Department Club may hint at her own views on these issues.[24]

French took a few absences from the club during the time she was involved with it. She went home to Kentucky in 1920 to be with her mother during her final illness. Letters attest to the fact that her students appreciated her and fervently wished for her return.[25] She did so after her mother's death and recommenced her lectures. She took or considered taking other breaks from the club and apparently even considered leaving; each absence or any threat thereof was greeted with impassioned letters from her students imploring her to stay. "You have enriched my life beyond my power to ever express," wrote one student. Another pleaded: "Surely you will not go? What will we do without you? What will the Department Club do without you? We all know that your unselfish work, your gifts of mind and heart have made the club. You have endeared yourself to this entire community, by the charm of personality, your many gifts of rare quality—your Christian virtues and graces—and the thought of having to give you up, brings sorrow to all of us."[26] One student even wrote an ode to her that began:

When French dons her Doctor's hood and gown
We see the earnest woman's eyes betray
A fond expectancy. She holds a sway
More sure than any queen with blazing crown.[27]

Two things are evident from these writings: that French's students adored her and that she was a powerfully gifted teacher who succeeded in awakening in her students a yearning to connect with knowledge and enlightenment.

It was typical for French to receive gifts at the end of every lecture season. Her diary notes the grateful receipt of flowers, china, drawings, paintings, and silverware. Her lectures were always well attended; she noted that three hundred women attended a lecture in 1920, an observation supported by a statement in the *Shreveport Times* the same year: "Dr. French and Mrs. Ellerbe are planning the lectures again in the Council chamber, but I don't know, those who came late last year stood up, and this year everybody is coming back—and then some." Largely by dint of French's charisma, women joined the Woman's Department Club in droves. By 1941, it claimed a membership of one thousand. Membership may have been as high as sixteen hundred during World War II.[28]

Such adulation must have been hard to walk away from, and, indeed,

Katherine Jackson French at the Woman's Department Club of Shreveport. Courtesy of Katherine Tolbert Buckland.

French did not. She continued her work as a lecturer with the Woman's Department Club for a total of eighteen years, and she served in other capacities as well: life member, vice president, chairman of literature, member of the board of directors. The twenty-fifth anniversary yearbook applauds her "joy and passion of the natural teacher" and states: "Her interest and cooperation have been felt throughout the club. A bronze plaque on the rear wall of the auditorium attests to the esteem in which Dr. French is held by this group of 1000 women." It was presented to French at the close of her lecture series in 1936 and remains hanging today.[29]

The Professor: Centenary College and the AAUW

French's light found other ways to shine. In 1924, a great opportunity came her way: the position of professor of English at Centenary College in Shreveport.

French began working at Centenary College in September 1924. She was to stay there for twenty-five years. Strangely, her diary contains no details

Centenary College. Photograph by Elizabeth DiSavino.

about her hiring, noting only the date she began. The hiring process remains a mystery. It is possible that members of the college attended her lectures, realized what an outstanding teacher she was, and initiated the process that led to her hiring. It is also possible that her social skills and activities had something to do with it. She entertained and called on people frequently. Her "guest" list takes up five columns in her diary for 1919–1920, her "call" list two. Finally, she was active in the First Methodist Church in Shreveport, taught Sunday school, and belonged to the Ladies Missionary Society and the Junior League. The Shreveport First Methodist Church had deep ties to Centenary and had helped bring the college there from Jackson thirteen years earlier. Those ties probably worked to French's advantage. Her prodigious social skills would have allowed her to network and to lay the foundation for her employment at Centenary.[30]

When she first arrived at the lush and verdant Centenary campus, only five of the twenty faculty members were women (including two of the music teachers, one of whom was married to the director of music, and another professor who carried the title "Director of Expression"). There were only three professors who held doctorates, and only one of those—French—was a woman. Once again, French found herself in the position of breaking barriers. She proved to be outspoken, especially for a new hire, and lost no time advocating for the cause of educating the underserved. At a 1924 luncheon with fellow Centenary employees, the newly minted professor gave an impassioned speech about how Centenary should not be "a rich man's college" and should help "not the few, elect, who have always gone" but also the less fortunate get an education.[31]

French's teaching left a deep impression on her students and colleagues alike. One of her students, Charles Brown, remembers her as "a great teacher": "She lived Shakespeare. She pantomimed Shakespeare. In one play, she pantomimed a snake all the way across the length of the classroom. I don't know if she killed him, but she stomped on him! She did that a lot." Brown recalls that she loved English literature and tried to get him to memorize Chaucer's *Canterbury Tales*, but he was "a World War II vet who was not too hot to trot for school anyway," so "she was not real successful." Brown also recalls her as "tall for a lady, then, probably five-seven, five-eight." She enunciated clearly, he notes, and did not have an overly loud voice, but everyone could hear her "over all the class." Hers was "not a soft little ladylike voice" but more like "a 'years-of-getting-students-to-listen' type voice." "Everybody liked her," he continued. "Definitely not overbearing. She did not try to make you do anything; she tried to *get* you to do things." Occasionally, French would sing, though Brown could not recall what. "I guess you could say she had what you would not classify as a singer's voice," he recalls wryly.[32]

A colleague, Dr. Betty Spears, remembers French toward the end of her career. Spears arrived at Centenary to teach at the age of twenty-two. She recalls going to a faculty picnic her first year, and that to her surprise, a gray-haired French jumped up and read Shakespeare to all in attendance: "She did an excellent dramatic job. Very entertaining! I was impressed by this entertainment at a faculty picnic." Spears recalls the faculty being "very respectful of French." She also somewhat ruefully recalls French talking her into running for president of the Louisiana chapter of the American Association of University Women (AAUW). She won. "I shouldn't have [run], but she was very persuasive," recounts Spears.[33]

French was still talked about even after her career was over. Dr. Lee Morgan, who taught at Centenary after French's retirement but heard lingering memories of her, recalls a story about her devoutness coming into conflict with her teaching duties. "She would read a great deal to her classes," he recalls. "She would read up to a word like 'maidenhead,' read right up to it and simply omit it . . . a real old-fashioned prudish person—an oddity in her personality. I do remember she was well-respected as a teacher."[34]

French served on committees, often more than one a year. She rarely missed a faculty meeting. Among the motions she made were one for the college to join the AAUW (in 1941) and another to elect two women to membership on the board of trustees (in 1942). Both motions carried unanimously, which again speaks to her communication and social skills. In another instance, French suggested that the faculty work on plans to "get the students more actively engaged in chosen churches." The dual issues of religion and women remained constants throughout her time in Shreveport.[35]

The Frenches were very much at home in Shreveport. Katherine taught during the week; Frank pursued a variety of business opportunities, including drilling oil wells and government appointments. Sundays were spent at church, usually followed by a fried chicken lunch and then visiting neighbors. "I don't know of anyone that didn't love her," says Kay Tolbert Buckland. "I can remember at Christmastime my father would take me and we would go and deliver presents . . . there in Shreveport because [all the recipients] were all good friends of my grandmother. And my grandmother didn't have any money. She was a schoolteacher! But they all wanted to be her friend." French was a "friend of the wealthiest people and the poorest people": "They all loved her."[36]

As noted, French often played hostess to a wide range of people in her home. A favorite tradition was the Christmas morning eggnog party. French made a brew, imported from her native Kentucky, called "Henry Clay eggnog." The recipe involved two dozen eggs, a lot of milk, and a lot of cream plus a quart of bourbon and a quart of rum. Her teetotalist guests "would come to her eggnog party, not knowing all the booze that was in the eggnog": "They . . . never said a thing about it." These guests apparently remained blissfully ignorant of the alcohol-induced cause of their early morning Christmas cheer.[37]

French kept in contact with Science Hill Academy, the school that had opened so many doors for her. Her high regard for Science Hill was genuine, evidenced by the fact that she sent her own daughter there. In 1925, the school held a centennial celebration. French was chosen from among hundreds of graduates to represent students from the Wiley Poynter years. Her speech honored him, reflected her ongoing passion for opening up educational possibilities for women, and also paid homage to Poynter's wife and successor, Clara. "Tonight," she declared, "I come to place two wreaths upon two brows, upon the one a crown of service for seventeen years of marvelous beginnings; upon the other a crown for thirty-nine years of exampled carrying-on."[38]

French attained local recognition in the Shreveport community on a number of counts, many of which she appears to have engineered herself. She was mentioned frequently in the *Shreveport Times* for her work with the Woman's Department Club. The paper pointedly uses her proper title in a 1920 article: "And by the way, for our everyday saying, she is our friend, Mrs. French, but whenever she is doing any work along the lines for which she received her degree, she has been asked to use the title bestowed upon her and be called Dr. Katherine Jackson French."[39] (Whoever "asked" her is not stated.) In 1930, the paper began to publish her weekly lectures. That same year, she is quoted in an article, "What Music Means to Me."[40] In 1933, she is the subject of a lengthy feature article: "The proud boast of Centenary college that its English department is unexcelled by any college in the entire South is supported among other reasons by the fact that it has been fortunate enough for 10 years to have identified with it one of the foremost English scholars in the entire country, Dr. Katherine Jackson French." The article refers to her work in the British Museum and mentions hobnobbing with education leaders at the Columbia University Library during summers off. It also makes a point of noting that French had met distinguished speakers and performers through the Woman's Department Club and that with many "she has had delightful associations."[41] This collection of famous acquaintances is corroborated by her granddaughter, who remembers going to a Broadway play when she was a child and being introduced to Richard Rodgers, a friend of her grandmother's.[42]

Not surprisingly, French became active in the early organizational efforts of both the Shreveport and the state chapters of the AAUW. In March 1941, nine months before Pearl Harbor, she was elected president of the Louisiana chapter. Immediately following her election, she and her secretary-treasurer, Mrs. C. L. Mooney (also of Shreveport), traveled to Alexandria for the tenth state convention. The focus of the convention was "the place of women in the defense program." French also traveled to the national convention in Cincinnati in May, that year's theme being summed up in the statement: "The American Cause is again the cause of the creative human spirit, which no enemy has ever overcome."[43]

At the national convention French heard Erika Mann, the daughter of German ex-patriot novelist Thomas Mann, speak of the dangers of Hitler's youth education programs as outlined in her book *School for Barbarians* (1938). She took copious notes on Mann's speech, the main points of which lamented the "blind obedience" of the Hitler youth and outlined Mann's solution: the "battering rams" of group action and the inculcation of the democratic process in schools. Mrs. Edward R. Murrow also spoke (albeit from London), as did Ambassador Mary Craig McGeachy, the first woman ever to receive a British embassy appointment. Dr. Margaret Mead, who had not yet become a cultural icon, also delivered an address titled "What Women Might Contribute to Science." (She also spoke to the state chapter in 1947.) French's circle of acquaintances and influences thus grew to include some of the most prominent female thinkers of the time.[44]

French's election as president of the Louisiana chapter of the AAUW came at a time of great world turmoil. Europe was being overrun by Nazi Germany, England had been attacked, and the United States was torn over whether to enter the war. In October 1941, French wrote to her AAUW colleagues: "Another year lies before us, filled with terrific problems to be solved. We must not merely be another club, but must recognize the challenge to think, face our obligation to society, and encourage our members steadfastly in the search after Truth, which will bring to us the courage and rebuild or uphold our morale. 'We have within ourselves the power to conquer bestiality, not with our muscles and our swords, but with the power of the light which is always in our minds.' (*There Shall Be No Night*)."[45]

In 1942, French invited Ambassador McGeachy to speak at the AAUW Louisiana state convention in Hammond, where she spoke on the subject "British University Women in War." An article in the *Shreveport Times* attests that McGeachy stated that British women were happy to be involved in the war effort and were part of an overall feeling of national unity. It quotes her as proclaiming: "Plato stated three things that save us . . . justice, self-demand, and truth, and I would add a fourth, love."[46] A photograph in an unidentified newspaper article shows McGeachy with French and the vice president of the Alabama AAUW.[47] French stands in the middle, as though bringing the two

Dr. Ellen Agnes Harris, Dr. Katherine Jackson French, British ambassador Mary Craig McGeachy. Courtesy of Kay Tolbert Buckland.

together. The visit was facilitated by Lord Halifax, to whom French wrote afterward: "[McGeachy] brought to us a message that is rarely heard. . . . You are making a great contribution to our civilian defense when you furnish such a marvelous speaker."[48] Other topics at the 1942 conference included the importance of the arts for preserving morale and culture and educating for times of peace.[49]

Perhaps partially spurred on by the enlistment of her son-in-law, Carl, French yearned for the AAUW to take a more active role in issues related to the war. She had been warned of the difficulties of this by her predecessor,

Lucy Lamb. Lamb's view proved to be correct. After Pearl Harbor, the war was in full swing, and everything else was put on hold. The national AAUW meeting in Dallas in 1942 "fell through," as did an attempt at a biennial in Kansas City. Still, French soldiered on. On behalf of the AAUW, she was appointed to the Louisiana Salvage for Victory Council in 1942. By 1943, she had visited every local AAUW chapter and in April 1942 reported to the state membership: "All [are] . . . flourishing, all busily engaged in civic defense work, social welfare, and educational projects in their communities. Many are furnishing teachers and leaders of all sorts, who are upbuilding and upholding the morale, conscious of having received especial gifts from life, and burdened with the responsibility of making honorable returns."[50]

French again wrote to the Louisiana membership in March 1943, advocating for a meeting of the leadership, and urgently asking each chapter to pay for its leaders to attend. "We have an unfinished task in the world," she proclaimed, "and as we now perform those assigned us, will we be able to share in the global policy of the post-war world, when questions of tremendous magnitude await us? A world society in security forever!" Writing in her last days as president, she took the bully pulpit in her closing: "Natchitoches, March 26–27: Please meet me."[51] Her letter with its tone of urgency succeeded. The AAUW did meet in Natchitoches. Topics addressed included "Our Part toward Tomorrow," "In International Relations, Survival of the Fittest," and "University Woman's Objections." While efforts toward concrete actions regarding the war effort do not seem to have coalesced as a result of this convention, the very act of meeting kept the organization active.[52]

French spoke at numerous local AAUW branches during her tenure. She served until 1943, when she was succeeded by C. C. Colvert.[53] The transition was facilitated by a past president, Sarah Clapp, who wrote to her: "In the helter-skelter of Saturday, you disappeared without my saying to you how great is my satisfaction in your administration from the first day to the last, how high a mark you have set for future presidents to aim at, and what a pleasure it is to work with you in any capacity whatever."[54] This view was seconded by Dr. Agnes Ellen Harris, who wrote: "You have been such an ideal and wonderful President."[55]

French was awarded an AAUW International Fellowship Grant for 1951–1952. She continued to attend state and national conventions. As was her custom, in her 1949–1950 conference program book she took notes on a lecture (likely that of Helen Dwight Reid) that particularly resonated with her: "1. Think for ourselves on every question. 2. Hold fast the spiritual, moral, and democratic ideals and values of our forefathers—the founders of America. 3. Must not hate men, but must hate wrong . . . hate war and end war for all time. 4. We must be stabilized and retain our ideals of peace and culture. 5. Get ready for tomorrow."[56]

The work of the AAUW at that time paved the way for the acceptance of women in academe and indeed, shone a spotlight on women's issues in general. French recognized the importance of this and lent her time and prodigious energy to that work. Her years with the AAUW as both member and as leader meant much to her. Her AAUW pin remained in her possession to the end of her days.

French was active in a number of other activities. She was a member in the Colonial Dames of America, she taught Sunday school at the First Methodist Church in Shreveport and at the London Methodist Church in the summer, and she was a member of the Shakespearean Society of America, Phi Theta Kappa and Chi Omega, the Modern Language Association, and the National Society of the Daughters of the Byrons of Runney.[57] Put all this together, and we have a picture of a committed, active woman. This is even more extraordinary in light of the health issues that French faced. She took numerous absences from the Woman's Department Club in the late 1920s, including one attributed to "continued illness."[58] We have an indication of what may have been wrong in an early letter from her sister Annie: "It is hard to get away with . . . that flu after having it. Hope your heart holds out better than before."[59] This is the first clue of the heart condition that later took French's life. She took a year off from the Woman's Department Club in 1929–1930 but apparently returned undaunted and resumed her lectures and busy schedule.[60]

Mother Katherine

French's daughter Katherine attended Centenary College during her mother's tenure there, graduating in 1935.[61] This must have been a complicated situation as French proved to be a concerned and somewhat overprotective parent. Young Katherine spent part of her first year at Mount Holyoke, apparently on some kind of transfer program, as she is also listed in the 1931 Centenary College yearbook. Correspondence from that time has French issuing orders to her daughter on virtually every issue from wardrobe to travel plans to study efforts. When Katherine struggled at Holyoke with both health issues and study skills, her mother attempted to help by sending material for her projects, including information for a paper on ballads:

> I have gathered up material for your Shakespeare and your ballad paper. Now Angel, this ballad material is absolutely new. Your teacher likely does not know half as much as I do. Not boasting, but I spent years at work on it. The only new book worth reading is Davidson's [*sic*] Traditional Ballads of Virginia[62] and I have gleaned the best of it. The article I send is one I prepared for the press and has never been published. You can use some of that as you had gone with me saying you as a child had accompanied your mother on your researches. Such a character as Aliza Bullard or Mrs. Watkins or your Aunt Nanny Bob's mother are the ones to use. Do you recall our trip to Columbus and can you remember Mrs. Branson. If you can remember her and her singing. . . . You do not need to do any library work as it is all here. You may have to omit a lot of the personal incidents as they may be too personal. Mrs. Foster knows I lecture on this and asked me to address her classes the last time I was there.

This is a very uncomfortable missive. French tells her daughter to use her material and claim she remembered things she clearly did not and instructs her as to how to pass off her work as her own. This overprotectiveness is tempered by another sentiment: "I hope deeply that this critical theme works the charm and gets you a good grade. I wish to help you in any honest way, but not for anything would I make it too easy for that would do you no good."[63]

Overestimating her daughter's modest academic efforts and abilities, French fruitlessly tried to get Katherine placed at Oxford. Either projecting her own wishes or hoping to provide inspiration, she wrote: "Every thing has its price, and the intellectual life demands a heavy one. However, you and I will sacrifice everything trivial for its possession."[64] Daughter Katherine was not a stellar undergraduate student, but it should be added that she went on to earn a master's in art from Columbia University in summer sessions between 1937 and 1941. French wrote to her daughter during her summers in New York, confessing to nostalgia for her own days there: "I well recall my similar experiences. After New York, one gets lonely anywhere. But shall we omit going to the big city for that reason? I get so lonely for it, and for you, and for life some days."[65]

French also explored the possibility of obtaining a position as president of Mount Holyoke, probably to be nearer her daughter. Here she hit a brick wall as the then president of the college, the iconic Mary Woolley, had no intention of resigning.

Like the rest of the nation, during the 1930s the Frenches were going through financial difficulties. Frank never struck it rich in oil, hoped-for appointments from the governor either did not pan out or did not pay much, and French often worked for long periods at Centenary without pay because of the toll the Depression took on the college's financial situation.[66] "This was the Depression," said Kay Tolbert Buckland. "She taught for nothing at the college. She got very little. Nobody had any money to pay anything. . . . They worked for nothing. . . . Mom said they ate pancakes morning noon and night. They had friends jumping out of windows. A lot of their friends were these very wealthy people and they're the ones who got hurt the worst."[67]

Prior to and during the Depression years, Frank traveled a lot for work, trying to strike it rich in oil. A frequent word in French's 1929 diary is *lonely*. There are several times she mentions spending nights alone because he was working. She also noted that he came to his mother-in-law's funeral in 1920 ninety minutes late. Whether or not these entries indicate trouble within the marriage, they do indicate at least routine periods of separation as Frank and Katherine pursued their own careers.[68]

Briar Lodge: Old Kentucky Home

Despite deep financial problems, French managed to travel. In 1938, she sailed for England aboard the steamer *Bienville,* a trip made with her sisters and friends. She also made a point of staying in touch with her Kentucky roots. She was often a guest of honor at events in London. In 1933, she gave a speech near her childhood home at the dedication of a new state park, known today as Levi Jackson State Park. She attended the first Laurel County Homecoming in London in 1935, gave a speech about mountain ballad origins, and introduced Millie Phelps, who sang "Barbara Allen." She continued to travel to London for summer homecomings and wrote "A History of London" for

The Jackson Cabin in London, Kentucky. Courtesy of Kay Tolbert Buckland.

the town's Founder's Day celebration on August 17, 1940. At this celebration, her great-grandparents, the London founders John and Mary Hancock Jackson, were reinterred at the new Dyche Cemetery. Six thousand people attended the event.[69]

Summer visits to London became yearly events. Though her sister Annie was still living there, the Frenches stayed in a cabin in the hills of South London built on land that belonged to her oldest sister, Lou, in the mid-1930s. (The deed was transferred to Katherine and Frank in 1949.) The cabin was off in the woods on an eight-acre parcel of land that backed on a pig farm. It had no heat, running water, or electricity. Water came from a well, and the outhouse was down the path. There was a wood stove and a true icebox in the kitchen.[70]

A *Shreveport Times* article featuring French describes the cabin, citing its name as "Briar Lodge": "[It is] in the foothills of KY on the Daniel Boone Trail . . . [a] quaint old-fashioned cabin built on land deeded her family in 1789 when KY was part of VA. . . . [It] is filled with antiques of the farm-type, such as wheels for wool and flax, rifles, powder horns, bullet forms, candle molds, cooking utensils for open fires, and much interesting furniture."[71]

Kay Tolbert Buckland has vivid memories of summers spent with Grandmother Katherine:

She loved to play cards at night, 'cause we could light the lanterns. We would pop popcorn in the basket . . . over the fire. . . . At the big fireplace at the end of the room, . . . she would sit in this little school desk, and she could write at it, and she could play cards on it. I remember eating her raspberries, blueberries, she would make wonderful pies. My mother loved them. With the pies, she would serve a little brown sugar and butter mixture, you know you mix up and just put a little scoop on the pie . . . that was their version of ice cream. . . . I guess they just liked to get away from the city in the summer and go out to the cabin."

They would also visit Annie, who lived in the big old Jackson family home, with a sprawling porch and a grape arbor and (by then) a mostly vacant upstairs where the children would run and play.[72]

French's diaries reveal a quiet devoutness with regular attendance of church and various Christian organizations. Both she and Frank were active in the Methodist church in Shreveport during the year and in London during the summers. Frank was a member of the Board of Stewards in Shreveport; French's diaries note regular teaching of Sunday school classes in both locations. She was also a constant attendee of the Missionary Society. Her language in her diaries is not overly religious, but, as we have seen, religion was a constant in her life.[73]

Retirement and Later Years

French became head of the English Department at Centenary College in 1945. In 1948, she attended her last conference of the Louisiana chapter of the AAUW. It was the organization's eightieth anniversary, and the group met, fittingly, in Shreveport. French retired from Centenary later that same year at the age of seventy-three with bouquets of accolades. Dr. J. Mickle, the president of Centenary, wrote: "Perhaps no teacher in the whole history of Centenary College has left a finer and deeper impression upon student life both within and without the classroom than you have done. The fine quality of your mind and spirit has been matched with a co-operative and constructive attitude on all matters pertaining to the development of Centenary College. Furthermore, your contribution to the Shreveport community as a whole has been tremendous. It has raised the intellectual, cultural, and spiritual level of the entire city."[74]

A proclamation from Mickle and the Board of Trustees declared: "[French] has created in her students a love of language and literature, and for two generations she has made Shakespeare live. She has had a lasting influence on the college and on the intellectual life of Shreveport. The Woman's Department Club owes much to her efforts; she has given unstintingly of her gracious personality and her stimulating mind. Centenary College and Shreveport will long feel the far-reaching influence of Dr. Katherine Jackson French."[75]

The 1948 *Yoncopin* yearbook was dedicated to her and describes her as "a woman of profound scholarship, gracious charm, and splendid Christian character—a humanitarian in the fullest and finest meaning of the word": "Hundreds of students have known, loved, and respected the value of so gifted a woman and would well appreciate the tribute of the student who recently said, 'Dr. French transforms the tasks of education into a challenging adventure in learning.'"[76]

French's Centenary career can be traced through three photographs. The first photograph of "Mrs. Katherine French" appears in the 1930 yearbook. There were thirty-nine faculty members that year. French is one of eleven female teachers and the only one with a doctorate. In fact, of the men, only five have doctorates. Yet French is not referred to as *Doctor*. Her photograph appears on a page with those of two other female teachers. They wear earrings and pearls. French wears her academic regalia, robes and hood. The other two women bear soft, gentle gazes. One's head is tilted down; the other gazes shyly at the camera through her makeup. French's chin is lifted, her head uptilted, she wears no makeup, and her eyes are steely with a glint of humor. It is the kind of gaze that might be taken as condescending. Perhaps it was. We are looking at a woman who is proud of her accomplishments, unapologetic for her presence, and likely quite demanding of her charges. In short, we are looking at one tough woman who at the age of fifty-five is quite cognizant of the achievements of her life and the obstacles she has had to overcome.[77]

The 1934 yearbook contains an even haughtier picture of French. It is in full profile, the only faculty photograph in which the subject does not deign to look into the camera, rather staring off into the distance as though with a far-seeing eye. It also bears an interesting comparison to her daughter's picture in the same volume. This younger Katherine French was voted "Most Popular." She has her mother's long, somewhat horsey face and large lips, but her expression is softer. Indeed, she is a member of "the Maroon Jackets," a club of college hostesses described as "overflowing with Southern hospitality." She was a member of Chi Omega, like her mother, and served as treasurer. She looks like a well-adjusted, happy coed, with no trace of her mother's hard expression.[78]

The final picture, from the school paper *This Is Centenary* in August 1948, accompanies an article about French's upcoming retirement. The older woman faces the camera. Her chin is still lifted, and she looks past the camera to the side. Her expression is softer, the eyes gently amused. The mouth holds a faint smile. Gone are the robes: she is wearing a jacket, blouse, and brooch. She is a woman whose battles are behind her, and she wears an expression of bemused contentment.[79]

Dr. and Mr. French remained in Shreveport after her retirement. French settled into retirement, moping with loneliness, missing her grandchildren:

Lodestars of my life!
Two angels great and small
Why are you so lingering
And come not to me at all?

For light is drawing on
And after that the night!
Hark, now, I hear you softly
All is joy and bright.[80]

The family continued to reunite in Kentucky in the summer and for some holidays as well. In July 1953, French was asked to be guest of honor at the 1954 Laurel County Homecoming.[81]

Other than one important incident that will be detailed in part 2, French did not seem to have had much in the way of excitement in her last years. In fact, to relieve her boredom, she spent time cataloging her huge personal collection of *National Geographic* magazines by volume, date, and subject matter on index cards. She lacked goals and adventure for the first time in her life. "My work is all over," she wrote, "and I am lost."[82]

(*Above, left*) Katherine Jackson French, 1930. Courtesy of Centenary College of Louisiana Archives and Special Collections. (*Above, right*) Katherine Jackson French, 1934. Courtesy of Centenary College of Louisiana Archives and Special Collections.

(*Left*) Katherine Jackson French, 1948. Courtesy of Kay Tolbert Buckland.

On Christmas Eve, 1955, a fine winter night, twelve-year-old Kay Tolbert went to bed looking forward to Christmas festivities the next morning. Instead, she was wakened by a neighbor and told that her grandfather Frank was dead. His passing was a shock; he had been in seemingly fine health the day before, helping the family with holiday preparations. The body was returned to London and laid out in Annie Pollard's home. The funeral service was held there two days later. The family attended, as did sixteen honorary bearers. French kept the ceremony book, making detailed notes of the hymns sung, scripture read, who the pallbearers were, who called (over 140 people), and what family and friends attended. She noted that "Crossing the Bar" was read at the grave and also took notes on the sermon, writing "Integrity, honor, justice, mercy, love for God and Man, happiness and usefulness to end" under the heading "Lessons from a good life."[83]

By the time Frank died, French's son-in-law, Carl Tolbert, had already changed occupations and begun working for an insurance company, deciding that it would pay the bills better than teaching music and playing the clarinet and better enable him to provide for his family. In 1954, he accepted a job as an assistant manager for the firm and moved his family to Atlanta. French, her husband gone and her career over, went with them. Prior to her departure, the Woman's Department Club of Shreveport awarded her a life membership: "No one in Shreveport has contributed so generously of both time and talent as have you, and now that you will be away from us part of the year we feel that we cannot pass up this opportunity to say a hearty 'thank you' from us all."[84]

After a short time in Atlanta, Carl accepted a promotion to the position of manager and moved the family to Columbia, South Carolina, during the summer of 1957. Columbia was a good-sized city by then, and Kay Tolbert Buckland remembers the family living across the street from a lake in a neighborhood with many pine trees. The house had a large porch, and neighborhood children would sleep out on it on cots during the summer while the adults played cards.[85]

"The Rose Still Grows beyond the Wall"

By this time, however, French had started to ail. Past useful work, separated from her sister Annie, who was "so alone and not well," and away from the two cities she loved (Shreveport and London), she began to succumb to the heart ailment that had plagued her for decades. She was bedridden almost from the day she moved with Carl and Katherine to Columbia. Her daughter tried to care for her, and a Dr. Miller made house calls, but she worsened. She was able to come downstairs for Christmas dinner, which Jackson's niece Eloise Jackson Pennington says "made [them] all feel better." But French was not to heal.[86]

French's daughter, Katherine, called R.Z., the African American woman who had worked as a servant for French during her many years in Shreveport. R.Z. came to Columbia, staying between six and nine months and tending French. The time came when even R.Z.'s ministrations were not enough, and French was placed in a nursing home in Columbia. According to Kay Toland Buckland, Carl and Katherine had "a huge battle": "My father insisted. . . . And I remember how upset my mother was because she did not want to put Grandmother in the nursing home. . . . It was a very difficult time for her."[87]

French suffered several heart attacks during her stay at the rest home. Her daughter visited her there "all the time," Kay Buckland remembered. "I went some with her. . . . She [French] was just laying there, almost not even aware."[88]

On Monday, November 10, 1958, Katherine Jackson French passed from this world. And thus the family gathered one last time in French's beloved London.

"Grandmother wouldn't have wanted us to cry and be sad," said Kay Buckland. "She would have wanted us to sing and be happy." And sing they did: "There was some member of the family, and I couldn't tell you who it was, probably someone Mother's age or maybe one of their children, could play the piano and could play by ear. And so we sang all night long. . . . I don't remember the songs. Everybody sang. . . . I don't remember whose house we went back to, but it was after the ceremony and all. I just remember for several hours we all sang . . . all songs that everybody knew but I couldn't tell you what they were."[89]

Services were conducted on Thursday, November 13. Over seventy friends signed the "Those Who Called" book. There were forty-seven floral tributes. As at Frank's funeral, Tennyson's "Crossing the Bar" appears in the program:

> But such a tide as moving seems asleep
> Too full for tide and foam

> When that which drew from out the boundless deep
> Turns again home.[90]

Katherine Jackson French was laid to rest next to her husband, Frank, in the Jackson family founders' plot in the Russell Dyche Cemetery in London. Her grave lies less than a mile from where she grew up.

Tributes poured in from Shreveport. Books were placed in libraries in French's honor, charities given money in her name. Several boxes of letters in regard to her death still exist. "You'd think everybody in Shreveport knew my grandmother," said Kay Buckland.[91] One letter reads: "Think of all the people whose lives were enriched because she passed their way." Another notes: "She was such a wonderful woman that it is difficult to put into writing what we, her friends, feel. Erudite, stimulating, yet down to earth and interested in the minutest bit that affected people and particularly her friends, which are legion. Public spirited, gregarious, deeply spiritual, and a great inspiration to so many both in the cultural and religious life of our community, her name will ever be enchrined [sic] in the hearts of her friends, the church, the organizations to which she belonged."[92]

Cecelia Ellerbe, her fellow cofounder of the Shreveport Woman's Department Club, had the last word on Katherine Jackson French. At the club's tribute to French the following January, she read a poem she had written in honor of her friend:

> Let this be said, for honor is her due,
> She was a teacher, one who loved this art
> That was the highest privilege she knew
> By right of knowledge, that she could impart
>
> The meaning of a life is in its thought
> And in the measure of the mind its test
> The good she knew, the wisdom that she sought
> These were the substance of her last bequest
> To keep when strength had failed and breath was spent
> To be her final wish and testament.
>
> The years have gone, and life has reached its end,
> Now Peace belongs to her, scholar and friend.[93]

Dr. Katherine Jackson French. Courtesy of Kay Tolbert Buckland.

Katherine Jackson French lived many lives in her one life: daughter, sister, wife, student, schoolteacher, professor, mother, writer, traveler, friend, neighbor, community member, dean, genealogist, Sunday school teacher, scholar, founder of an important women's department club and inspiration to the women of Shreveport, leader of university women, and pioneer ballad collector. Despite an ongoing heart condition and a world unaccustomed to the achievements of women, she accomplished all this on her own terms.

The opening page of the service book for French's funeral reads: "If life is sacred, it should not be allowed to perish. . . . We are not dead until we are forgotten."[94] Sadly, Katherine Jackson French has indeed been forgotten.

Traces of her are impossible to find in her birthplace. No one there remembers any mention of her. Only a few echoes linger in Shreveport. There is no mention of her at Centenary College, no statue, no plaque, no marker, although a framed photograph and an inscribed gold plaque of Dr. Stewart A. Steger hangs outside the office of the chair of the English Department.[95] There are no markers to her at the Shreveport First Methodist Church, though she taught Sunday school there for thirty-one years. Streets bear the names of other founders of the Woman's Department Club—Ellerbe, Wilkinson—but the only monument to her is the lonely plaque that hangs in the back of the auditorium of the Shreveport Woman's Department Club, thanking her for sharing her gifts and changing the lives of thousands of women.

This remarkable pioneer—the first collector, male or female, to attempt to publish a large scholarly collection of southern Appalachian ballads, a mover and shaker in the Louisiana AAUW, the cofounder of the Shreveport Woman's Department Club, a beloved professor at Centenary College, and a proud daughter of London, Kentucky—has been consigned to obscurity by the passing of years and a seemingly willful ignorance on the part of her time and ours regarding the accomplishments of such women. That her feats have largely been ignored or forgotten makes them no less glorious. She was a giant, and like many other forgotten giants, she paved the way for other women who followed, breaking down walls that might still be in place without her efforts. Indeed, "honor is her due," and hers is a name worthy of remembrance.

PART 2

"THE STURDINESS AND TRUTH OF SONG"

They have lived because they have been loved.
                                    Katherine Jackson French

4

"A Fortnight of Balladry"

Jackson had studied medieval literary balladry while at Columbia University, so it was natural that she was intrigued by the idea of old ballads of the sung variety being kept alive in the Kentucky mountains.[1]

The ballads that Jackson's classmates told her about and that she eventually sought were descendants of the same ballads that Francis Child had collected in Great Britain and immortalized in *The English and Scottish Popular Ballads*.[2] These songs left the Old World, sailed with immigrants to New England or Virginia, and then clambered over the mountains from eastern Virginia or Pennsylvania into Appalachia. These musical fables are old; some date back to the thirteenth century and, as Ron Pen reminded me, give a sort of eternal window into issues of "race, gender, class, power relationships, identity, and memory."[3]

The early collectors—and Jackson was no exception—focused on these British Isle ballad escapees. Though some of the collectors may have had a variety of motives, they held one thing in common: they thought these ballads to be worthy of their efforts, eschewing other kinds of music from other kinds of people. It was a bias that was sometimes manifested in a condescending and explanatory racism ("[The Negro's] . . . mental processes are not adequate to the burden which some scholars have imposed upon him"),[4] derisive dismissiveness ("When we reached the cove, we found it peopled by niggers . . . all our troubles and spent energy for nought"),[5] or wishful racial identification ("This little booklet . . . will represent the life and spirit of a people in whose veins runs the purest strain of Anglo-Saxon blood to be found anywhere in America.)[6]

The last quote brings up a paradoxical circumstance: the ballads discovered in America were determined by the early collectors to be of both English

Berea College president William Goodell Frost.

and Scottish origin, but the ballads themselves were invariably referred to as being *Anglo-Saxon*. Of the immigrants who fled the Scottish Lowlands for northern Ireland and then wound up in southern Appalachia, most were actually Scots, not Englishmen. This is a case of trying to jam a square peg into a round hole. The Scots were, in fact, neither Anglo nor Saxon; their ancestry was largely Celtic. Yet the claim of the ballads' exclusive and unblemished Anglo-Saxon origin was to continue unchallenged for close to a century.

The social conditions that led to the establishment of that claim are double-edged, and no one exemplifies that better than Berea College president William Goodell Frost. Berea's original mission was interracial and coeducational education; when the segregationist Day Law was passed in 1901, Frost took on a new focus: recruitment of mountain young people.

The stereotype of "mountain people" prevailing at the time was that they were white, ignorant, dirty, and dangerous. On the one hand, Frost sought to redeem them from that stereotype by exalting them as "of pure English and Scottish stock" and giving them a chance to better themselves through a Berea education. On the other hand, he viewed the population of the southern mountains as utilitarian "reserve forces for the coming battles of America and of Protestant Christianity" against "the foreign born and hyphenated population." This notion of the white race being overrun by Catholics, Jews, and other non-Anglo foreigners was a prospect that many white people feared.[7]

Exaltation of Angloness went neatly hand in hand with that fear, and the collecting of Anglo balladry was a part of that. The fact that ballad collectors in those same mountains were finding a wealth of supposedly pure, ancient Anglo song implied, by extension, a superior and eternal value to Anglo culture. The very longevity of these songs in the face of hardship indicated, in this view, the inherent superiority of the culture from which they sprang and promised the continued dominance of that culture in the future.[8]

Jackson's own interest in these ballads came from a variety of motives. First, as a scholar of English literature, Jackson was interested in and appreciated them for their own sake and expressed a kind of awed delight at experiencing them firsthand. Second, she was out to make a name for herself in academe, and this seemed a handy way to do so. Third, she was a woman acquainted with and proud of her Scottish heritage (though, like Bradley Kincaid, she equated that to being Anglo-Saxon) and therefore felt a personal connection to the ballads. Finally, she was a believer in the power of English literature and English culture. As with other early collectors, this resulted in a bias of omission against other musics of the mountains.

We are fortunate to have the adventure of Jackson's 1909 ballad-collecting trip detailed by Jackson herself in a manuscript entitled "A Fortnight of Balladry." An abbreviated version of this was published as "A Fortnight in Ballad Country" in *Mountain Life and Work* in 1955, three years before her death.[9] In both the manuscript and the published versions, she describes riding off at dawn with a wagon, a team of three mules, and a companion named Lizane, "a carefree widow of sixty." Lizane was to serve as Jackson's guide and go-between. "Convinced of the honesty of my journey," Jackson writes, "she freely

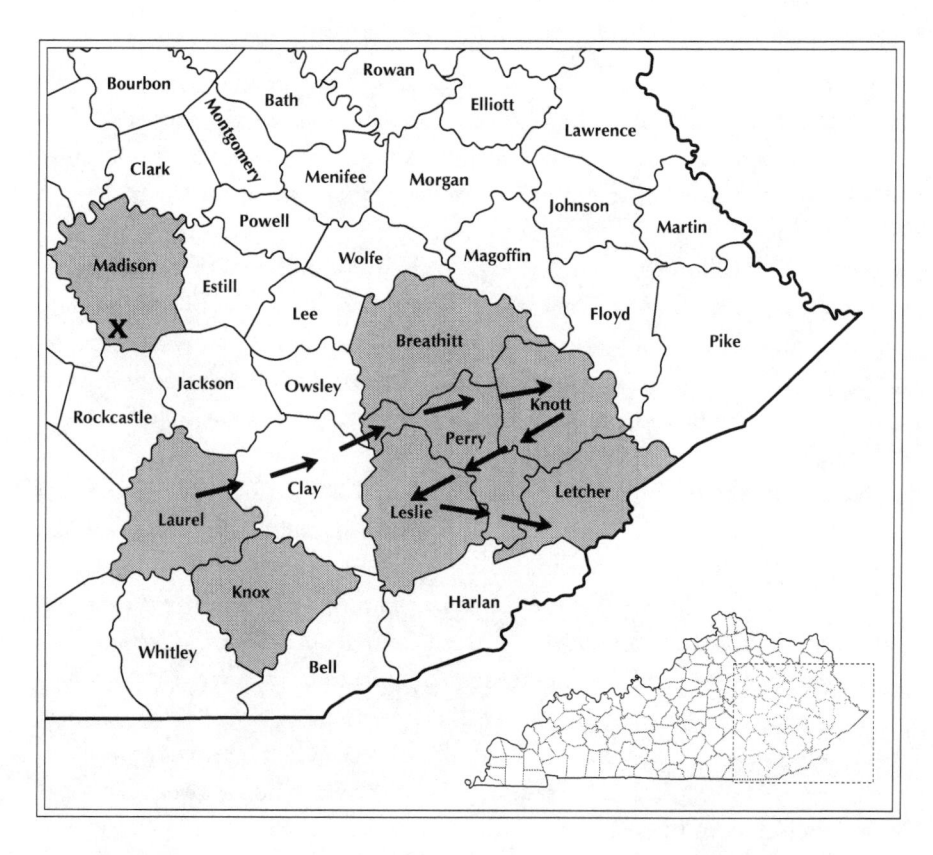

The areas in eastern Kentucky visited by Katherine Jackson and directions traveled on her 1909 trip into the mountains. She also collected later in Berea and in Madison County; that trip too has thus been highlighted. Map by Dick Gilbreath, independent cartographer.

offered me her friendship and assistance, which pre-ordained my success." The selection of Lizane as a companion was sheer dumb luck. Jackson had heard that a wagon loaded with merchandise was to head into the mountains; Lizane was a passenger and had no objection to another woman climbing aboard.[10]

Jackson admits that, at the journey's beginning, she was not familiar with the ballads she eventually found but "fully realized that they were an immemorial record of the pure ancestry of the singers, and an undoubted proof of the sturdiness and truth of song."[11] In this, she seems to concur with Frost and other early collectors: the existence of the ballads went hand in hand with the pure Anglo-Saxon bloodline of Appalachians and the lengthy ancestry of the both the songs and the singers.

In the manuscript version, Jackson lovingly describes the autumn morning of the trip's first day. She reminisces: "The first frost had colored the leaves, ripened the apples, the persimmons, and the pawpaws, and had given a crisp tinge to every variety of mountain life."[12]

Jackson tells us that the initial leg of the journey was sixty miles into the mountains to Lizane's house, "where I was made comfortable." The trip took three days. Lizane would take no money from Jackson for her keeping, though Jackson did pay for the white and bay mules to be used on their journey. The first house visited was "Sister Marthy's" (Lizane's sister, Martha Begley), fifteen miles up a dry creek bed, as there was no road. They were greeted by two boys, whom Katherine describes as "fatherless," and were welcomed "heartily." After a simple supper of corn pone bread, bacon fat, and coffee, the singing began. "Of course the guest sang first, and obtained their confidence," Jackson records. "After some persuasion and assurance of friendship, the family unlocked its word-horde, and for two days we had a feast of song." As the host, Marthy held court most of the time, "swaying back and forth in her low, straight chair, singing loudly and clearly." Jackson asked her hosts to sing the songs more than once, no doubt to transcribe them, remarking that "they were glad to repeat them" and that they seemed pleased by her interest. Ever the academic, Jackson noted "the usual landmarks of the ballads—rapidity, change from narrative to dialogue, alliteration, overflow, impure rhyme and assonance, many recurring phrases and epithets, frequent use of the numerals three and seven, a barbaric profusion of silver and gold, and always simple thought, direct and distinct, with that emphasis that springs from the need of expressing in a few words, some deep passion."[13]

Marthy and Lizane sang "Lord Thomas" together, and, when they sang "Sweet William and Lady Margaret," Jackson was "almost overcome with the transport of the centuries":[14]

Sweet William arose one May morning
And dressed himself in blue
"Oh, tell me about that long, long love
That's between Lady Margaret and you."[15]

Indeed, the song invoked for her the presence of Chaucer, Shakespeare, the

"Sweet William and Lady Margaret," collected by Katherine Jackson French. Manuscript.

British Isle collectors John Dryden and Thomas Percy, Sir Walter Scott, and Queen Elizabeth. "These were my invisible companions," she said later.[16]

The boys also displayed their musical ability and played banjo together. Jackson noted their "force and decision expanding into rough jollity." However, like most collectors of the day, she was interested in ballads and did not spend much time or energy making note of anything else. Except for a few adjectives describing the boys' playing and a description of one boy striking the neck of the banjo with knitting needles while another "played upon the usual part of the instrument," it is overall a disappointing loss of an opportunity to learn about banjo styles of the mountains in 1909 and corresponding incarnations of those melodies.[17] Jackson did note the tunes the boys played:

> The Jacobite airs to Prince Charlie
> The Swapping Song of Jack Straw
> Sourwood Mountain
> Hawk and Chicken
> Long Yeared Mule
> Rosin and Bow
> Nubbin Ridge
> Forked Deer.[18]

The boys also sang "Callahan's Confessions." Jackson is the first collector to make note of this song in the Appalachians. She thought that it was modeled after "McPherson's Farewell" or "Lord Maxwell's Goodnight." She considered it to be a "goodnight" ballad, modeled after a long line of Scottish songs supposedly composed by a rebel outlaw who is about to be hanged. (As with many folk songs, numerous places claim it as their own.)[19]

Jackson noted the existence of fiddle tunes but was not impressed with the singing of the men she encountered. She was seeking ballads, and men did not seem to sing them, gravitating instead toward eighteenth-century hymns and songs like "Annie Laurie," "Ben Bolt," "Blue Bells of Scotland," and "Maid of Dundee."[20]

Two days after the visit to Marthy, Jackson and Lizane got invited to an all-day quilting bee, which involved twelve women using a wooden frame to make a sun-dial-design quilt. Jackson describes a sort of potluck of sewing equipment and food; everyone brought gifts for the hostess, and the food included sour milk, molasses, and honey. She describes the gathering as "strikingly homogenous, breathing one unlettered atmosphere, one habit of thought and life, one measure of support and sympathy."[21]

One wonders whether some of this communal feeling was because her subjects were mostly women. In remote settings, women were often less powerful than men, more subject to the ravages of life. Every pregnancy was a chance at new life, but it was also an equal chance at death. Women of the mountains—all women of the mountains—were bonded by this circumstance regardless of race or heritage. They were thus more prone to pursue collaboration than competition and to understand that they counted on each other.

The community Jackson visited on this trip was cut off from modernity, such as it was in 1909. She reports that the women were familiar with no modern stories but knew about the headless horseman, a figure from Celtic mythology predating Washington Irving's appropriation of it. Thus isolated, she infers, they made their own entertainment, as had been done since the earliest days of settlement.[22]

Singing at the quilting bee started with "Barbara Allen." Jackson talks of hearing British schoolchildren carefully taught to sing the song. In contrast, she proclaims: "Here, in these backwoods, mothers and children sang it voluntarily and with great avidity, without any suggestion from the world." Jackson relates some of the "crude" elements of the version she heard that day, including the phrases "hick'ry buds a-swellin'," "sweat on him a-streamin'," "ricamember the other day," and "murty drinkin'." These images seem mild to the twenty-first-century ear, but, to a refined, educated woman of 1909, and according to the mores of the day, they were graphic and shocking. Jackson also notes that the hero's name changed from singer to singer and that the names used included Sir Jeems Graham, Sweet William, Johnny, or William Green and that the final two verses had their origin in ballads like "Lord Lovell" and "Sweet William and Fair Margaret."[23]

Jackson lists nonsense refrains heard in that day's songs, including "sing lay the lilly lo," "down by the greenwood side," and "bow down, bow down." She also notes an air played by a woman on dulcimer. Her description of the instrument indicated that it was "shaped somewhat like a violin, only with two swells, and a short neck," and that it gave "a smooth, flowing sound, with a sort of weird, melancholy cadence, and the tenderness of a wind, wailing in a mountain cave."[24]

As to the melodies of the ballads heard that day, she again gives us detail: "The airs to the long ballads, not intended for dancing, and different from the ditties, are expressive, tender, plaintive, sometimes cheerful, more often morose. The last note falls gradually to the keynote at the end. Another peculiar feature, difficult to express in written music, is the long interval after each phrase—well-calculated for recitation and for recovery of breath. All exist in only one part, although capable of exquisite harmonies."[25]

One woman brought "all her ballets"—written on sheets of paper "yellowed with age and difficult to read"—to show Jackson. A *ballet* was what the women called any type of song that had been written down. This particular woman said some of songs had been given to her "by her grandmother, who had taken them down from her pioneer grandmother," meaning that they dated from the time of the settlement of Kentucky in the early nineteenth century. Jackson does not mention copying these down or borrowing them, so in all likelihood the old papers remained with their owner and crumbled to dust in someone's attic. She did, however, notate many of the melodies she heard that day.[26]

Jackson provides a partial list of ballads from her visit, which included the following:

Barbara Allen
Lord Lovel
Lord Randall

"A Fortnight of Balladry"   67

We're met, we're met, my own true love, We're met, we're met cried she I've just re-turned from the salt salt sea and it's all for the love of thee. and it's all for the love of thee.

"The House Carpenter," collected by Katherine Jackson. Transcribed by Elizabeth DiSavino.

> Wealthy Young Squire
> Lord Vanner's Wife (Matty Groves variant)
> Pretty Polly
> Seven King's Daughters (Lady Isabel and the Elf Knight)
> Loving Henry (Young Hunting and Lady Margaret)
> Lord Bateman (The Turkish Lady)
> Two Brothers
> The Cruel Mother
> Twa Sisters
> Edward
> Lovers Farewell (Lass of Loch Royal).[27]

After the quilting bee, Jackson and Lizane spent some days traveling about. Jackson lists Viper, Sassafras, and Cut Shin Creek as towns they visited and talks about going to several funerals. One was for someone who had died during the winter; the body had been buried, but the service had been held off until the "pleasant weather."[28] Jackson and Lizane also visited Troublesome, stopping in on a young newly wedded woman who was living in an unfinished cabin. The young woman sang "The Bailiff's Daughter," which Jackson wrote down. A neighbor, Bettie, visited, "spread her collection out before [them]," and sang "The House Carpenter" ("The Demon Lover"). Bettie swayed as she sang, "looking directly out the door and apparently unconscious of the listeners."[29]

There are a number of colloquialisms in Bettie's version of "The House Carpenter" that replace the original British phrasing, including "we're met" for "well-met" and "I'm sure she woulda married me" for "and fain she would have married me." This supernatural tale, in which the lover returns as a ghost to his beloved, has had many powerful incarnations, and Jackson says of Bettie's version: "Never did I enjoy hearing it more than at this time." A lonely song sung in a lonely place on a lonely mountain—there is a power in such things, a sense of rightness, of coming home. As Jackson put it: "[Ballads] stir one in a strangely intimate fashion, to which artistic verse can rarely attain. . . . The ballad is not dead, but alive and appealing, not as an individual call, but as an outcry from a community of lonely people."[30]

Jackson was hoping to find a song from the days of Chaucer, "Little Hugh of Lincoln" (the story of "a little chorister . . . who is murdered by the Jews for his devotion to the Blessed Virgin"), and stumbled on it while visiting a woman who wove "coverlids." It was a rainy day, and the woman, trying to recall the song, murmured: "It rains a mist." The rest of the song followed easily. "Two Sisters" was collected from a very old lady who called it "The Lord of the Low Country." "Lady Gay" ("The Wife of Usher's Well") was collected "from a pathetic old woman, who walked a long way to see me," which prompted Lizane to sing "The Greenwood Side" ("The Cruel Mother").[31]

Lizane deserves some attention. The daughter of Mary and Farris Begley, she was born in 1857. Her husband was Hiram Napier of Perry County. The Napiers were a musical family, but, more to the point, Lizane was born a Begley, and that was also a highly musical family. There are a number of Begleys who figure into the history of Appalachian music. The "Singing Sherriff" of Perry County, Justus Begley, recorded for Alan Lomax in the 1930s, and a "Big Hiram" Begley recorded in the 1930s in Clay County; both were likely kin to Lizane. Lizane's mother was a York, which is of interest as balladry often passed down the matrilineal side of families, but no further information about her is available.[32]

Jackson did not grow up a mountain woman. She was an upper-class, educated town woman. Her father's affluence afforded her gowns to wear to dances, music lessons, private tutors, foxhunts, and the privilege of attending college. One wonders whether she would have found so many mountain women eager to share their songs had she ventured into the mountains alone. Referring to her own 1930 collecting trip, Dorothy Scarborough speaks of initial reticence on the part of some of her informants. Similarly, Ada Smith might never have sung "Barbara Allen" in 1907 to Olive Dame Campbell had Katherine Pettit, Campbell's host, not encouraged her to do so. Outsiders like Jackson needed an intermediary. Lizane Napier was accepted by all the households she and Jackson visited, and, thus, so was Jackson. Her presence guaranteed Jackson an open door wherever they went.[33]

A warm relationship developed between the old mountain woman and the young scholar while the two tramped about the mountains together. When it was time for Jackson to go back home, Lizane sang "The Lover's Farewell" (based on "The Lass of Loch Royal"). The friendship and fondness shared by these two women is evident in Lizane's choice of this song. The third verse is not common:

> The time draws near, my dearest dear,
> When you and I shall part
> How little do you know the grief
> Of my poor aching heart
>
> Lord that I could go with you
> Or you could tarry here
> Your company is so charming love
> So charming is to me
>
> It will make me think when you are away
> That a day is three and an hour is ten
> It makes me weep, when I might sleep
> And say I've lost a friend.

With this song of parting, Jackson returned to London.[34]

In the end, it was not the English or the Scottish who were most exalted in Jackson's view but rather the women of the mountains. In her travels Jackson encountered forty-four singers: thirty-one women and thirteen men.[35] She strongly felt that women should be credited for keeping Appalachian balladry alive. "I realized [on that initial trip] that to the women is credit of this preservation due," she declares, and she finds the reason obvious: "The women, in their constant intercourse with the children, come nearer the heart of the tales, and are keener at picturing the tragic situation and in sympathizing with the crying out of the soul of the woman in the ballad. The mother's monotonous environment and condition of life make the story seem both natural and true."³⁶

Jackson describes what she encounters in blunt terms. Her portrait of mountain women is unsparing. She describes one young woman, recently married, living in "an old log house, ceiled with undressed lumber, and blackened by smoke from the open fire. In order to make it more habitable, the woman had pasted fresh newspapers all over the walls and ceiling of the one big room."³⁷ She also talks about a "pathetic old lady who walked a long distance" to see her and, in a later newspaper article, is quoted as referring to a visit to another woman as spending the night in "a rather horrible hovel."³⁸ She depicts both the despondency and the resiliency of the women she saw. She describes the abject poverty she encountered but praises the women for their communal ways and for keeping the art of ballad singing alive. She finds a kind of transcendence exhibited by these women in their insistence on beauty in the midst of lives of despair. It is to women, "the singing mothers of Colonial America," that she dedicated her collection of ballads.³⁹

At least twenty-three ballads from nine sources were collected on this trip. Jackson kept no record of other collecting trips, though in her later life she refers to *trips* in the plural and to informants not mentioned in her extant collection or in her account of this trip. In a later newspaper article, she is quoted as saying she spent five months in the mountains.⁴⁰ We also know that she collected from students and townspeople in Berea during her visits there. In later letters, other trips are alluded to, but no details are given. Altogether, Jackson compiled a collection of over sixty ballads and an unknown number of variants from an undetermined number of sources. Of these, forty-three variants of twenty-eight ballads from seventeen informants still exist today in either lyric or lyric with music form.

In a sense, we are fortunate that Jackson was new to ballad singing. This allowed her to view it with a clear eye and describe details that someone raised in the tradition might take for granted. And what did her description of those details tell us?

A great deal, it would seem:

- That ballad singing was done as communal entertainment at gatherings and in the home in 1909 and that the practice was both greatly valued and entered into with no sense of pomp or ceremony.

Mrs. Lucy Banks of Madison County, Ky, who weaves coverlids and sings ballads of the long ago.

Lucy Banks of Madison County, one of Jackson's informants.

- That such sings could go on for long periods of time and that these sometimes occurred at working social events like quilting bees.
- That some of the ballads being sung were lyrically the same as or very similar to the British versions previously collected by Francis Child (in his monumental *English and Scottish Popular Ballads*) and others.
- That the dulcimer was being played in the Kentucky back mountains, as was the banjo.
- That old Scottish and English ballads were being sung as a matter of course.
- That some of these versions, both melodically and lyrically, were different than any other versions collected.

- That people did not always pass on everything orally but in fact had written collections of ballads.
- That one written collection of ballads dated back four generations.
- That, at least in Katherine Jackson's experience, women were more interested in singing ballads than were men.[41]
- That fiddle tunes were alive in the mountains at that time and that at least one style of banjo playing was being taught.
- That ballads were usually sung unaccompanied, either by one person or by a roomful of people together, that the dulcimer was used occasionally to accompany ballads, and that the banjo was used to play tunes.
- That women sometimes swayed back and forth in their chairs when they sang, as if davening.
- That there were elongated notes at the ends of phrases when ballads were sung.
- That songs were sung at important occasions, like partings.

Thus, we learned a great deal just from Jackson's first foray into the hills, seven years before the publication of Campbell and Sharp's *English Folk Songs from the Southern Appalachians*. It is all here, all in one place, collected, notated, and commented on by a still-unknown young woman from London, Kentucky.

5

Berea Beloved

After making several collecting trips, Jackson began to search for ways to publish the material she had gathered. Her thoughts immediately turned to Berea College. Thus ensued a five-year, confusing, frustrating, and ultimately futile attempt to publish "English-Scottish Ballads from the Hills of Kentucky."[1]

The broad strokes of this effort have been known for some time, thanks to Sidney Saylor Farr's "Appalachian Ballad Collectors," written under the tutelage of Loyal Jones. Jackson asks for Berea's help; William Goodell Frost says yes; things seem to move forward; two years down the road things have gotten stuck, much to Jackson's despair; and finally, in 1915, she asks for the collection back.[2]

It was logical for Jackson to assume that Berea would be interested in her collection since lecturers it sponsored first brought the subject of balladry to her attention. Besides, she had heard of collecting efforts going on at Berea, and, in fact, the month before she contacted the college, the *Berea Quarterly* published a five-page article on mountain songs that included five verses from and a synopsis of "Lord Thomas and Fair Ellender." Jackson may also have heard of the work of James Watt Raine, a professor of English and theater at Berea whose own collecting efforts began in 1908.[3]

In fact, Berea's commitment to all things Appalachian was quite well-known by Jackson's time, owing in large part to President William Goodell Frost's constant travels and fund-raising efforts in which he highlighted Appalachian culture and history, with special attention paid to the crafts and music of the Appalachian people. As the Berea College archivist Harry Rice points out, however, not all Berea faculty thought that the study of traditional Appalachian music had a place in the curriculum. Some held that it had "little literary or musical value."[4]

Berea College. Photograph by A. J. Bodnar.

Frost and several other faculty members, including Raine, did not concur. They believed that the music of Appalachia should be taught and honored along with conventional Western classical music. (This dichotomy has existed throughout Berea's history, a century-old tug-of-war that has reached a happy equilibrium in the past few decades.)[5]

Given all this, it made sense for Jackson to approach Berea College cheerfully and with the full expectation of its interest. In October 1910, she wrote directly to President William Goodell Frost:

> As I am very interested in the publication of the early English ballads, as sung in the mountains of Kentucky, and having heard that you are likewise concerned, I presume to address you. I want to edit and publish, this winter, my collection,—some familiar, ancient ones, with striking variations; others, remarkably preserved; some direct imitations made in colonial days, and some modern imitations,—giving an introduction concerning ballad history, traditions, preservation, . . . and critical notes of a literary and philological character.

My reason for doing this now is because of my being at liberty from pressing work,—having given up my duties as Lecturer in English Literature at Bryn Mawr College, to be with an aged mother, who resides in this village. Should we be able to unite forces, I wish you to realize in the beginning, that my interest is purely scholarly, that I care for no pecuniary returns, but should be happy to dedicate the royalty to your work.

If you feel at all inclined to consider this,—your allowing me to use your ballads and data, my adding my own and doing the work,— due credit being given to every one, who has contributed to the enterprise, with the royalty to be donated to Berea College, to be used as you direct,—will you please address me at once.

Yours faithfully,
M. Katherine Jackson.[6]

This project had to appeal to Frost. Jackson's letter makes it clear that she was accomplished in the field of English literature, that she had taught at an important college, that she was willing to bring to print not only her own ballads but the college's as well, that she wished no financial remuneration, and that in the end the royalty and ownership of the publication would go to Berea College. Berea would risk nothing and gain everything. An invitation to visit was proffered. A month later, Miss M. Katherine Jackson was en route to Berea College from her home in London, arriving on November 28, 1910.[7]

Eleanor

It was to Eleanor Marsh Frost, Berea's First Lady, that the management of Jackson's visit fell. Mrs. Frost, like Jackson, was an educated woman. Her lineage—old New England stock—was in its own way as exalted as Jackson's. She met William Goodell Frost when she first worked for him as a housekeeper while attending Oberlin College. After his first wife died, Eleanor Marsh completed her schooling and promptly married her employer one week after graduation. She quickly became a vital helpmate to Frost in his work at Berea.[8]

According to a contemporary account, Mrs. Frost's character was one of serenity, a trait in direct contrast to the temperament of her husband: "She was a balance wheel for an impetuous, red-headed husband. I never saw her ruffled." Eleanor attended suffragette meetings, sometimes bringing her somewhat reluctant husband with her. She was very active in working with women in more conventional roles as well.[9]

Mid-1909 found Eleanor despondent over the death of a baby niece. She wrote of a "strange, aimless, indifferent existence" during this time. In mid-1910, she had a bicycle accident that left her bedridden for a prolonged period of time.[10]

Enter Katherine Jackson, an accomplished, poised woman who had an ambitious project on the table and was requesting Berea's help. One would have expected that Jackson was exactly the kind of woman Mrs. Frost would have embraced and held up as an example for the young women of the college and that Mrs. Frost would be excited about her project. Surprisingly, however, she was not immediately enthused with either the idea of Jackson's visit or her collection. She initially viewed the visit as an intrusion and an unpleasant duty, one that would fall solely on her shoulders owing to her husband's absence. "A week from today, the ballad collector comes," she wrote resignedly to her husband, who was in New York at the time, "and I shall have to give some time to her. . . . I had planned my social on Dress for Saturday afternoon, but the reception for Miss Jackson will have to take its place."[11]

It is possible that Eleanor was still depressed by the death of her niece, still in pain from her accident, or exhausted by her trip to England and Scotland that summer, but she may also have absorbed some of her husband's lackadaisical attitude. Despite his proclaimed interest in the importance of Appalachian ballad collecting, William Goodell Frost was not optimistic about Jackson's upcoming visit. His initial discomfort was due, however, not to his attitude toward balladry, but to ongoing feuds among the Berea faculty and the accompanying personal vanities and self-interests that might hinder or disrupt Jackson's visit. He told Mrs. Frost:

> I fear the Ballad Collector will not find an appreciative or sympathetic atmosphere in Berea. Even Raine has showed but light interest, and all the material Raymond has collected has been lost in his rubbish heap. It is a crying shame. There is a good chance among our students to collect and collate but that cursed ignorance of the half enlightened man like Seale often seals up those sources. Miss Douglas, when she is under our influence, can do much. I am grateful that

you are in Berea, and hope we can really annex the lady from Bryn Mawr and London. Her coming may help to give confidence to Miss Douglas, and the hostile element can be concealed, and our work concealed from them.[12]

This is intriguing. The impassioned collector James Watt Raine seems uninterested in his fellow ballad collector from London. C. Rex Raymond is too flighty to court interest. Alice K. Douglas (who was a teacher and the head of the Ladies' Hall) seems timid, easily manipulated, and without a clear opinion of her own. Ellis Seale (who taught Latin and mathematics through the advanced academy program) appears to be downright hostile to the idea of ballad study altogether, discouraging and perhaps even suppressing student interest in the subject. In fact, he wanted references to and the inclusion of ballads dropped from all Berea publications. Frost's letter further refers to the hostile element in the plural, meaning that Seale was not alone in his antagonism. Finally, the idea that a college president would feel the need to keep this sort of endeavor hidden from those who might oppose it points either to a simple desire to avoid conflict or to the fear that those hostile elements could derail Jackson's visit. In short, Jackson was walking into a hornet's nest of preformed opinions, prejudices, self-interests, and egos.[13]

Eleanor Frost was cognizant of all this and tried her best to lay some groundwork before Jackson's arrival, musing: "I believe it will be better received after I have gotten into closer relation with more people as I have with a few."[14] Exactly what this wooing consisted of and how she went about it are not spelled out. She was fairly close to Raine by this point in time; a friend recalls him attending her and William's wedding, and her diary speaks of visits and dinners with him, so he was certainly among the "closer relations" to which she refers. Others may have proved less amiable.[15]

Katherine Jackson arrived in Berea on November 28, 1910. Any ennui from which Mrs. Frost might have suffered evaporated completely during the fortnight that Jackson stayed at the Frost residence. Eleanor quickly came to see her as a kindred spirit and potentially a great asset to the college. She sent her husband the following account of Jackson's visit:

> As the Gortons departed, Miss Jackson arrived. She was "born and raised" in Laurel County. Her family and relatives are there, grandfa-

ther was there. So she is a bonafide mountain woman. She prepared for College with tutors and at Science Hill, Shelbyville, took A.B. and A.M. degrees at Ohio Wesleyan, taught two years in South. Studied at Columbia and took Ph.D. degree. Taught literature in Holyoke three years, and in Bryn Mawr one. / On first afternoon, she talked with Professor Raine. Her trip through the back countries had been much more fruitful than his, she having secured there fifty genuine ballads. I think he felt the contrast. In evening, Miss Collette gathered mountain girls in her room and Miss Jackson had "sing" with them. Yesterday morning I took her to Miss Douglas's Report Division which I have charge of in her absence. I wish you might have heard her talk and have seen the result. At the mention of certain ballads, the hands went up, a goodly number. Her presentation of the subject was perfect and adapted. / Next on my program, was our Mountain teacher. In a long talk I had with Seale some time ago, he mentioned the ballads as an unnecessary feature in our publications. That was just as he was leaving, and I had no discussion on that point, but I knew of his attitude and wondered how it could best be managed. On Sunday afternoon, I had a long and most satisfactory talk with Mr. and Mrs. Faulkner. His horizon is much broader than Seale's. As I was leaving, I asked his judgment of the ballad question and told him of Miss Jackson's scheme. He approved at once. Yesterday morning, I arranged interviews with Seale, Lewis, Dizney at different hours, so that she had each man alone. Seale was the first, and she enlisted his enthusiastic support. Told her that if she would be in a room in the library this forenoon, he could send students to her all day who he knew could sing ballads! Lewis and Dizney likewise promised cooperation. Mr. Lewis invited her to lead Normal chapel this morning, and Mr. Dizney secured an appointment for Model Schools[16] chapel tomorrow. She has yet to see May and Hunt. . . . Friday evening she will speak to Faculty and wives at President's House. She will tell a little of life at Holyoke and Bryn Mawr and then proceed to the main subject, singing ballads in illustration of her subject. / I have invited her to come back in winter term when she will have new people to work with and at that time she thinks she can work up a ballad entertainment among the students which shall be given in the Chapel. She is masterful and will make it go. I think she will prove a real godsend to us. I have grown deeply interested in the matter of the thorough enlisting of our mountain teachers. Like so many other "problems" here, time is the main element needed. These conversations with these two men has opened up a most profitable vista to me which I hope I can share.[17]

In short, Jackson impressed not just Mrs. Frost but the entire contingent of Berea College faculty and students. Charles Lewis and Elijah Dizney,[18] two faculty members whom Mrs. Frost held to be important in the scheme of things, gave their support immediately. Even the curmudgeon Seale was charmed. Once again, this speaks to Jackson's excellent skills with people as well as her knowledge of her subject matter. In addition to wooing faculty and their wives, she ran a ballad sing with some of the girls and led chapel. It is likely that it was at this time that she collected ballads from Bereans/Madison County residents Mrs. Ollie Huff, Nathan Ambrose (a student at Berea), Lucy Banks, Jennie and Bettie Combs, and Mrs. James Baker. This process both added to her collection and helped her develop relationships with students, faculty, and townspeople. In a mere fortnight, she went from being a threat and a bother to being a "godsend."[19]

Jackson's initial visit was a booming success, to the great relief of President Frost. In a letter from Boston (where he had coincidentally met with John C. Campbell, the husband of famed song catcher Olive Dame Campbell),[20] he thanked his wife for her part in the experience: "Your management of the . . . Jackson visit and other things was masterful. I admire you more than ever, even, but my prevailing sentiment is something warmer than admiration."[21] Given the success of Jackson's visit, it would be logical that Frost would jump at the chance to publish her ballads and, indeed, to have her continue to participate in the life of the college community. All seemed on track for her dream to be realized: publication of her ballad collection.

In a letter likely written in 1910, Jackson instructs Frost: "When East, you might see that Mr. Bradley of Harper's Magazine and . . . get estimates of the ballad book. However if you are too occupied for that, I can write Linus. He is already interested and offered his services. Meanwhile, I shall try to get the mss into better shape." Frost acquiesced to this request, but the situation played out later in ways Jackson did not foresee.[22]

In another letter, probably from 1911 (according to Farr), Jackson informs Frost that she is sending him the ballads because she is too far away to meet in person: "My reason for doing so is that this the publication [sic] might not be delayed." She envisioned the ballads being published as a booklet, "prettily formed [and] neatly bound . . . with an illustrated frontspage [sic] from an Elizabethan Ballad." She also suggested that Frost get the opinion of the noted ballad historian Francis Gummere of Haverford, Pennsylvania, "the American authority on ballads." She reiterated that she requested no money for her work: "Any arrangement you make with publishers will be satisfactory to me—the royalty is yours; I only request a neat edition and the right to read the proof and correct the copy."[23]

Jackson visited Berea again for at least five days starting Friday, March 10, 1911.[24] An unsigned handwritten note reads: "Miss Jackson of London March 16 1911 visiting with Frosts. Getting a collection of old English ballads."[25] This is puzzling. If the ballads had already been sent, what was she bringing? Perhaps she had additional material, or maybe she was borrowing ballads from Berea's collection for comparison or potential inclusion in her publication. Also important is the use of the plural *Frosts*. This implies that William was there and that Jackson and he met face-to-face at this point. She had at least five days to charm him and win his support. We know that they dined together on Saturday night, when they ate "lettuce, radishes, sweet peas . . . [and] White Leghorn eggs."[26] We do not have any more information about what passed between them or what Jackson did in Berea. At any rate, the ballads were certainly in Frost's hands by this point in time, and Jackson had made her case to him in person.

In May, Frost visited the Sue Bennett Memorial School in London, and Jackson conscripted the president of the School, J. C. Lewis, to extend a dinner invitation on her behalf, no doubt to discuss the ballad collection. It is unknown whether that meeting came to pass, but it would have given Jackson another chance to urge on Frost's efforts toward publication.[27]

Despite Jackson's stated desire that the book appear in print in the winter of 1911, January 1912 found it still unpublished. Jackson writes anxiously to Frost: "In most especially that Prof. Gummere give the ballads his stamp of approval,—by writing a foreword,—even a page would suffice to introduce the work to his many readers on ballad matters. . . . I am not particular about a second introduction, whose value would be in advertising purposes. While it would be very beneficial to have the names of H—— or James appended, I really do not think the collection sufficiently important to ask their assistance. . . . Should Prof. Gummere. . . . think the book should be so re-arranged, one thing all comments, on collecting all in a preface, for free to return to me. Let me put in order."[28]

Stolen Thunder and the Ballad Wars

It is at this point that Katherine Jackson unwittingly entered the Ballad Wars, a twisting maze of academic territoriality and jealousy, intrigue, social and musical ideology, political connections, cultural assumptions, miscommunications, stature, and fights over ballad origin and primacy of material. The choices she made during this time, combined with shifting circumstances, caused her to begin to lose control of the opportunity to establish herself as an expert on Kentucky balladry.

As word of Jackson's ballad project with Berea spread, it reached the ears of Katherine Pettit, the cofounder and codirector of the Hindman Settlement School in Hindman, Kentucky. Pettit was acquainted with Berea and the Frosts, who had likely mentioned the project. She was also a ballad and song collector and had published an article in the *Journal of American Folklore* in 1907 entitled "Ballads and Rhymes from Kentucky" in which she included seventeen songs, including eight Child ballads, that she had collected primarily from her students.[29]

In March 1911, Pettit wrote to Olive Dame Campbell, the young woman who had collected ballads while traveling the Appalachians with her husband. (Campbell had visited Pettit's Hindman Settlement School in 1906, and the two women were on friendly terms.) She said of Jackson: "She is a wonder for a mountaineer." She also urgently advised Campbell: "Get yours [i.e., her ballad collection] out as soon as you can. . . . Miss Jackson and Dr. Frost at Berea are planning to get some [ballads] published right away." It was Pettit's impression that Jackson's publication was imminent, and she was trying to help Campbell beat her to the punch.[30]

That same year, Hubert G. Shearin put together a descriptive synopsis of ballads that came to be called *A Syllabus of Kentucky Folk-Songs*. Shearin was a professor of English philology at nearby Transylvania University in Lexington, Kentucky, about forty miles from Berea. (He was also the president of Hamilton College for Women.) He was known for his work on language, publishing arcane and vehement articles on topics like the proper use of the word *that*. By his own account, his awakened interest in balladry coincided with Jackson's; he too began collecting in 1909. His first article on Appalachian balladry, "*The Glove* and *The Lions* in Kentucky Folk-Song," was published a month after Jackson's visit.[31]

Shearin was assisted with the *Syllabus* by his protégé Josiah H. Combs. (Combs would go on to put together a large collection of ballads on his own for his 1925 doctoral thesis, a copy of which, ironically, sits on a shelf in the Berea archives near Jackson's ballad collection. In 1911, however, he was a lowly twenty-five-year-old bachelor of arts graduate of Transylvania University.) The *Syllabus* was a small booklet that listed, summarized, and categorized over three hundred ballads. It was concerned only with lyrics, not the music accompanying those lyrics. Information for each ballad included a synopsis of the story, the number of verses, the rhyme scheme, and the number of stressed beats per line.[32]

Jackson had given Shearin permission to include in the *Syllabus* information about the ballads she had collected and met with him during her second visit to Berea in March 1911.[33] According to an article in the *Louisville Courier Journal*, she stayed with the Shearins while she was in Lexington, by which point Shearin had collected "about 325 typical folk songs."[34] When the *Syllabus* was published later that year, it contained 333 songs and drew on 111 variants.[35]

The *Syllabus* does not, with one exception, identify the sources from which the ballads came. In the table of contents of her own copy of the book, inscribed by Shearin, Jackson carefully put a check mark next to every ballad she had collected—twenty-two of the twenty-nine described in the first section, which consisted of "survivors of English and Scottish originals"—a possible indication that these were among the ones she had turned over to Shearin.[36] She received credit for "The Jew's Daughter"—and, in fact, was given a separate listing under the title—but did not get individual credit for any others. In addition, six more of the songs she had given to Shearin appear in other sections in the book. Combs himself was a ballad resource, so it is probable that he and Shearin had drawn on his knowledge for a good bit of their material, but the commonality of ballads as well as the nearly identical descriptive scholarship suggest that they utilized Jackson's work to at least some degree beyond the inclusion of the one ballad.[37]

Jackson's name is listed at the beginning of the book as part of a lengthy introduction—in a paragraph that begins, "Kind words and letters of appreciation, and in some cases, suggestions . . ."—as "Katherine Jackson, formerly of Bryn Mawr, who has generously given the use of her manuscript collection." Her name appears among those of some mighty company, including John Lomax, George Lyman Kittredge, and Harry Belden.[38]

Shearin and Combs increased their academic visibility by virtue of their authorship of the *Syllabus*. Jackson's considerable contribution was not as well-known as she was mentioned only in passing. And so the genie was let out of the bottle, and early on Shearin and Combs became regarded as experts on Kentucky balladry, rather than Jackson.

Shearin was able to use the *Syllabus* as a basis on which to build. In October 1911, he published "Kentucky Folk-Songs" in the *Modern Language Review* and "An Eastern Kentucky Word List" in *Dialect Notes,* furthering his status as a Kentucky expert, and further diminishing Jackson's profile as an expert in the study of Kentucky music and folklore. Sidelined by Frost's delays, Jackson was no longer the sole pioneer of Kentucky balladry.[39]

Shearin's fame and Jackson's lack of it persist to this day; Henry D. Shapiro in 2011 states, "At the end of the first decade of the century, Hubert Gibson Shearin demonstrated that Raymond's 'British' ballads were, in fact, versions of the canonical 'Child ballads'—the ur-texts of Anglo-American culture," which is exactly what Jackson had set out to prove, contemporaneously.[40] Like Shearin and later Campbell and Sharp, Jackson cited the Child version of each ballad along with the Kentucky title. In addition, however, she also referenced other collections of British ballads, like Percy and Scott,[41] broadside ballad editions, and the famous Samuel Pepys hearing of "Barbara Allen" in 1666,[42] making her scholarship more thorough than Shearin's. She further included full versions, that is, lyrics and melodies. Nevertheless, Shearin was published, so his name has enjoyed a century of fame while Jackson's was doomed to a century of obscurity.

Jackson gave Shearin permission to use synopses of her ballads in the *Syllabus.* "Kentucky Folk-Songs" is another matter. The degree to which Jackson felt Shearin capitalized on her work ("stole," she later lamented bitterly), likely in both this article and the *Syllabus,* must be mentioned.

There is no absolute proof of this, but there are a number of items that could be taken as circumstantial evidence. In "Kentucky Folk-Songs," Shearin states that he had collected over three hundred ballads over the course of two years (the same number as appear in the *Syllabus*) but that, of those, "only 37, or 56 if variants of the same ballad" are counted, were British. This corresponds with the number of ballads (over fifty) that Eleanor Frost says Jackson brought to Berea in November 1910. On examination, we see that eighteen of the nineteen "British" ballads listed in "Kentucky Folk-Songs" were in the collection Jackson lent Shearin for the *Syllabus of Kentucky Folk-Songs*. And, in the article, Shearin also cites exactly the same comparative British sources that Jackson did (Child, Percy's *Reliques,* and the British Museum). Further, four other ballads from Jackson's list are also included, although she listed them as songs, not ballads. While the bulk of "Kentucky Folk-Songs" dwells primarily on songs not included in Jackson's collection, it is significant to note that twenty-two of the thirty-seven songs quoted or cited as "discovered" by Shearin were among those given to him by Jackson. The number comes to twenty-six if we include variants. Finally, while in the *Syllabus* Shearin credited Jackson for "The Jew's Daughter," an obscure ballad that one would not expect to find in Appalachia, he did not do so in "Kentucky Folk-Songs."

A chart of the correlation of repetition of ballads between Jackson's work and Shearin's two publications makes clear the correspondence not just of ballads, but of regional titles as well. The concordances of local ballad variants and colloquial titles are clear. For example, both use the "Lord Vanner" and the "Lord Daniel" versions of the Matty Groves story ("Little Musgrave and Lady Barnard"). There is also concordance of analysis. Both relate "McAfee's Confession" to the tradition of goodnight ballads. Both point out that "The Green Willow Tree" is an adaptation of "The Golden Vanitee." Both point out that "Loving Henry" is a New World variant of "Young Hunting." Both differentiate between "Barbara Allen" and "Barbara Allen's Cruelty." In addition, both refer to the use of the word *ballet* for *ballad,* with Jackson explaining the meaning of the word in this context and Shearin using the phrase *song-ballet*.[43]

There are other possible explanations besides outright theft. Shearin worked with Josiah Combs and was familiar with other singers, so Jackson was not his only source. Both Shearin and Jackson collected in Kentucky, so, while other titles were in use, perhaps they collected in the same regions. *Ballet* was a term used by other academics by 1911. Both Shearin and Jackson referred to Child's titles, but, as they both acknowledged Child as a touchstone, that is to be expected. The similar total number of ballads could be a coincidence. Shearin may have thought that Jackson was giving him the ballads and maintaining no proprietary interest. He may, as an esteemed male professor, have thought that, as a woman, Jackson did not have the right to any claim on her songs. There is no clear answer. What is clear in light of Jack-

Francis Child, *The English and Scottish Popular Ballads* (Title and Number)	Jackson, "English-Scottish Ballads from the Hills of Kentucky" (1910 Manuscript)	Shearin, *A Syllabus of Kentucky Folk-Songs* (1911)[a]	Shearin, "Kentucky Folk-Songs" (1911)[b]
Lady Isabel and the Elf Knight, No. 2	Six Pretty Fair Maids, Pretty Polly, Lady Isabel and the Elf Knight, May Colvin,	Six Pretty Fair Maids, Pretty Polly, The King's Daughters	Lady Isabel and the Elf Knight
Earl Brand, No. 7	Fair Ellender, Earl Brand, The Douglas Tragedy	Fair Ellender	Earl Brand
The Twa Sisters, No. 10	The Lord of the Old Country, The Twa Sisters	X	The Twa Sisters
Lord Randal, No. 12	Lord Randal, Lord Randall	The Rope and the Gallows	Lord Randal
Edward, No. 13	Edward	Edward	Edward
Cruel Mother, No. 20	The Greenwood Side, The Cruel Mother	The Greenwood Side, Three Little Babes	The Cruel Mother
The Three Ravens, No. 26	The Three Crows, The Three Ravens	X	X
Two Brothers, No. 49	Little Willie, The Twa Brothers	Little Willie	The Two Brothers
The King's Dochter, Lady Jean, No. 52	x	The King's Daughter, Six Pretty Fair Maids (misattributed)	X
Young Beichan, No. 53	The Turkish Lady, Lord Bateman, Young Beichan and Susie-Pye	The Turkish Lady, Lord Bateman,	Lord Bateman (Beichan)

Table 5.1. Comparison Chart of the Work of Hubert G. Shearin and Katherine Jackson

Table 5.1. Comparison Chart of the Work of Hubert G. Shearin and Katherine Jackson

Young Hunting, No. 68	Loving Henry, William and Ellender, Young Hunting	Loving Henry, Sweet William and Fair Ellender	Young Hunting
Lord Thomas and Fair Annet, No. 73	Lord Thomas, Lord Thomas and Fair Annet	Lord Thomas and Fair Ellender	Lord Thomas
Fair Margaret and Sweet William, No. 74	Lady Marg'et and Sweet William, Fair Margaret and Sweet William, Sweet William and Lady Marg'et	Fair Margaret and Sweet William	Sweet William and Lady Margaret
Lord Lovel, No. 75	Lord Lovely, Lord Lovel	Lord Lovely	Lord Lovel
The Lass of Loch Royal, variant, No. 76.	Lover's Farewell	Cold Winter's Night, Bosom Friend, Lover's Farewell	Cold Winter's Night
The Wife of Usher's Well, variant, No. 79	Lady Gay	Lady Gay and a close variant[c]	X
Little Musgrave and Lady Barnard, variant, No. 81	Lord Vanner's Wife, Lord Daniel's Wife	Lord Vanner's (Daniel's) Wife	The Little Musgrave and Lady Barnard
Bonny Barbara Allen, variants, No. 84	Barbara Allen, Barbara Allen's Cruelty, Bonny Barbara Ellen	Barbara Allen	Barbara Allen's Cruelty
The Bailiff's Daughter of Islington, No. 105.	The Beggar Girl, The Bailiff's Daughter of Islington	The Bailiff's Daughter of Islington Child, No. 105.	The Bailiff's Daughter of Islington
Sir Hugh, Child, No. 155	The Jew's Daughter, It Rains a Mist, Sir Hugh	The Jew's Daughter[d]	The Jew's Daughter

Table 5.1. Comparison Chart of the Work of Hubert G. Shearin and Katherine Jackson			
MacAfee's Confession, No. 195	McAfee's Confession[e]	MacAfee's Confession from the section[f]	X
The Daemon Lover, No. 243	The House Carpenter, The Daemon Lover, The Old Salt Sea, The Salt, Salt Sea	The House Carpenter	The Demon Lover
The Wife Wrapt in Wether's Skin, variant, No. 277	x	Dandoo	The Wife Wrapt in Wether's Skin
The Golden Vanitee, variant, No. 286	The Green Willow Tree[g]	The Green Willow Tree[h]	The Golden Vanitee
----------	X	The Driver Boy (Young Edwin)	x
Trooper and Maid, No. 299	Pretty Peggy, O	Pretty Peggy O	X
The Merchant's Daughter of Bristow[i]	The Wealthy Merchant of London, Jackaro	Jackaro	X
X	A Wealthy Young Farmer, The Golden Glove, The Squire of Tamworth	The Golden Glove	X
X	William Hall, John Reilly	William Hall	X
X	The Serving Maid	X	X
X	(Summer Is a'Cumin' In)[j]	X	X
X	X	The Fan[k]	X
X	X	The Apprentice Boy	X
X	X	The Rich Margent [Merchant]	X

		Table 5.1. Comparison Chart of the Work of Hubert G. Shearin and Katherine Jackson	
X	X	Beneath the Arch of London Bridge	X
X	X	Jack Wilson	X
X	X	The Old Woman of London	X
X	X	Shearfield	X
X	X	Fair Notamon [Nottingham] Town	X
X	X	Lovely Caroline of Old Edinboro [Eddingsburg Town]	X
X	X	Who'll Be King but Charlie?	X
X	X	Cubeck's [Cupid's] Garden	X
X	X	Rosana	X
X	X	Mary of the Wild Moor	X
X	X	Betsy Brown	X
X	X	The Romish Lady	X
X	X	X	Irish Molly O
X	X	X	William Reilly

a. From the first two sections, listing ballads and songs of British origin.
b. Shearin here used only Child's titles.
c. From North Carolina.
d. "Communicated by Dr. Katherine Jackson."
e. Jackson's introduction links this to British goodnight songs.
f. The songs of this group are of the goodnight type.
g. Jackson's notes link this to "The Golden Vanitee."
h. Shearin's notes link this to "The Golden Vanitee."
i. Child A, appendices, page 328. This source lacks a number.
j. Not a ballad, but in her collection.
k. Published by Shearin, Mod. Lang. Notes, 26. 113. For the British originals, see Belden, *Sewanee Review*, April 1911, p. 218, and Kittredge, Mod. Lang. Notes, 26. 168.)

son's later comments ("Professor Shearin stole much of my thunder"; "others stole my work") is that, in her view, Shearin had used or at least capitalized on her work, gaining the recognition that she felt should have been hers and marginalizing her own achievement.[44]

Another hint of this dynamic is given in William Aspenwall Bradley's *Harper's* magazine article "Song-Ballets and Devil's Ditties," written in 1915. Bradley quotes Jackson by name in the article, but later she also appears there anonymously: "Another mountain woman, who had studied and taught in Eastern colleges, told me that when she informed a well-known authority on the subject of ballad literature what she herself had heard in the hills about her home, he at first utterly refused to credit her." He hastily goes on to infer that in this case *credit* meant "believe."[45] This was clearly Jackson speaking, unless Kentucky was teeming with women who had studied and taught at eastern colleges and collected ballads, which it was not. This was a statement, then, that Jackson, not Combs, was the first to draw Shearin's attention to Appalachian balladry and that the whole concept was so new to him that he doubted her information. Yet Shearin writes that he began collecting ballads in 1909, two years before Jackson's trip to see him. This would counter Jackson's claim that she was Shearin's gateway into Appalachian balladry, unless she had already communicated with him in 1909, and we have no record of such a visit or correspondence.

Whether Shearin actually stole Jackson's ballads cannot be proven. His papers apparently no longer exist. From Jackson's viewpoint, however, he stole the study of Kentucky balladry in its entirety, capitalized on her work, and did not give her the credit she deserved. She could only watch as, from the comfortable vantage point of his professorial perch at Transylvania University, he published and basked in the glow of recognition, respect, and admiration of scholars and students.

Jackson married and continued to wait on Frost.

The Reason for My Generosity

Stories of stolen work and stolen credit were probably as rife in academe in 1911 as they are now. Sharing her work with Shearin, in retrospect, was a misjudgment on Jackson's part. It seems odd that an academic would so carelessly disseminate her work, unless she were certain that it was about to be published. In fact, Jackson *was* sure her work was about to be published.

Unfortunately, she was wrong.

In an April 16, 1912, letter found at Berea, not in the Katherine Jackson French Ballad Collection, but in the D. W. Wilgus Collection, Jackson writes:[46]

> My Dear Mrs. Marshall,
>
> Your . . . letter awaiting my arrival home, makes me deeply regret that either it had not come sooner, or that your club did not meet later. My mss. are all in the Lodge and the caretaker would not know a ballad from a bull-finch—and I shall not return to Perry Co., our present abode . . . for a month.
>
> I have hastily written out from memory three airs;—the originals you can find*—I should suggest that you read the ancient versions of each of these, these . . . being in the modern rendering. The words of Barbara Allen's Cruelty (most popular, sung by school children) . . . are as in Child's Ballads . . . one thing the first stanza, using the intro verse for the hero. I have many variants, but you cannot use those now.
>
> The words for The Salt, Salt Sea, is [sic] enclosed, not for any other reason, than that I happen to find a copy at Laurel. The original The Demon Lover, you must read. The air for Lord Thomas is quaint. . . . Insist that your soloist be a real minstrel . . . and tell the whole story in song—the story in each case, being the necessary point, the reason for its existence.
>
> I could so easily have sent you many more of these, had I known it a bit sooner. The reason for my generosity is that my little volume of words and airs has gone to press. I'm not afraid of stolen thunder. . . .
>
> With every good wish, believe me
Katherine Jackson French
>
> *Chappel's Ancient National Popular Airs of England.

"My little volume of words and airs has gone to press." This is the key phrase that indicates that, by April 16, 1912, Jackson believed the collection had been sent to a publisher and gone to press, just as she had planned. There is only one person who could have told her this: William Goodell Frost. This is why she agreed to let Shearin and Combs use her work. This is why she sent these four songs (copies of which she still had in her possession) to Mrs. Marshall in Louisville. She seemed to think she could be gracious and generous and still beat everyone else to the punch.

But the book had not gone to press. There are two possibilities for this grievously erroneous conclusion on Jackson's part: either Frost had told her it had been sent when it had not, or she simply assumed that everything had fallen into place and the book was already at the publisher's. Unfortunately, there is no documentation that might clarify the situation. But, whatever the reason, Jackson had opened the floodgates prematurely.

A week after she sent ballads to Mrs. Marshall, Jackson received a letter from Frost revealing that the book had, indeed, not yet been sent to a publisher. She wrote back with considerable surprise and agitation: "Your letter of April 4th was returned to me only last afternoon—The Mss, with the airs, is the one to present . . . containing, as it does, all ballads in the first group, and . . . systematized according to a logical place." She concludes with an urgent nudge: "Unless a change is suggested by the critics, I'm ready for this Mss to be shown the publisher." (This suggests that they had agreed on a publisher.) She also indicated that she was planning to include other ballads, but in another, later volume, and not until she had "spent a season in the British Invasion, discovered the originals," presumably meaning older British sources.[47]

We can assume Jackson took her trip to England at this point or a little later, doing some genealogical research along with her ballad work at the British Museum, as she did on some of her other trips there. She sailed off across the Atlantic, confident that "English-Scottish Ballads from the Hills of Kentucky" was going to be published soon.[48]

But, by February of the following year, the situation had stagnated. The ballads still had not been published. Jackson wrote Frost in February 1913, a communiqué that began, not with her usual pleasantries, but with a curt "May I inquire what of the whereabouts of the ballads, which I left with you some time ago?" She then asked for her manuscripts to be returned to her if he had "not found a suitable publisher." Her sharpness and brevity suggest that her patience with Frost was at an end; he had not done what he promised, and she wanted the ballads returned.[49]

But the ballads were not returned. She wrote to Frost again in August 1913, and this time her words came as ultimatum and also as complaint:[50]

My Dear Mr. Frost,—

A few days ago, I had a call from Mr. Bradley of Harper's, interested in things pertaining to the mountains, and also, in ballads. From the reading of my manuscript, he had gleaned a good many facts, and had he known more fully the subject matter, much of my thunder would have been gone. I cannot give him free use of what I have collected; you may know that Prof. Shearin stole much of my thunder a year ago, and published in his bulletin, and while he recognized my authority, yet, the information has weakened my manuscript. In July, Mrs. Campbell wrote, asking for the whole thing, that it be turned over to the American Folk-Lore Society,—which I refused. These people imagine, I presume, that I am not intending to publish, and they might as well have the results of my work.

Now, I want you to please write Prof. Gummere, Haverford [College], Penna., asking him if he will give the manuscript a few hours this vacation, long enough to read and get an opinion of its worth. A note from him will do every thing [*sic*] toward getting it before a publisher. Please do not wait to do this, while you are East, but write him, and then mail at once the collection. I gave Mr. Bradley the ballads I wish him to use, except Lord Thomas, which is in the first collection, I sent you. He may copy it from that group. If you should wish to have him present it to Harper's, a business contract will have to be arranged. I cannot allow every one, who claims an interest in ballads, to have access to this, and had I known it sooner, he would have been refused. What cost me hours and hours of labour, as well as a good deal of expense and endless fatigue, is made popular, in a magazine article, along with humorous stories, and pictures.

If, with your many claims on time, you cannot give this any thought or attention, then I shall ask you to return it to me; two years have passed with nothing accomplished.

In the hope, that you and Mrs. Frost are having a most restful vacation, and with very best wishes, believe me

Very Truly,
Katherine Jackson French

Her signature on this letter was particularly large, written in very dark pencil with a hand so forceful that its imprint still can be felt on the underside of the paper a century later. There is no question that, by this point in time,

> If, with your many claims on time, you cannot give this any thought or attention, then I shall ask you to return it to me; two years have passed with nothing accomplished.
>
> In the hope, that you and Mrs. Frost are having a most restful vacation, and with very best wishes, believe me
>
> Very Truly,
>
> *Katherine Jackson French.*

Katherine Jackson French to William Goodell Frost.

Jackson was angry. Her frustration with Frost's delay is chiseled into every line of this letter.

Jackson was also displeased with Bradley's desire to use her ballads. Though she had initially suggested contacting the *Harper's* writer for "estimates of the book," his desire to use her ballads in the magazine did not please her. She wanted this work that she cared about so deeply to be published in its entirety and taken seriously in the academic world. Instead, it was to be perused as though it were mere entertainment in a popular magazine. In addition, there is evidence that Jackson did not give Frost permission to share her work with Bradley or Bradley permission to use it ("had I known it sooner, he would have been refused"); she seems dismayed that he was given the opportunity to view her manuscript at all. There is no evidence of any kind of business contract either, as she had requested. In short, Bradley, assisted by Frost, helped himself to her work. Jackson nonetheless did not veto the use of her material in Bradley's *Harper's* article outright, designating only that specific ballads were to be used. Most of all, Campbell's request that her collection be turned over to the American Folklore Society galled her. She had had enough of other people getting credit for her work and perhaps feared that Campbell was planning the same sort of shady credit-grabbing move that Shearin had executed earlier.

Six more months passed with no movement on publication of the collection. In February 1914, Jackson tried again and wrote to Frost, sending him a January 22, 1914, newspaper clipping entitled "Popular Songs of Olden Times." The article states that the "Federal Bureau of Education" had instituted a nationwide search for versions of old ballads under the supervision of Alphonso Smith, all the while, as Jackson pointed out, her collection sat "in [Frost's] vault." Full publication having slipped away, Jackson wanted her ballads included in Smith's collection and requested Frost to act. He did not. Jackson's letter apparently did finally prompt him to contact Francis Gummere in March (unless it was Jackson who did the contacting). Gummere wrote to Frost to ask how many ballads there were and how large a collection he intended, indicating that Frost either did not send Jackson's collection to him at all or sent only a few pieces. Gummere said that he would be at Chautauqua in upstate New York in March and intended to network there and try to "generate enough interest to justify . . . printing the collection": "Surely Mrs. French's collection must be printed!" Still, Frost did not send them to Smith or to a publisher. At this point, he may have been waiting in the hope that at Chautauqua Gummere would find a party interested in publishing the collection as a whole. At any rate, the ballads went nowhere.[51]

Despite Gummere's proclamation, and despite the surge of interest in ballad collecting, Frost did nothing with the collection. In November 1915, five years after Jackson initially approached Frost for help, it still sat untouched at Berea College. At that time, Jackson wrote to ask that it be returned to her for a presentation for the Cumberland Valley Teacher's Association. She ended with: "I do want you and Mrs. Frost to come see me this winter. Could you—would you? With every good wish, believe me, Faithfully, Katherine Jackson French."[52]

The letter was written on half sheets of Sue Bennett Memorial School stationery. Jackson had become dean there in 1914. She seemed to harbor no hard feelings and appeared anxious to heal any discord between her and Frost on the issue. She did, however, still want her ballads returned to her. The visit to London did not happen, but Jackson visited the Frosts in December of that year, inviting herself. In May 1916, the Frosts did, indeed, visit Jackson in London, a visit she coordinated enthusiastically and happily.[53]

By that time, Jackson had given up. In the end, she and Berea College parted ways. This estrangement would last forty years. No one of scholarly import would connect the words *Katherine Jackson* and *ballads* for nearly a half century. "English-Scottish Ballads from the Hills of Kentucky," the work that had been the passion of Jackson's youth, would never see publication. There is reason to believe that she never completely got over that disappointment. Forty years later, she was to write: "Others stole the work I had done. . . . I had had my fill and did not seek the glory."[54] Gifted, creative, and practical, she did the only thing she could have done. She acknowledged her defeat, picked herself up, and moved on.

Jackson did take a few last stabs at getting out word of her work as a ballad collector after moving to Shreveport. A 1921 article in the *New York Post* recounts her ballad-collecting trip into the Kentucky mountains and contains much of the information later found in "A Fortnight of Balladry." It states that she was "waiting to verify [some songs] from the annals of the British Museum before presenting them to the public."[55]

Jackson attempted to memorialize her ballad collecting in another form as well. At some point after moving to Shreveport, likely the late 1910s or the early 1920s, she wrote a play called "Lizane of Leatherwood" the action of which coincides almost exactly with her later description of her 1909 trip into the eastern Kentucky mountains. The play takes place in Leatherwood (a real town, most famous for the Blue Diamond Mine), "a mountainous country, sixty miles from a railroad." Two of the characters bear the same names as people who figured prominently in her own journey. The characters sing, and, in fact, one sings the same version of "Barbara Allen" that French heard at the quilting bee. A number of men are portrayed in a negative light, invoking the image of the lazy, drinking mountaineer. The women are rough and earthy but are the soul and conscience of the community. Colloquial dialect is employed. The plot centers around two visiting developers, one ruthless and one ethical, who have different schemes for the resources of the area. The ethical one wins out in the end, love prevails, and a raucous "Sourwood Mountain," sung and danced by the company, finishes out the story. This foreshadows both the movie *Songcatcher* and the 1950s Berea College production *Wilderness Road* that served as the capstone for French's reconciliation with Berea College. "Lizane" never appeared in print despite attempts to land it with at least one publisher (the *Saturday Evening Post*). Sadly, life in the real Leatherwood did not have the happy ending and economic growth that French wrote about in her play. Though at one point it was a large coal camp town, there is little of that heyday left. The most recent available figures list barely one thousand people living there, with over half the population earning under $30,000 a year per household and over half unemployed. A 1989 photographic project by Shelby Lee Adams shows members of the Napier family (likely latter-day relatives of Jackson's guide Lizane) living in extreme poverty in Leatherwood but proud of and content with their way of life.[56]

French did some minimal collecting in later years but did not put much effort into publishing. She herself later wrote: "In 1911, I married, and never did much more about [trying to get the collection published]."[57] "I don't know," says Kay Tolbert Buckland. "Maybe she just didn't want to outshine my grandfather."[58]

Undoing the Tough Knots

In tracing the physical journey of the manuscripts, Sidney Saylor Farr assumed that they were returned to Jackson when she requested them in November 1915: "[Jackson] was [by 1915] on very good terms with President and Mrs. Frost. (Perhaps she knew that he had done the best he could to get the ballads published.) . . . From the correspondence and especially from the November 3, 1915 letter, from French to Frost, a conclusion can be drawn about the whereabouts of the manuscript collections from 1915–1955. When French wrote this time to Frost, apparently he returned the ballads to her."[59] But Farr was wrong. Frost never returned the ballads. Then where were they? What did Frost do with them?

Those questions were answered when one Mrs. Elizabeth Peck, the Berea College historian, ventured into the "mountain room" where things had been "put away." There she discovered, as she wrote Jackson, "a package, much wrapped and tied with tough knots, labeled 'K. Jackson—hold,' in President Frost's handwriting, which I know so well. Because of my position, I assumed the right to undo those tough knots, and no longer hold." She unwrapped the package and found "something precious in my sight—a typed manuscript with introduction and music."[60] It was, in fact, Jackson's "English-Scottish Ballads from the Hills of Kentucky." The year was 1954. The package had sat, wrapped on that shelf, tied with tough knots, since March 1911, for forty-three long years.

In a five-page letter to Jackson, Peck gleefully describes how she surreptitiously engineered Gladys Jameson (a prominent Berea College music professor) to take an interest in Jackson's work. No name was on the manuscript itself, only the mysterious "K. Jackson" on the accompanying note, so Peck

Elizabeth Peck to Katherine Jackson, 1954. Courtesy of Kay Tolbert Buckland.

did some detective work, reading countless letters and journal entries. Finally, she deduced that the "K. Jackson" of the attached note was in fact one Katherine Jackson of London, Kentucky. She kept quiet about the manuscript, feeling that the right thing to do was to find Jackson and return the package to her, not exploit it for her own gain. One day, without mentioning the manuscript, she causally asked Jameson whether she knew that Jackson's work had preceded Cecil Sharp's by a decade. As Peck wrote to Jackson: "this put [Jameson] on the trail, and the result was her trip to London to find you."[61]

By the date of Peck's blow-by-blow letter, Jameson had, in fact, gone to London, talked with Jackson's sister Annie Jackson Pollard, and gotten Jackson's married name and address. She wrote to Jackson in August of 1954 and asked her to donate "a representative number" of ballads from her work to Jameson's Berea College 1955 centennial songbook *Wake and Sing*.[62]

Elisabeth Peck's initial letter gratefully thanks Jackson for her "great generosity" in giving Berea her ballad materials: "It seemed to me almost a miracle."[63] It is unclear exactly what materials these were. Peck mentions that a package from her ("with its very precious content") had arrived that very morning, probably containing at least several more ballads for Jameson's use. (It may also have included later drafts of the ballad collection as there are four extant.)[64] She also notes that she wants to put Jackson's entire collection, including the correspondence, into a formal collection—giving her assurances that there is nothing embarrassing in the correspondence—and expresses her hope that Jackson will say, "Berea can keep all." Then she thanks her for her "precious gift—already given," referring to the manuscript at Berea and whatever she had received that morning.[65]

Jackson agreed to this second request. All four versions of the ballad collection, some photographs, correspondence, her original "Fortnight of Balladry" manuscript, a typed one-page vita, and a one-page handwritten letter of bequest became the Katherine Jackson French Ballad Collection at Berea College in 1955.[66]

This led to a happy ending of sorts. Jackson helped Jameson edit the centennial collection *Wake and Sing*, and Jameson included Jackson's version of "Lord Bateman" in it, giving her full credit.[67] Her version of "Fair Margaret and Sweet William," which had enchanted her on her collecting trip so long ago, was incorporated into the outdoor Berea College musical extravaganza *Wilderness Road* by Paul Green. Jackson came to Berea in 1955 to see the performance and kept the playbill.[68] It was then that she met Peck and Jameson, her champions, and the three got on famously. Peck mentioned Jackson in her quintessential Berea history, *Berea's First Century, 1855–1955*, and Jackson kept an autographed copy given her by Peck.[69] Finally, the rediscovery of Katherine Jackson French led not only to the formation of the Katherine

Jackson French Ballad Collection at Berea College but also to the belated publication of an expanded version of her account of her first ballad-collecting journey, the 1955 *Mountain Life and Work* version of "A Fortnight of Balladry," which incorporated some observations and conclusions from the introduction to the never-published "English-Scottish Ballads from the Hills of Kentucky." In this way, just three years before her death, Katherine Jackson French finally had a little bit of the glory she had not sought and got back a little of her stolen thunder.

The Story between the Lines

Finally, we come to the question of why Frost agreed to help publish the collection and then instead placed it on a shelf where it sat for forty-three years. As with most difficult questions, there is no simple answer, but rather an unfortunate conjunction of circumstances, miscommunications, and personal reactions.

Miscommunications

There were many misunderstandings during this process, most notably Jackson's belief that her book had gone to press when in fact Frost was still confused as to which version to publish, whether to include all the ballads, and whether he should wait for Gummere to write an introduction. Because she mistakenly believed the printing to be in progress, Jackson allowed her work to be disseminated. Much to her chagrin, this weakened her singular authority on the subject, fueling her anger about Frost's handling of the matter. Frost, of course, may have thought the misunderstanding to be Jackson's and may not have appreciated what he perceived to be her lack of clarity or prickliness over his own indecision. This dynamic may have tempered his enthusiasm for the project.

Campus Jealousies

Frost had to keep peace on the Berea College campus. In her correspondence, Eleanor Frost hints at professional jealousy from Raine and a wave of negativity regarding ballads in general from Ellis Seale and others. Keeping peace among faculty members, all with their own agendas, is not an easy task. William Frost would have to deal with all these people long after Jackson returned to London. Perhaps he could not find a way to publish her ballads without alienating his staff to a degree that he considered too costly.

Frost's Changeable Interest in Balladry

William Frost's own interest in ballads waxed and waned. James Watt Raine complained several times that Frost would ask him to institute ballad courses and collecting activities and then change his mind. For example, in proposing a ballad course in 1920, he spoke of the college eliminating "the new course in Ballads which the President had previously asked [him] to introduce" and also referred to his "unheeded suggestion of several years ago." He reiterated elsewhere: "A suggestion that I made years ago, still seems to me good tho it has received no encouragement from the President."[70]

For a man who claimed to have discovered Appalachia and championed Appalachian ballads, Frost appears to have displayed lackluster interest in including balladry in the Berea curriculum. This suggests that his interest and belief in the importance of ballads might not have been fully sustained during the time Jackson was attempting to publish and that what he considered more important matters took precedence.

Delays

Delays can be deadly to any project, and this particular endeavor was full of them. Jackson herself instituted several of them: when she went to England to check other sources, when she was fussing about the foreword, when she sought an endorsement from Gummere, and when she was deciding which version of the collection was to be published. Then there were the delays caused by Frost's misunderstanding of various aspects of the project and, finally, by waiting for Gummere to come up with a foreword and a publisher. The way in which these delays piled up slowed momentum and probably cooled Frost's interest in the project.

Loss of Primacy

Another possible negative in Frost's view was that exclusivity and primacy were lost when Shearin and Combs published the *Syllabus of Kentucky Folk-Songs* and Shearin published his other articles in 1911. Jackson referred to the appearance of these works as *stolen thunder,* and it was just that. Frost may have felt that Berea had lost dibs on the ballads by virtue of this development, and with good reason. Once Shearin had established himself as the foremost authority on Kentucky folk song, and especially once he had claimed to have collected exactly the same ballads Jackson had, the cutting edge had been forever dulled. Frost might have seen Jackson's collection as redundant at that point.[71]

Another major voice in Kentucky balladry whose work further diminished Jackson's claim to primacy was that of Josiah Combs. Not only did he publish with Shearin in 1911, but he also went on to publish *The Kentucky Highlanders* (1912) and *All That's Kentucky* (1915), making him another leading authority on Kentucky culture, and further undercutting Jackson's importance.[72]

Harper's *Magazine*

Regarding the *Harper's* magazine matter, Frost may have thought he was doing Jackson a favor by arranging for Bradley to use her ballads in an article. He never saw publicity he did not like and was interviewed regularly by newspapers and magazines to exalt the causes of Berea College and Appalachia. He may have thought that *Harper's* would be good publicity for Jackson and Berea both. If so, he would not have taken kindly to her icy letter in response to what he considered a kindness.

"Mr. Bradley," the mysterious *Harper's* contact, bears some consideration here. Peck tantalizingly wrote Jackson: "I have some of your correspondence and a letter of Mr. Bradley's. I think I know the story that is contained between the lines."[73] Unfortunately, she does not state what that story is, and the Bradley letter in question cannot be located.

The "Mr. Bradley" who was working for *Harper's* in Kentucky during this time (and from whom Jackson beseeched Frost to get a publishing estimate) was William Aspenwall Bradley, who later went by William A. Bradley. This William A. Bradley was later to found one of the most influential literary agencies of his day. But, in 1913, he was a reporter on assignment for *Harper's* in Kentucky. Indeed, he spent large amounts of time in the state from 1912 to 1918 and became well-known for his writings on Appalachian America; "Hobnobbing with Hillbillies," "Song-Ballets and Devil's Ditties," and "In Shakespeare's America" were all written for *Harper's* as a result of his posting to Kentucky. These articles garnered him fame as an expert on the southern mountains. It was "Song-Ballets and Devil's Ditties" for which he had wanted Jackson's ballads.[74]

Bradley later wrote an article on Katherine Pettit, May Stone, and the

Hindman School called "The Women on Troublesome." He therefore knew and was interested in the woman who urged Olive Dame Campbell to publish her collection before Jackson and Frost had a chance to publish Jackson's.[75]

Bradley settled in Paris in 1921 and went on to work with expatriate authors in France, including Gertrude Stein, Henry Miller, James Joyce, and F. Scott Fitzgerald. He reappeared in the history of American balladry in 1925 when he translated Josiah Combs's Sorbonne doctoral thesis into French for *Vient de paraitre*.[76] As we have just seen, Combs was Shearin's partner in the *Syllabus of Kentucky Folk-Songs* before Shearin went on to write "Kentucky Folk-Songs," the article that Jackson felt borrowed so liberally from her own work. Bradley, then, kept up ties with both Pettit and Combs, who were in a sort of rivalry with Jackson.[77]

The Ballad Wars

The rivalries just described were part and parcel of the aforementioned Ballad Wars. The term *Ballad Wars* was first used by D. W. Wilgus in 1954 to refer to the virulent feud over the communal (Gummere) versus individual (Louise Pound) origins theories of ballads that went hand in hand with opposing views of balladry as a dead as opposed to a living thing. Wilgus describes the argument of the Emersonian (balladry as alive) side of the Ballad Wars thus: "The ballad, no longer a corpse to be lamented and dissected, was found living in tradition side by side with possibly related but non-canonical songs. The ballads refused to die, the folksingers refused to sing what the scholars said they should, and the scholars refused to stay within the limits Gummere had set. The result was confusion, thirty years of acrimonious controversy, and the beginning of considered and reasonable study of traditional songs."[78]

The term was extended by Scott B. Spencer to include the ongoing struggle for supremacy by followers of various ballad collectors and the ongoing battle for primacy, authenticity, and bona fides established by links to collectors higher up in the pecking order: "The . . . academic scattering, reinterpretation and redefinition of the Child ballads by his acolytes came to be known as 'The Ballad Wars.' . . . As scholars fetishized the work of particular folklorists and ballad collectors, an assumption arose that the inherent musical authenticity might be partly tied to the stature of the collector himself (and it usually was a him). Similarly, as Olive Dame Campbell proved through her ballad collecting efforts in Appalachia, authenticity could also be associated with region or even era."[79]

The early Ballad Wars were somewhat brutal; every collector was trying to elbow every other collector out of the way and lay claim to primacy of sources. Elizabeth McCutcheon Williams states: "Ballads were viewed as a scarce and endangered species, and collectors sought them (and guarded their sources) as jealously as an antiques collector on the trail of the last John Townsend blockfront."[80] In light of this, it is not surprising that some questions arise regarding the cast of characters and their actions and motives.

This brings us to the matter of Frost's developing relationship with John C. and Olive Dame Campbell. We know that the Campbells visited Berea in 1908 and that Frost met with Campbell in Boston during the time that Jackson made her initial visit to Berea College. Frost and Campbell had a great deal of common cause in the matter of Appalachia's welfare. Perhaps Frost thought his goals for the elevation of the region were in better hands with a woman he already knew and admired and with whom he had more common cause than with Jackson. But this seems unlikely. According to Shapiro, by 1913 Frost and Campbell were bitterly battling over whose Appalachian strategy would prevail, so the possibility of any kind of influence at this time seems unlikely (unless it occurred early on and was abandoned later).[81]

The question of whether George Lyman Kittredge—Francis Child's successor at Harvard—had an invisible hand somewhere in this story is worth addressing as well. At the very least, he did have a presence. Harvard was "the unofficial center of folk song study" at the time, and Kittredge was the kingmaker when it came to future ballad scholars, training the next generation. This illustrious group under his tutelage included Helen Hartness Flanders, Phillips Barry, John Lomax, Harold Thompson, and Arthur Kyle Davis Jr. Kittredge saw to it that his protégés were well versed in the omnipotence and authority of Francis Child and, by extension, Kittredge himself. He encouraged this perception, using it to elevate his already illustrious stature in the field.[82]

Kittredge was also a long-standing member of the Board of Syndics of the Harvard University Press and, for all practical purposes, *was* the press. Involved from the beginning, and serving longer than any of his colleagues, he had a huge amount of control over which ballad collectors were published and which were not. He spent much time "looking over manuscripts, making editorial suggestions, on occasion proposing a happy change of title, sometimes concerning himself with typographical arrangement, and almost invariably arguing over proofs of the books he had specially recommended."

This is a very clear picture of someone who enjoyed being in control and micromanaged to a fault.[83]

At the time Jackson was trying to get her collection published, Kittredge was also the go-to man at the American Folklore Society's *Journal of American Folklore,* the primary venue for early ballad and song collectors seeking to publish their finds. He became president of the society in 1904, served as its vice president from 1911 to 1918, and helped edit the *Journal* from 1909 to 1940. Esther K. Birdsall declares: "In his editorial capacity in the *Journal of American Folklore,* he undoubtedly read most, if not all, of the ballad manuscripts." In fact, he served as Katherine Pettit's editor when the *Journal* published her "Ballads and Rhymes from Kentucky" (twelve songs, not all British-origin ballads, and six rhymes) in 1907. Note that he edited the work, though he did not officially hold the title *editor* at the time. This is representative of the influence he exerted over *Journal* publications.[84]

Kittredge enjoyed his stature and had his chosen circle of students and acolytes. Jackson was definitely outside that circle. It is probable, however, that Shearin was not. As a doctoral student at Yale from 1899 to 1902, he might have known Kittredge, a fellow New Englander, and been conscious of his focus on Child. There was certainly direct contact between the two after the appearance of a 1911 *Modern Language Notes* article on the ballad "The Den of Lions" in which Kittredge extolled Shearin's scholarship on the same topic.[85] Shearin happily quotes a letter Kittredge wrote to him in his July 1911 "British Ballads in the Cumberland Mountains" and recommends Kittredge's and Child's collections to his readers, a bit of politicking in a public forum.[86] There may have been even earlier contact as Shearin published in *Modern Language Notes*—to which Kittredge was a frequent contributor—as early as 1907.[87] It is interesting to note that Kittredge and Shearin were corresponding precisely when Jackson was (or thought she was) solidifying publication efforts with Berea. Kittredge did, as we have seen, throw his weight about in early Kentucky balladry. He would have favored Shearin's cite-Child-faithfully approach over Jackson's multisource comparative one as his stature depended greatly on his own link in the Child line of succession. Shearin also contacted Kittredge for input on the *Syllabus* and credited him in the introduction. In the end, we cannot know whether Kittredge ever even heard of Jackson, but he knew Shearin, and at the very least this relationship lent a gravitas to Shearin that Jackson did not have.

Olive Dame Campbell had the good fortune to have John Glenn of the Sage Foundation contact Kittredge for her with a collection of ballads and songs she had gathered. Glenn saw to it that Kittredge had a copy early in 1910. Kittredge pronounced it "a remarkable collection . . . which ought to be printed." As with Jackson, Campbell had difficulty publishing and also encountered delays. Nevertheless, Kittredge's imprimatur lent heft to her collection when she presented it to Cecil Sharp in 1915.[88]

Jackson's attempt to enlist the support of Francis Gummere, the Child protégé, was an attempt to enlist a powerful ally of her own. It may also have been an effort to establish a line of contact with Kittredge himself, along with the *Journal of American Folklore* and the young Harvard University Press. Gummere was a close personal friend of Kittredge's; his 1909 translation of Beowulf was dedicated to Kittredge, "keenest of critics, kindest of friends."[89] Gummere and Kittredge were also trench buddies in the early Ballad Wars, both holding to the communal theory of ballad origin (i.e., that a ballad came about by a community of people shaping it together) instead of the individual theory (i.e., that a ballad had a sole creator). It seems strange today that this was such a sticking point, but, as noted, this clash of theories was at the heart of the Ballad Wars. Like Gummere and Kittredge, Jackson clearly took the side of the communalists. Not only does she talk of the singers as being of "one unlettered air"; she closes her introductory essay to her collection with, as we have seen, that beautiful line about ballads living, "not as an individual call, but as an outcry from a community of lonely people." At any rate, if she was hoping to get Kittredge's attention through Gummere, the ploy did not work. Further, Josiah Combs published "Sympathetic Magic in the Kentucky Mountains" in the *Journal of American Folklore* in 1914, helping cement his reputation as a Kentucky culture scholar. His editor was George Lyman Kittredge, establishing him as a member of the Kittredge circle with all the advantages thereof.[90]

In short, Combs, Campbell, and Shearin were better connected to Kittredge, the center of gravity in the Ballad Wars, than Jackson was. As each of these achieved a degree of repute not shared by Jackson, Kittredge's influence remains a matter of interest. It would be impossible to weave all the threads of the Ballad Wars together in relation to Jackson's story without mentioning Kittredge, who was the key connection between the Child and Pettit networks. The resultant interactions resulted in a web in which Kittredge published Pettit (who capitalized on Combs), and later edited Combs, who worked with Shearin, who "stole" from Jackson, who tried to publish but was beaten to the punch by Campbell, who published first partly because she had Kittredge's endorsement, which helped with Sharp, and because Pettit warned her about the imminent publication of Jackson's collection, which was used by Bradley, who wrote about Jackson and Pettit and Shearin and Combs and wound up translating Combs.

The Ballad Wars were a messy mix of motives and interactions, and the full nature of the relationships among Jackson, Shearin, Kittredge, Gummere, Combs, Pettit, the Campbells, and Bradley has been lost to time. The precarious balance of power shifted as each exerted their efforts and power, and in this way, the battles of the Ballad Wars were won or (in Jackson's case) lost.

A full timeline of the Ballad Wars can be found in appendix C.

The New Bride

Another fly in the publication ointment was Jackson's marriage to William Franklin French in 1911 and the arrival of her daughter a few years later. "I know among other things it was the timing that was bad," says Jackson's granddaughter, Kay Tolbert Buckland. "She was not married at the time of the collection of the ballads. Then my grandfather came back, and they got together, . . . and they decided to get married, so Mom said that's why she never totally followed up on it. . . . That's just the feeling I got about it from my mother."[91] Jackson had to fulfill the roles of wife and mother, both new to her. These would have been time-consuming and unfamiliar endeavors. She also became dean of the Sue Bennett School in 1914. She no longer had the time to keep chasing down President Frost, and ultimately she gave up. She forgave Frost, not because he had tried to help her, but out of the strength of her own spirit and character—"the spirit and sap of the stock," to use her own words.[92]

Gender Roles and Sexism

The question of gender and sexism must be examined, yes, even at Berea, the first coeducational college in the South, but also in the broader culture of the time.

I use the term *sexism* gingerly. Sexism can be measured only against the lack of it, and, in the world of 1910, there was no lack of it. It would have been difficult to find men of that time who were not, by today's standards, sexist. Yet, to judge them by today's standards puts us in peril of historical presentism. It may be more accurate to acknowledge that the views of 1910 America, and especially American academe, and certainly the American South, were simply manifestations of an overall male-dominated society in which the inferiority of the intellectual and social capabilities of women was a given.

This societal hierarchy led to the necessity of men's sponsorship of ambitious women. It was hard at that time for a woman to get anywhere without the assistance of a man, especially in the South. Katherine Jackson knew this. So did Olive Dame Campbell, who had the good fortune to attract the support and attention of Cecil Sharp, John Glenn, and George Lyman Kittredge. Had she not, we may never have heard of her ballads. Jackson was not as lucky in her choice of patron. Her doctorate from Columbia, her postdoctoral studies at Yale, and her teaching experience at Ivy League schools did not carry enough weight by themselves for her work to gain publication, and her sponsor proved ineffective.

Gender roles may also have played a part in Shearin's alleged liberal use of Jackson's research. Shearin modestly referred to himself at least once as "a mere collector."[93] It is doubtful that he really thought of himself in this way, but he may have thought of Jackson as "a mere informant" rather than an academic colleague. In 1910, male college professors did not have many female colleagues and may not have been prone to consider those they did have as equals. One of Shearin's female colleagues at Transylvania held a PhD in history, so Jackson would not have been the first woman with a doctorate in Shearin's experience. Still, the ratio of male to female faculty at Transylvania was two to one. The male/female ratio of the administration was even more skewed, twelve to one.[94]

The actions of William A. Bradley were more egalitarian, though perhaps not entirely so. As we have seen, he was given access to Jackson's work by Frost. Whether gender played into the assumption of right of access on the part of both Frost and Bradley is unclear. However, we must give Bradley credit: he had corresponded with and spoken with Jackson and asked permission, though only after seeing her collection.

Bradley mentions Jackson in another context in which he not only uses her title (and states both her given and her married names) but also describes viewing her collection: "One collector, Dr. Katharine B. Jackson [sic] (Mrs. Wm. F. French), whose manuscript I had the privilege of examining at Berea, told me later that she had gathered some sixty separate specimens (exclusive of interesting and important variants), of which thirty could be positively identified as old British ballads through Child and other printed sources, while the rest, she was confident, could be identified equally by referring to the British Museum manuscript collections." He continues: "Nearly as good a showing is made by Professor Shearin in his and Josiah Combs's *Syllabus of Kentucky Folk-Songs.*"[95]

Jackson seems to be a notch above Shearin and Combs in Bradley's estimation here (in "Song-Ballets and Devil's Ditties"). Later, however, Bradley quotes the closing paragraphs of Shearin's "*The Glove* and *The Lions* in Kentucky Folk-Song" as well as Alphonso Smith's 1915 bulletin for the Department of Education.[96] Jackson is not quoted at all and, thus, does not appear as a full character in the story, a quote serving to make a subject flesh and blood, real, and authoritative. The fact that Jackson limited Bradley's use of her material contributed to this perception; he could quote none of her work, as he could with Shearin and Smith. The situation was of Jackson's making, then, not Bradley's. Still, her presence is diminished in comparison to that of Shearin, Smith, and Combs. (Combs is not quoted either, but his stature is enhanced by lengthy quotes in Bradley's later "In Shakespeare's America.")

With regard to William Goodell Frost's relationship with Jackson, we must ask about his personal reaction to this unusually (for the time) assertive woman. It is possible that his attitudes toward women and gender roles may have played a part in his response to her requests.

One passage from Eleanor Frost's diary provides a window onto her husband's views on gender equity. Mrs. Frost was, as already noted, prosuffrage, but there was apparently something of a divide between her and her husband on this issue. She notes that, one morning, they stayed in bed and had a "long talk before getting up": "Women's Suffrage, etc. Came close together in sympathy and understanding. Exhausting, distressing, comforting."[97] This diary entry hints that they were not of one mind on this issue. It is easy to forget how contentious the question of female suffrage was. It was a thorny issue that threatened that era's entire societal structure. Men—even progressive men—had difficulty understanding why women found the long-accepted gendered distribution of power objectionable. President Frost appears to be a case in point.

Mrs. Frost also paints a picture of her husband's limits on taking advice from women or at least from her: "When you spoke bitterly of my assuming an attitude of superior wisdom there was ground for the charge. I do feel that I can more quickly get the other person's point of view, and I count it a necessity to know it, while you will prescribe without one thought of the other man's ability to get the point, and dismiss him without trying to know his thoughts." This is an important insight into not only how Frost took criticism from at least one woman but also his quickness at making assumptions, which may have come to play in the *Harper's* magazine affair. Eleanor continues: "I will try to be quiet and self-controlled when counsel is not followed. At the same time I will try not to be indifferent to anything that affects your interests."[98] (One wonders whether Jackson might have been one of the things about which they were quarreling.)

Frost's view of the role of women is made even clearer by his elegy for Matilda Fee, John G. Fee's wife. He says of her: "She was an old-fashioned heroine. She made no public harangues, asserted no 'rights,' sought no 'emancipation' from the duties of home, and never regretted the fact that her name and fame were bound up in those of her husband. She never knew that she was confined, or oppressed, by the narrowness of woman's true sphere. . . . It was worth much that with that grim encounter with relentless foes Mr. Fee and the Berea champions had among them a beautiful woman's smile, and a bright spirit's jest and laughter."[99] History does not record what Eleanor Marsh Frost thought of this speech. However, if a compliant, homebound woman was Frost's ideal female, he would have found Jackson to be the opposite.

We must also consider the overall status of female teachers on the Berea campus during Frost's tenure. There is at least one record of a woman who expressed frustration at Frost's unequal treatment of women. In a 1908 letter, Katherine S. Bowersox agrees to return to Berea if Frost will grant her increased pay to go along with her title *dean of women*. A later letter makes it clear that Frost granted her that raise, but it also makes it clear that her duties are more exhaustive than those of the male deans. In this 1914 letter, in which she pleads for a vacation to go home and tend a sick mother, Bowersox details the many duties she performs as dean of women students. She also mentions the fact that, unlike the male deans, she is not allowed to go home in the evenings but must reside on campus with the girls in her care.[100] Some of that may have been due not to any unusual view held by Frost, but to the standing sexist idea of the time that young ladies needed constant chaperoning whereas young men did not. To be fair, Bowersox knew the demands when she took the job. Still, it is clear that the women at Berea were not granted the same privileges or held in the same regard as the men and that any change in the status quo had to be fought for.

In light of all this, Frost may have had a problem on some level with Jackson's occasional assertiveness, outright bossiness, and other not so docile and ladylike behaviors. He may even have had a problem on some level with such a project as the ballad collection coming from a woman. He did believe in educating women, but the available evidence indicates that he would not have taken kindly to a woman educating him or at least issuing him directives and ultimatums.[101]

Personalities

We must take into account the overall personalities of both Frost and Jackson. As noted, Jackson could be assertive, she could possibly have been perceived as overly aggressive, and she was prone to micromanagement. Frost had a history of reacting badly to such personality traits. But, if Jackson's personality played a role in this story, then we must also mention the general temperament of William Goodell Frost. To say that he was high-strung is an understatement. By many accounts, he was easily offended, quick to anger, often ready to jump to conclusions, and prone to holding grudges. Correspondence from close friends urged him to keep his temper in check. The music teacher Ira Penniman resigned in 1899 over negative statements made about him in public by Frost and public accusations of conspiratorial conduct, saying that he admired Frost but could not "abide [his] treatment."[102] William E. Barton, a close friend and colleague, admonished Frost in 1901 for omitting a faculty member's address from the *Berea Quarterly* simply because he was angry with him.[103] In 1895, Berea founder John G. Fee told Frost that his language was "harsh."[104] Frost was a man with whom a number of people had personal conflicts. Put this together with Jackson's aggressive admonishments for the delays her ballad project experienced, and it appears probable that he reacted in a negative manner and strongly. He did not have a record of going out of his way to help people with whom he was angry. Thus, his excitable and unforgiving personality combined with Jackson's own assertiveness may have played a role in the fate of Jackson's collection.

Mr. President

Finally, there is the matter of Frost's situation as president of Berea College. Jackson herself says: "Other matters pressed too heavily upon him." Frost was overburdened from the day he took up his post. He inherited a school that was in deep financial trouble, and half of his strenuous schedule was spent on the road, at the cost of family and health, raising money to keep the college afloat and publicize the college's mission. He did this with great success, raising the endowment from $200,000 to $12 million over a twenty-year period. It is not an exaggeration to say that Berea College exists today because of him.[105]

Frost had a lot to deal with. Kentucky's 1904 Day Law outlawed interracial college education (Berea's prime mission) and was, in fact, prompted by Berea. Half the town of Berea hated Frost because they thought he was for the law, and half hated him because they thought he was against it. Nevertheless, the college expanded greatly under him in terms of attendees and physical size. In his first twenty years, he oversaw not only this growth but the institution of the labor program as well.[106] His pace was one of continuous fever pitch.

As a result of all this, combined with his naturally high-strung temperament, Frost worked himself several times into what was politely called *nervous exhaustion*. He and Eleanor both had instances in 1916 where they collapsed from overwork and exhaustion. And this was before they were dealt the terrible blow of their son Cleveland's death in World War I in 1918, just six weeks before the Armistice. This was a devastating loss to them both. Eleanor spent days in bed, unable to do anything but reread her son's letters; William's final breakdown in 1919 led to his gradual relinquishment of duties as president.[107]

In short, though Frost was an imperfect man, he operated with absolute devotion to the cause of Berea College at a breakneck pace in a horrendously difficult time. One could argue that he deserves to be given the benefit of the doubt. Unfortunately, his actions, or more precisely, inaction, affected the history of balladry in America. For all the good that he did Berea College— and that good was monumental—he did not see through on his promise to a young ballad collector from London, and it is on such small things that history often turns.

6

A Comparison of the Ballads of Katherine Jackson and Olive Dame Campbell/Cecil Sharp

I now turn to the question that fueled this study: Just how much did history turn on the suppression of Jackson's ballad collection? In what ways were Jackson's and Sharp's depictions and collections of Appalachian balladry the same, and in what ways were they different? Would it have mattered if Jackson, not Sharp, had published the first large scholarly collection of Appalachian balladry?

We cannot, of course, say for certain. Given his distinguished reputation and the fact that he was a man, Sharp might have outshone Jackson even if she had succeeded and published first. The fact that his overall collection was so much larger might have erased any initial influence she might have had as well.[1] But we do know that his *English Folksongs from the Southern Appalachians* (and Maud Karpeles's expanded 1932 revision)[2] became the yardstick against which all other Appalachian collections were measured. The question then becomes, What if Jackson's collection had become the yardstick instead?

A word is in order for the ballad neophyte at this point regarding Cecil Sharp: he was one of a handful of well-respected British collectors and scholars who wanted to preserve British folk song before modernity extinguished it. While several people had written about Appalachian balladry in scholarly journals like the *Journal of American Folklore* as early as 1893 and some smaller groupings of songs had been published, it was Olive Dame Campbell who first alerted Sharp to the presence of British ballad survivals in the southern Appalachians in 1915. She had begun collecting them in 1906 as she traveled with her husband, John C. Campbell, through Appalachia to ascertain the condition of the mountain people. She knew Sharp's reputation and thought that he would be interested. She hoped that the ballads would evoke sympathy and respect for Appalachians among the general public. Since she had been turned down by the Russell Sage Foundation in a previous attempt at publication (in a situation parallel to Jackson's, the foundation initially intended to publish but got distracted by other matters), she may also have realized that having a scholar with Sharp's reputation on board was an advantage. Once alerted by Campbell to the presence of these ballads, Sharp was intrigued. Assisted by Maud Karpeles, he spent the summer and fall of 1916 collecting ballads, publishing them in 1917, as we have seen, as *English Folk Songs from the Southern Appalachians*.[3]

Though the 1917 collection was published mainly to raise money for more trips and a future expanded book, it attracted enough attention that it helped inspire others to follow in Sharp's path. John Harrington Cox followed suit in 1925 with *Folk-Songs of the South*, as did Arthur Kyle Davis in 1929 with *Traditional Ballads of Virginia*. As late as 1939, Jean Thomas dedicated her *Ballad-Makin' in the Hills of Kentucky* to "the Kentucky Ballad Makers Who Have Kept Alive the Art of Their Anglo Saxon Forbears."[4]

As Ann Ostendorf notes: "[Sharp's] attitude and approach pervaded scholarship for fifty years." The system followed by subsequent collectors was based on Sharp's method and entailed a scholarly connection of Appalachian ballads and songs to British versions, use of titles identical to Child's, and preservation of music as well as lyrics. His theories about the musical aspect of Appalachian balladry have likewise been passed down by subsequent collectors and are held as found wisdom even today.[5]

Sharp's footprint was large. Jackson's was nonexistent. While we cannot say for certain what the results of the publication of her collection would have been, we can compare his collection to hers. We can examine whether Jackson had a different view of balladry and ballad keepers in the southern Appalachians than the one that Sharp passed down to us. We can compare the ballads presented by each, postulating the effect on the history of Appalachian balladry had Jackson's collection set the standard.

The Role of Women as Ballad Keepers

Sharp's and Jackson's views clearly diverge on the role of women as ballad keepers, with Jackson highlighting it much more than Sharp does.

Sharp

The picture Sharp gives us of the typical Appalachian singer is a consistently male one. Although he and Olive Dame Campbell found that the ballads were being sung mostly by women, he did not discuss this in the twenty-three-page introduction to *English Folk Songs from the Southern Appalachians,* in which he espouses his theories about Appalachian balladry. In fact, despite the fact that fifty-eight of his seventy-seven informants were women and 144 of his 188 ballad variants came from women, and despite the fact that his star informant, Jane Hicks Gentry, gave him over 60 songs, he invariably uses the word *he* when describing ballad singers. For example, he writes: "I never saw one of them close his eyes when he sang." Also: "The genuine folk-singer is never conscious of his audience—indeed, as often as not, he has none—and he never, therefore, strives after effect. . . . [H]e is merely relating a story in a peculiarly effective way which he has learned from his elders." He does mention female informants in a paragraph listing singers, but any discussion of these singers is restricted to men: "These are often of great interest and significance and sometimes show an inventiveness on the part of the singer that is nothing less than amazing, as, for example, in Mr. Jeff Stockton's version of 'Fair Margaret.'" He also mentions collecting tunes from two fiddlers, both male.[6]

Thus, the image of the Appalachian musician that dominates Sharp's introduction to the bedrock collection of Appalachian balladry is male, this in spite of the fact that half again as many woman as men were informants and that three times as many women as men provided variants. It should be pointed out that the use of *he* when referring to mixed genders was normal for the time. Still, Sharp did not consider the overwhelming preponderance of female singers important enough even to mention, however briefly.

In fact, it can be argued that Sharp's marginalization of women extended to Campbell herself. In his introduction to *English Folk Songs from the Southern Appalachians,* his own experiences, not Campbell's, take center stage. Campbell gets only a brief mention. For that matter, of the 325 songs in the collection, only 31 (including the 10 Kentucky ballads) came from Campbell's prior collecting trips. This may be simply because Sharp felt more comfortable with the accuracy of songs he collected himself, but the result is still the minimization of Campbell's contribution. Most of the rest of Campbell's songs were not published until Maud Karpeles's 1932 revision, though in that edition Campbell's name was left off the cover, appearing only in the front matter.[7]

Jackson

As were Sharp's, most of Jackson's informants were women—sixteen of seventeen. Of the still-existing forty-three ballad variants in her collection, twenty-two of the twenty-three credited ones are from women. Unlike Sharp, Jackson considered the role of women to be central to American balladry. She wrote at length in the introduction to her collection about the role of women in keeping ballads alive in the mountains. "To the women of the community, is the credit of the preservation due," she declared. And her dedication reads: "To the Singing Mothers of Colonial America." In both the introduction to "English-Scottish Ballads from the Hills of Kentucky" and "A Fortnight of Balladry," she discusses at length women ballad singers and their motivation for keeping the ballads alive. She also consistently refers to the ballad singer as *she*, painting the archetype as female rather than male:

> Thus, oral transmission has retained ballads of the purest type, although the singer is unconscious of the antiquity of her song, and the possibility of finding it in print. To her, a "ballet" is what it was to her Elizabethan forebears,—a written-down copy, or a broadside, of anything sung. . . . To the women of the community is the credit of this preservation due. When the older men sing, they rarely go beyond 18th century hymns, or such songs of the homeland as Annie Laurie, Ben Bolt, Blue Bells of Scotland, or The Maid of Dundee; the younger men most often sing a banjo or fiddle tune, perhaps of British origin or influence,—as the Jacobite Aire to Prince Charlie, or the Swapping Song of Jack Straw,—airs, thought frivolous and unbecoming for any mother. The reason for this is easily explained;—the women in their constant intercourse with the children, come nearer the heart of the tales, are keener in picturing the tragic situation and in sympathizing with the crying out of the soul of the woman, in the ballad. The mother's monotonous environment and condition of life makes the song seem both natural and true. In addition, she feels a loyalty to her own mother, in continuing this unbroken line of song, for the accomplishment of her daughters and the social plea-

sure to her family and friends; companie are [*sic*] invited and asked to join in the refrains, which, however unintelligible and meaningless, are, none-the-less, emotional, expressive, and communal. In such a gathering, the original intent of the word, ballad,—the huc et illud inclinare vacillare,—impresses one as the leader sways backward and forward in her low, straight chair; or walks to and fro . . . expressing in her face the thought of the stanzas sung.[8]

In this manner, and unlike Sharp, Jackson attempted to shine a very bright light on the role of women in Appalachian balladry.

Scope: Ethnic Focus, Agendas, and Perceptions

Sharp

As the saying goes, Sharp went looking for ballads, and that is what he found. He paid little initial attention to tunes that were played on the banjo or the fiddle. He was trying to follow in the footsteps of Child and, thus, came harvesting English-Scottish ballads, tossing aside the (to him) useless flotsam of tunes, dances, bawdy songs, drinking songs, hymns, spirituals, camp revival songs, minstrel songs, popular songs, and any music of African Americans that he may have encountered. Such a limited scope was not unusual; most collectors had a singular focus. Child himself had no interest in broadside ballads, for example, considering them to be "veritable dung-hills, in which, only after a great deal of sickening grubbing, one finds a very moderate jewel."[9]

Mike Yates, however, suggests that Sharp's cultural and racial beliefs were a possible motivation for his exclusion of other kinds of music in general and African American music in particular. He gives as evidence the fact that Sharp used the word *nigger* derogatorily and nastily several times in his journals, particularly in an account of leaving Winston-Salem earlier than planned because it was "a noisy place and the air impregnated with tobacco, molasses, and nigger!" (Karpeles was even blunter: "Glad to leave Sylva. Did not like town. Too many negroes.") Sharp did collect ballads from one mixed-race woman and one African American, however, so his exclusion of African American music was not absolute, though, as Yates points out, it did not seem to affect his notion that the Appalachians were peopled only by those of English and Scottish descent. Benjamin Filene concludes that Sharp was probably not unusually racist for his time, that there was a "racial undertone" to most of the early collectors' focus and methods that presumed that anything other than music that originated in the British Isles was somehow less worthwhile, thus delegitimizing the music of other ethnic groups.[10]

Sharp's own words do not necessarily indicate motivation for the Anglocentrism of his collecting, but they do infer that the Appalachian keepers of the ballads should themselves be held in esteem on the basis of race: "They have one and all entered at birth into the full enjoyment of their racial heritage. Their language, wisdom, manners, and the many graces of life that are theirs, are merely racial attributes which have been gradually acquired and accumulated in past centuries and handed down generation by generation."[11]

It should be mentioned that Sharp's *English Folk Songs from the Southern Appalachians* includes fifty-five songs that are not related to the Child ballads and twelve children's songs. While some of these songs contained wandering verses related to British ballads, most were clearly homegrown, written on the North American continent. "Omie Wise," for example, told of a local murder in clearly colloquial musical and lyrical language and was based on a true North Carolina crime.

Jackson

Jackson does not spend much time and ink examining any other kind of music than survivals of British ballads (although a few native ballads are to be found in her collection).[12] Like Sharp, she makes the case for the Anglo connection, stating that the ballads are "peculiarly Anglo-American, most characteristic of the traditional history and spirit of their composers of the 14th, 15th, and 16th centuries, and likewise, after generations of contact, made to be a part of the blood, bone, and sinew of the settlers in the remote land." She refers at one point to the people in question as "Saxons." She basks in the fact that the women she visited were "strikingly homogeneous, breathing one unlettered atmosphere, one habit of thought, one measure of defence and sympathy." The homogeneity she paints here appears to focus on common experience and culture ("one unlettered atmosphere"), however, rather than on race. Her main interest seems to be in the power of the songs themselves. "They have lived because they were loved," she says simply, "and with this excuse for existence, they have played for ages upon free, generous, and impulsive minds. This, then, becomes an immemorial record of sentiment, loyalty, principle—a conserver of their love for poetry of song." She stresses that the singers of these songs are part of a community, but she does not dwell on the particulars of their heritage.[13]

It is hard to say whether Jackson's racial views were different than those prevailing at the times, those expressed by the Englishman Sharp and held by most white people in America. Unlike Sharp, in no diary entry or any correspondence did Jackson ever use the usual ugly word *nigger,* unfortunately in common use at the time. Absent the remarks about "the spirit and sap of the stock" and the ballads themselves being "peculiarly Anglo-American," she did not seem as driven as Sharp was to prove that the existence of British balladry in Appalachia somehow helped establish the Angloness of the Appalachians and, therefore, their inherent superiority.

Style of Ballad Singing

Both Jackson and Sharp found that the ballads were sung unaccompanied, with rare exceptions. When it comes to style of delivery, however, their descriptions differ.

Sharp

Sharp speaks of ballads delivered without overt emotion and motionlessly, in a "straightforward, direct manner, without any conscious effort at expression, and with the even tone and clarity of enunciation with which all folk-song collectors are familiar": "Perhaps, however, [these singers] are less unselfconscious, and sing rather more freely and with somewhat less restraint than the English peasant; I certainly never saw any one of them close the eyes when he sang, nor assume that rigid, passive expression to which collectors in England have so often called attention." He also mentions the practice of dwelling on more weakly accented notes, which makes the tunes sound freer.[14]

Jackson

In contrast, Jackson describes the female ballad singer delivering her songs as swaying back and forth, as if keening, or walking around, or singing while doing tasks. And she finds expression in the singing itself, noting that the typical female ballad singer's face is "expressive of the thought of the stanzas sung."[15] As we have seen, she also depicts listeners joining the leader on refrains. Unlike Sharp's picture of the solitary ballad singer, Jackson's account has an element of communal participation.

Discussion

There are several possible reasons for the divergence between the descriptions that Sharp and Jackson give. Sharp did not collect in Kentucky for the 1917 edition of his book, whereas Jackson collected entirely in Kentucky, so it is possible that their descriptions are the result of regional differences in style and ethnic background (English vs. Scottish). It is also possible that Jackson was more focused on the women and Sharp on the men. It could be that the deep mountains of Kentucky, where Jackson based her study, featured a different style of singing than that prevailing in the areas around the towns and villages (primarily in North Carolina) to which, for health reasons, Sharp was largely limited. Finally, it is possible that the mostly female singers behaved differently around a female collector than they did around a male collector.

A word should also be said at this point about the limitations of the music transcriptions themselves. Unlike Phillips Barry, who collected in Maine, neither Sharp nor Jackson (nor Campbell, for that matter) notated anything other than pitches and rhythms. Bent notes, scoops, falls, changes in tone, catches at the end of phrases or on a high note, vibrato or the lack thereof, when notes were slightly elongated in a phrase—these features were not recorded. Their existence in southern Appalachian ballad singing must be left to faith in regional traditions and the documentation to be found in early recordings.

Roles of Women and Men in Ballads

The female characters that appear in the ballads of both Sharp and Jackson are by and large not positive figures, and their fates are similarly constant cases of misfortune. There were, of course, ballads in the British Isles where the women were heroines and came out victorious: witness the collection of Mrs. Brown of Falkland and certain songs of the Travellers. But songs like "Jock O'Hazeldean" and "True Thomas" did not seem to make their way to Appalachia. Instead, in the Appalachian versions of British ballads, women were typically characterized negatively: as powerless creatures ("The Beggar Girl"), evil creatures ("The Cruel Mother"), or unfaithful mates ("Little

Musgrave and Lady Barnard"). Often, they were the victims of foul deeds, usually murder.

It should be pointed out that, as poorly as the women fare in these ballads, the men fare little better. In fact, in both collections, more men than women wind up dead. Happy endings were not the norm in the ballad collections of either Sharp or of Jackson.

Jackson and Sharp both claim that women passed these ballads down to their daughters. Offering a reason why mothers would want their daughters to hear such tales of violence and murder against women, Polly Stewart suggests that these songs served as a sort of negative template for young girls—what not to do.[16] Jackson offered a different reason, that in the mountains ballads were kept by women because of a certain kinship they felt with the unfortunate characters in the songs. The fact that throughout Appalachia the ballads were called *love songs* is an uncomfortable indication that violence was accepted as part and parcel of male/female relationships and human relationships in general. In over half the ballads in each of these collections, someone is killing someone, often in relation to love, and men and women both die.

The Ballads Themselves: North Carolina and Kentucky

Here, we reach the crucial question: How were the lyrics and music of the ballads collected by Jackson and Sharp different, and would those differences have resulted in an alternative early view of Appalachian balladry had Jackson published first? To examine this, we need to examine characteristic differences between Jackson's Kentucky ballads and Sharp's mostly North Carolina material.

First, we need to be very clear: *English Folk Songs from the Southern Appalachians* is very much a North Carolina collection, and Kentucky is almost completely unrepresented. One hundred seventeen ballads and variants came exclusively from North Carolina, and fifty-one of the fifty-five ballads had at least one version collected in North Carolina. Only ten ballads and variants in that first edition were from Kentucky, fewer than came from any other state. This is likely due, as noted, to the fact that Sharp himself had not collected in Kentucky at that point and the only ballads at hand from that state were those previously collected by Campbell.

English Folk Songs from the Southern Appalachians thus gives us a good look at the heart and soul of North Carolina ballads. Since two-thirds of

Table 6.1. Comparison, Location of Informants for the 1917 *English Folk Songs from the Southern Appalachians*

	Informants (N)	Ballad Variants (N)	Ballad Variants (%)
North Carolina	37	117	64
Kentucky	9	10	5
Georgia	9	116	6
Tennessee	11	22	12
Virginia	11	24	13

the ballads it contains hail from that state and define the overall character of the collection, I have focused on those ballads and compared them with the Kentucky ballads of Katherine Jackson to determine how the body of ballads Jackson presented differed from those that Sharp presented.

Comparing the Ballads of Sharp and Jackson

Lyrical Similarities

There are some lyrical similarities between the collections.

The *story lines* do not change very much from version to version or collection to collection. In fact, despite time and distance, they remain remarkably similar. There are occasional twists and omissions, and the use of colloquialisms varies. People love, lose, and die in each collection in a similar fashion.

In terms of *lyric devices,* the collections are quite similar. There are no significant differences in prevalent lyrical forms and lyric accents. Both collections' ballads are significantly wedded to form, Jackson's almost totally and Sharp about 80 percent of the time. A higher instance of condensation of story line in Sharp's songs results in more persistent wandering rhyme schemes (i.e., schemes that are not maintained throughout).

The same overall rhyme schemes are often used in the ballads of both collectors. The iconic ABCB[17] is the prevalent form; it is used half the time in Jackson's ballads and about half the time in Sharp's if we include variants with wandering schemes. Songs with refrains occur with great frequency as well. The use of the familiar accent scheme of 4 / 3 / 4 / 3 is used by both at approximately the same rate, 50 percent of the time; 4 / 4 / 4 / 4 sees the next greatest use.

Neither collection uses simile or personification very much. All this bears witness to long effort over time to preserve that which was handed down lyrically in both locales.

Lyrical Differences

There are, however, significant lyrical differences between the collections.

In terms of *tone,* the overall language of Sharp's ballads is more colloquial than is that of Jackson's. It is difficult to ascertain whether the particular colloquialisms used are the result of individual choices or overall local linguistic mores. They differ from locale to locale, but they can also differ from person to person within the same locale. Overall, Jackson's ballads seem to be less affected lyrically by local influences than are Sharp's.

In terms of *poetic devices,* the language of Jackson's ballads is consistently more poetic, evinces greater use of archetypes, metaphors, archaic English, imagery, and alliteration, and is closer to the more archaic language of ancient English/Scottish balladry than is that of Sharp's ballads. Again, this would indicate less change at the local level.

Musical Similarities

The *melodic form* AA'BC[18] is the prominent form for each, though not by much; ABB'C and ABCD figure prominently in Sharp's collection, and ABCD and ABCA' figure largely in Jackson's. Other forms are also used in both.

As for *modes,* a similar percentage of ballads examined in this sample from the two collectors are in pentatonic mode—32 percent for Jackson and 32 percent for Sharp. Differences will be discussed later.

Melodies in both collections are mostly conversational in phrase shape in that they rise in the first phrase and fall in the last. There is a similar frequency of angularity within phrases, but, mostly, the melodies are smooth.

The *beginnings and endings* of most melodies in both collection are in the low and middle range. Melismas are used with roughly the same frequency, with slightly more in Sharp's.

Musical Differences

When it comes to *differing overall variants,* about half the ballads in Jackson's collection have related versions in Sharp's. However, the others do not. Of this latter group, one version of "Barbara Allen" is the standout. Its upward sweep sets the stage; its repetition of the second phrase, resolving downward on the last note, is wholly satisfying. ("Barbara Allen," "Lord Vanner's Wife," and "The Lord of the Old Country" were collected by Katherine Jackson and transcribed by Elizabeth DiSavino.)

In Scarlet Town, where I was born, There was a fair maid dwelling And ev'ry youth cried, "Well-a-day-," her name was Barb-'ra All-en

"Lord Vanner's Wife," Jackson's version of "Little Musgrave and Lady Barnard," has an unrepentantly cheery Ionian melody, in stark contrast to the usual Appalachian pentatonic stereotype so championed by Sharp.[19]

1. The first came down were lil-ly-white, the next were pink and blue, The next came in, Lord Vanner's wife, the flower of the view.

"Two Sisters" ("The Lord of the Old Country"), "Lord Thomas and Fair Ellender," and "Lord Randall" are likewise unrelated to anything in the Sharp collection. Here is "The Lord of the Old Country" from Jackson.

1. There was a lord lived in the Old Country, bow down, There was a lord lived in the Old Country, these vows were given to me — There was a lord lived in the Old Country, and he had daughters, one, two, three, I'll be true, true to my love, If my love will be true to me.

Somewhat different *melodic ranges* are used in the two collections. The ballads in Jackson's are slightly easier to sing owing to their more limited range, most often an octave. The most often-occurring ranges in the Sharp ballads are ninths and tenths.

Melodic devices in Jackson's ballads include scalar melodies, walking quarters, and text painting. Sharp's also use walking quarters and text painting. His differ from Jackson's in the use of fermatas midphrase (indicating held notes as executed by the singer) and a more consistent use of eighth notes on the second and fourth beats of the measure, with almost no notation of Scottish snaps.

As to *meter,* Jackson's ballads are evenly split between duple and triple. Sharp's are more slanted toward duple over triple at a rate of 5.3 to 3.2.

Modes: Sharp's Pentatonic Doctrine and the Pure Anglo Connection

Sharp's theories on the use of the pentatonic and gapped scales in Appalachian music have resonated through the years down to our day, so they bear some examination. Sharp postulated that, in addition to the clear migration of lyrics, the use of gapped scales and particularly pentatonic modes helped prove that the ballads he found in southern Appalachia were English in origin. The notion that gapped modes, and particularly the pentatonic scale, indicate a direct tie back to Britain, and particularly to medieval England, persists to this day in elementary music textbooks, college classrooms, books and articles, and the found knowledge of the general folk community.[20]

In his introduction to the 1917 edition of *Folk Songs from the Southern Appalachians,* Sharp outlines what I have dubbed *the pentatonic doctrine:* "Personally I believe that [the pentatonic] was the first form of scale evolved by the folk." He adds: "If the prevalence of the gapped scale in the mountain tunes is any indication of the ethnological origins of the singers, it seems to point to the North of England, or to the Lowlands, rather than the Highlands of Scotland, as the country from which they originally migrated. For the Appalachian tunes, notwithstanding their 'gapped characteristics,' have far more affinity with the normal English folk-tune than with that of the Gaelic-speaking Highlander. . . . The tunes in question would quite correctly be called English." He further notes that, "for all we know," eighteenth-century

English folksingers still used the gapped scale because their musical understanding had not yet advanced to using a full scale and advances the supposition that those were the melodies they brought with them to America. If this supposition is accurate, there should be copious proof of eighteenth-century (and earlier) British folk song rife with pentatonic modes and other gapped scales.[21]

While it is impossible to investigate all sources, an analysis of a large sample of British song from four major collectors/publishers (368 melodies, all sources cited by both Jackson and Sharp, from Chappell, Johnson, Bronson, and Playford)[22] does not support this theory,[23] showing instead the majority of melodies to be composed on the basis of neither pentatonic nor gapped scales of any kind. The majority of the melodies are in the seven-note Ionian (major) mode. The proportion is impressively large in all the collections except Playford's, where Ionian comes in 5 percent above other gapped scales. Further, the majority of gapped-scale tunes in the Bronson sample were Scottish, not English, and from the Aberdeenshire area, not the borderlands. There is also the issue of melodies that modulate or use multiple modes, which is characteristic of Renaissance music, a subject that Sharp avoids addressing altogether. Gapped scales are in the minority in all four collections. The pentatonic mode is strikingly absent altogether in Playford and barely makes a showing in the other three collections. Gapped scales in total barely crack 10 percent in the three song collections and are found in only a quarter of the Playford collection.[24]

Table 6.2. Modal Chart for English/Scottish Collections					
	Ionian	Other Gapped Scales	Pentatonic	Total Gapped Scales	Multiple Modes
Chappel, *Popular Music of Olden Time*	56.5	8.3	1.2	9.5	7
Johnson, *Scots Musical Museum*	58.5	10	1.1	11.1	13.8
Bronson, *Tunes of the Child Ballads*	40	2.9	7	9.9	4
Playford, *The English Dancing Master*	30	25	0	25	1.7

The breakdown of the modes in Sharp's collection does not coincide with that found in the comparison sample. If we examine the entire 1917 publication, we find that only 8 percent of the tunes are Ionian while a third are based on the pentatonic scale and three-quarters on gapped scales.[25]

Table 6.3. Modal Chart for the 1917 *English Folk Songs from the Southern Appalachian*s

Ionian	Other Gapped Scales	Pentatonic	Total Gapped Scales	Multiple Modes
8	39	33	72	7.5

Here is a side-by-side comparison with the previously mentioned English sources. The discrepancies are apparent.

Table 6.4. Modal Chart for English Collectors vs. Sharp

	Ionian	Other Gapped Scales	Pentatonic	Total Gapped Scales	Multiple Modes
Chappel	56.5	8.3	1.2	9.5	7
Johnson	58.5	10	1.1	11.1	13.8
Bronson	40	2.9	7	9.9	4
Playford	30	25	0	25	1.7
Sharp	8	39	33	72	7.5

In contrast to Sharp's collection, 32 percent of Jackson's ballad melodies are Ionian, 32 percent pentatonic, 5 percent Aeolian, 5 percent Dorian, and 26 percent gapped Ionian or gapped Ionian/Mixolydian (missing the seventh step). In short, Jackson found a much higher proportion of Ionian

Table 6.5. Modal Comparison between Jackson's and Sharp's Collections

	Ionian	Other Gapped Scales	Pentatonic	Total Gapped Scales	Multiple Modes
Jackson	32	50	28	78	0
Sharp 1917	8	39	33	72	7.5

ballads than did Sharp. However, they both found similarly high percentages of gapped-scale and pentatonic ballads.

The pentatonic doctrine was, then, incorrect. Sharp indeed found a great number of tunes using gapped scales and pentatonic modes in the southern Appalachians. But this does not prove a link to English music of the Elizabethan age or later years.

Something happened, then, to the melodies of these songs once they came to southern Appalachia. One possible explanation is that the pentatonic and other gapped scales were borrowed from or at least reinforced by their use by African Americans who hailed from West Africa and, perhaps to a lesser degree, certain Native American tribes. That is, their use may have been a conscious choice on the part of the ballad singers themselves, one influenced by the musical language of some of their "different" neighbors, a language that reinforced a small portion of their own musical vocabulary. This would be ironic given Sharp's holding that same musical language as proof of the purity of Anglo mountain culture.[26]

This is crucial. Sharp and early collectors were intent on proving the Englishness of Appalachians and argued that British ballads were being preserved in the mountains in their unspoiled and untouched form by an unspoiled and untouched Anglo population. Had anything put a dent in Sharp's theory, the initial impression of the racially pure ethnic makeup of Appalachia and its music might not have been so compelling.

One such dent might have come from the publication in 1911 of Jackson's collection, given the prevalence of the Ionian mode among the songs found in it, which would have countered Sharp's theory and laid a different foundation for the study of Appalachian balladry. On the other hand, Jackson did not engage in the kind of analysis and theorizing that Sharp did, so the difference in musical language might have passed unnoticed. Further, the frequency with which the Ionian mode appears in Jackson's collection might have reinforced the Anglo connection, rather than countered it, to those not yet swayed by Sharp's Pentatonic Doctrine.

Overall, Jackson's ballads used more triple meters, simpler melodies, and a good dose of Ionian melodies, whereas Sharp's ballads were characterized by duple meters, an extended melodic range, and the absence of the Ionian mode. Who knows how these differences might have been interpreted had Jackson published? A comparison of the two collections might have led to a more accurate picture of the relationship between English and Appalachian melodies, or it might have made no difference whatsoever.

The Ones That Got Away

All that having been said, consider the following scenario.

Katherine Jackson French, with the aid of Berea College and William Goodell Frost, publishes her "English-Scottish Ballads from the Hills of Kentucky" in late 1911. All honor is given to her, and to Berea College, for this landmark work. She is offered and accepts the position of professor of philology at her alma mater, Columbia University, only the second woman to serve as a full professor in the college's history.

Cecil Sharp hears of Jackson and is intrigued by her collection. He comes to America and focuses his own study on Kentucky on the assumption that the state is the center of balladry in America. The ballads he finds there have a large number of tunes in Ionian as well as pentatonic modes and are divided equally among double and triple meters. The language of the ballads is poetic and formal with only the occasional colloquialism. The presence of Ionian modes prompts Sharp to rethink his theories and investigate the source of pentatonic modes in Appalachian music, leading to early corroboration of musical crossovers between African Americans and the Ulster Scots.

Since such interest in Kentucky balladry has been generated, Frost sees to it that the ballads of the Berea collectors James Watt Raine and John F. Smith are published and disseminated. Their collections are accorded great acclaim, and the music of Kentucky becomes the foundation of America's understanding of itself through balladry. Because Jackson's collection makes the Anglo connection clear but is not intent on proving the superiority of the Anglo settlers and their descendants, and because the recently famous John F. Smith's collecting techniques are inclusive, new collectors begin compiling music other than British Isle survivals.

The first large Appalachian music festival, the Pinnacle Festival, takes place on a sunny day in May 1918 in Berea. Kentucky singers share their songs, and fiddlers share their tunes. Given the historic role regarding race and gender that Berea had played, African Americans and women are also invited to perform, though African-American performers play in a separate tent. Jackson, Raine, and Smith are honored guests, with Eleanor Frost presiding as the mistress of ceremonies. Eleanor gives a stirring speech, properly recognizing women for their role in preserving balladry in America. The speech hits the newspapers, and, because of this, when the recording industry is born, it is female Appalachian singers and performers who are sought out and whose immortality is first etched into wax cylinders. When Ralph Peer organizes the Bristol Sessions in 1927, he makes an effort to find Kentucky ballad singers and musicians, and they constitute the majority of artists on the Big Bang recording that resulted, shaping the direction of early country music.[27] Solo female Appalachian artists become the norm in the late 1920s, providing models of upward mobility for mountain women. African American string bands are likewise sought out as representative examples of mountain music and are big sellers in the field of early race records.

Or not.

Still, that imagined scenario illustrates the point that perhaps the biggest impact on Appalachian balladry was the one that never happened. I am speaking of those missing ballads and their singers: the ones that got away. What of those ballads that did not make it into the 1917 version of *English Folk Songs of the Southern Appalachians,* some of which never made it into the canon of American balladry at all? Would they support Jackson's or Sharp's picture of Appalachian music?

Kentucky ballads sung before 1916 but collected after can be found in a number of places, including (ironically) the 1932 edition of *English Folk Songs from the Southern Appalachians*.[28] Other published collections include Josephine McGill's *Folk-Songs of the Kentucky Mountains,* twenty songs collected at the behest of May Stone and published in 1917, and the 1916 *Lonesome Tunes,* which was put together by the entertainer Loraine Wyman and Harold A. Brockway and featured the piano accompaniments used by Loraine in her New York shows.[29] In addition, the Berea College Sound Archives at Hutchins Library has many fine recordings of Kentucky ballad singers who have kept alive generations-old versions of family ballads. The ballad collections of James Watt Raine and Josiah Combs (a contemporary of Jackson's) and John F. Smith (just after Jackson) are also excellent sources, although neither had the staying power and reputation that Sharp's collection did.[30] I used a combination of all these resources to look for the ones that got away.

One fine example of unknown Kentucky balladry is Jim Gage's archival sound version of "Dog and Gun" ("Golden Glove"), which was passed down in Gage's family and sung in 1977 at the Berea College Celebration of Traditional Music. It conveys the usual story but bears a very different melody, one in triple meter and sung slowly. The tune is Scottish in nature, complete with Scottish snaps, features a strong Ionian mode (including dwelling on the deliberately ill-tuned seventh-step midphrase), and has a third phrase reminiscent of several other Scottish songs.

"Dog and Gun" as sung by Jim Gage at the 1974 Berea College Celebration of Traditional Music. Transcribed by Elizabeth DiSavino.

Jean Ritchie recorded a version of "Fair Ellender" in Mixolydian mode in her 1949 recording for Alan Lomax.

"Fair Ellender" as sung by Jean Ritchie, 1974. Transcribed by Elizabeth DiSavino.

The melody of John F. Smith's "The House Carpenter" is mostly pentatonic (until the last phrase, when it becomes gapped Aeolian/Dorian minus the sixth step), and it uses an extended range.

A Comparison of the Ballads of Jackson and Campbell/Sharp 131

[musical notation with lyrics: "Well met, well-met, my own true-love, Well-met,-well met," cried she; "I've just re-turned from a for-iegn coun-try, And it's all for the sake of thee."]

"The House Carpenter," John F. Smith collection. Transcribed by Elizabeth DiSavino.

The Kentuckian Bradley Kincaid had yet another version of "The House Carpenter" in his *Favorite Old-Time Songs: Volume 2.* While Kincaid was popular for his work on WLS's *National Barn Dance,* he was also a devoted ballad collector who made numerous song-hunting trips into the Kentucky mountains. He published several volumes of ballads and songs. This version is clearly Ionian.

[musical notation with lyrics: "Well-met, well-met, my-own true-love, Well met, well met," cried-she; "For I've just re-turned from-the salt, salt-sea, and it's all-for the sake of-thee."]

"The House Carpenter" as sung by Bradley Kincaid. Transcribed by Elizabeth DiSavino.

John F. Smith, who deserves a book of his own, collected a large number of ballads and ballad tunes from his students that bear no resemblance to those appearing in other collections. All four of his versions of "Lord Bateman" are pentatonic, but one differs from most others in the upward sweep of its first two phrases.[31]

[musical notation]

"Lord Bateman," John F. Smith Collection. Transcribed by Elizabeth DiSavino.

Chappel Wallin was born in 1889 to a ballad-singing family in Madison County, North Carolina, but settled in Kentucky, where he raised a family and lived the rest of his life. It is not surprising that his version of "Lord Bateman"—recorded in 1984 in Pulaski County by Loyal Jones, weds the Kentucky and North Carolina strains.

[Musical notation with lyrics: "Lord Bates-man was a no-ble man, A val-ient sol-dier as you shall see; He gath-ered all of his funds and rich-es, Vowed some strange land he'd go and see."]

"Lord Bateman," from the singing of Chappel Wallin. Transcribed by Elizabeth DiSavino.

Wallin's version features a somewhat condensed plot. Unlike Jackson's rather formal version, his employs some creative colloquialisms. For example, Lord Bateman gathers "all his funds and riches"; once captive, he gets bread and water "oncet a day." Some of these phrases appear in other North Carolina tunes collected by Sharp; it would seem that they were retained in Wallin's version.

Still another lovely version of "Lord Bateman" (its melody closely related to one used by Jean Ritchie for "Barbara Allen" and also to some versions of "Come All You Fair and Tender Ladies") collected by Smith is unusual in its dramatic use of angular leaps and extended tessitura in the second half.

[Musical notation]

"Lord Bateman," John F. Smith Collection. Transcribed by Elizabeth DiSavino.

Note the use of multiple modes in Jean Ritchie and the Ritchie family's "The Wars of Germany."

A Comparison of the Ballads of Jackson and Campbell/Sharp

[Musical notation with lyrics: "There was a rich old merchant, in London he did dwell; He had one only daughter, the truth to you I'll tell, Oh, the truth to you I'll tell."]

"The Wars of Germany" as sung by Jean Ritchie. Transcribed by Elizabeth DiSavino.

Raine's version of the same song, "Jackaro," is from his 1923 *Mountain Ballads for Social Singing*, used for social singing at Berea. It lacks the multiple modes found in the Ritchie version.

[Musical notation with lyrics: "There was a silk merchant, in London he did dwell; He had one only daughter, the truth to you I'll tell, The truth to you I'll tell."]

"Jackaro," from James Watt Raine's *Mountain Ballads*. Transcribed by Elizabeth DiSavino.

In the foreword to *Mountain Ballads,* Raine gives thanks for the cooperation of Cecil Sharp, who let him use his melodies. In fact, several of the music manuscripts in the Raine collection are in Sharp's handwriting. Curiously, the collection also contains manuscripts of two sets of lyrics and eight tunes that bear the appellation "Miss Jackson." A ninth, "The Serving Maid," appears to be from Jackson as well. Perhaps she shared these during the time she was at Berea, or perhaps she and Raine collected together, or perhaps, like William A. Bradley, Raine helped himself to the ballads while Jackson's collection was sitting on the shelf in the mountain room.[32] In fact, a lot of Jackson's finds seem to have migrated into the hands of other collectors. Copies of ballads credited to her can be found, not only in the Raine collection, but also in the collections of D. L. Thomas, D. W. Wilgus, and Gladys Jameson.[33]

A transcription of a recorded version of "Lord Bateman" found in the Leonard Roberts collection and sung by Jim Couch of Harlan, Kentucky, in 1954 can be seen in figure 6.13.

"Lord Bateman" as sung by Jim Couch, 1954. Transcribed by Elizabeth DiSavino.

Finally, mention must be made of John Jacob Niles, whose collecting efforts were concurrent with Jackson's, though for a much longer period of time. His publications began appearing only later. Niles was an atypical collector in that he did not shy away from studying and collecting African American music. His first publication, *Impressions of a Negro Camp Meeting,* which included eight spirituals, appeared in 1925; his first collection of Appalachian song, *Seven Kentucky Mountain Songs,* was published in 1929.[34] Niles is also atypical in that he is known as much for being a performer as for being a collector.

Niles is, unfortunately, not an entirely accurate source of melodies. He changed and arranged what he found quite freely and did not always indicate when that was the case. Sometimes he claimed to have collected a song only to admit later that he himself composed the melody. Ron Pen states: "On the one hand, Niles was engaged in actively collecting music and text from folk sources. On the other hand, he was equally busy creating arrangements from these folk sources and writing original songs in the style of the songs he had been collecting. There would be nothing wrong—indeed, much that is right—about both preserving folk song and creating original song based on the model of folk song. There is only a problem when the collector-composer is less than scrupulous in declaring which is which. . . . [S]ubsequently he ambiguously labeled some of his work as the product of folk collection rather than personal invention."[35] Regardless of his methods, in the 1930s Niles became quite popular as an entertainer, and his repertoire, entirely traditional or not, became synonymous with Kentucky folk music in the public mind.

In summary, what we are seeing in these other Kentucky ballads is the following:

- Many pentatonic ballads, to be sure, but also ballads that are not pentatonic and more examples in Ionian, Mixolydian, and Dorian modes than Sharp's 1917 collection suggests.
- Instances of the Scottish snap rhythm in the Kentucky ballads.
- More melismas than notated by Sharp or Jackson, as evidenced by the ornamentation of singers like Jim Couch.
- Examples of mixed modes within a single song.
- Language that is more poetic, more formal, and less condensed than that of Sharp's North Carolina ballads.
- More devotion to preservation of lyrics in general on the part of Kentucky collectors.
- In the unsung persons of John F. Smith, Wyman/Brockway, and John Jacob Niles, songs other than the Old World ballads that are the meat of the 1917 Sharp collection, including songs of African American origin and popular songs.

Conclusions

Combining this information with what we have learned about the ballads of Katherine Jackson, some probable conclusions can be drawn.

Publication of Jackson's work as initially planned would likely have elevated the status of women as the keepers of Appalachian balladry. That work would have featured more tunes in Ionian and Mixolydian mode but also a large number in pentatonic. (Sharp's erroneous theory of the genetics of British and Appalachian music and the pure Anglo link between them might, therefore, never have gained hold or at least been relegated to the status of being one of several competing theories.) It would have featured an equal number of melodies in triple meter and in duple. It would have featured ballads with a greater adherence to archaic and poetic language and a lesser reliance on colloquialisms than did Sharp's collection. And it could have helped increase early interest in Kentucky balladry during the 1910s and shone a spotlight on Berea College and the work of other collectors there.

Had the Berean John F. Smith's eclectic collection been widely disseminated as a result of more focused early interest in Berea ballad collecting, or had his informants been utilized by others, attention might have been given early on to a wider variety of sources for and types of Appalachian music, including music inspired and performed by African Americans. Ballads birthed exclusively in the southern Appalachian Mountains (many of which showed clear African American influence), exemplified by later recordings of singers like Addie Graham and Mary Lozier like "We're Stole and Sold from Africa" and "Pretty Polly," might have gained early attention. In addition, hymns and the tradition of singing prevalent in the Primitive Baptist churches would have added rich musical, historical, and social dimensions to the overall picture of the region's music.[36] We might also have more extensive recordings of early Kentucky banjo and fiddle players. Finally, the body of instrumental and vocal music of the area's many African American musicians might not have been entirely ignored by the early collectors and, thus, lost to history. In short, Appalachian music as presented to scholars in the early 1910s might have appeared much more rich and diverse than was initially represented. The limited Anglocentric viewpoint that was established by Sharp and others would have been challenged by the recognition of other peoples and other musics.

Katherine Jackson herself might have gone down in history as the mother of American balladry. Olive Dame Campbell would have gone on to do her great and good work for the people of Appalachia, but *English Folk Songs of the Southern Appalachians* would not have been initially hailed as the first and most important collection of Appalachian balladry. It would have been only one of several or perhaps many such collections, though it still would have been held in great esteem for its size, breadth, and scholarship. It is also possible that Sharp still could have eclipsed Jackson owing to his prestige, his gender, and the sheer size of his initial collection, but at least Jackson and her account would have been part of the body of knowledge of southern Appalachian balladry and might have altered the initial understanding of the origin, practices, keepers of, and influences on Appalachian music in general.

It is, of course, impossible to know for certain what kind of impression Jackson's collection would have made if it had appeared as planned. Nevertheless, it can inform us still.

PART 3

"ENGLISH-SCOTTISH BALLADS
FROM THE HILLS OF KENTUCKY"

7

Introduction by Elizabeth DiSavino

By at least one account, Katherine Jackson had, by 1909, accumulated over sixty ballads (five more than were included in Campbell and Sharp's 1917 *English Folk Songs from the Southern Appalachians*) and set about compiling them in a scholarly manner. Sadly, a large number of those ballads were lost over the years, and fewer than half remain today. I have included everything that remains of the collection, a total of twenty-eight ballads (twenty-five of British origin and three native) in forty-three variants, one thirteenth-century song, and one Appalachian tune. Four versions of Jackson's ballad collection can be found in the Berea College Special Collections and Archives, and almost all the ballads printed in this book can be found in one of those four versions. A few had migrated to other collections, including those of Gladys Jameson, James Watt Raine, and E. C. Perrow. I have noted the collection or collections from which each song comes, and I have edited Jackson's introduction by weaving together parts from several versions of her manuscript.

I have ordered the ballads as Jackson intended (in the same order as given by Francis Child, the iconic British collector), though I have included some variants she did not list in, or eliminated from, her original table of contents. I have also included a few other pieces that she collected but did not originally list for publication and added only later. When applicable, Child's title is applied, followed by the colloquial name used by Jackson. Many ballads are similar to ones in earlier British collections, but informants are not always indicated, so it is not always clear whether some ballads were gleaned from other collections or were collected in the field and just happen to appear in other collections. All such instances have been duly noted.

Often, however, Jackson does note that a ballad also appears in an earlier collection in order to demonstrate its connection to its musical ancestors in the British Isles. She often refers to Sir Walter Scott's *Minstrelsy of the Scottish Border*, Robert Jamieson's *Popular Ballads and Songs*,[1] and Thomas Percy's *Reliques of Ancient English Poetry*, but her chief touchstone for comparison to "older original sources" from Great Britain is Sir Francis Child's massive ten-volume *The English and Scottish Popular Ballads*. She appears to have consulted two versions of Child's collection: the 1880 Riverside version and the 1882–1898 Dover version. The 1880 Riverside version combined two and sometimes three books per volume and started pagination anew at the beginning of each book; the Dover version also combined two and sometimes three books per volume but is paginated sequentially. I have dutifully replicated Jackson's citations, with *Child A* referring to the Riverside version and *Child B* the Dover. In instances where the edition is unclear and Jackson has given only the ballad number, I have left citations as she supplied them.

Jackson notated melodies with the first verse written underneath and the corresponding full set of lyrics on a separate sheet. In some instances, a notated melody in her collection does not have the same lyrics as any other version of the same ballad. In such instances, melody and lyrics are presented separately here, with two exceptions where external evidence indicates a match between lyric and melody. Jackson's notes are in italics, usually directly below the song title, unless the length of a comment demands relocation; my editor's notes are in roman and are found at the end of the song, as are the citations regarding sources. I have used the designation *v.* to indicate which version of Jackson's manuscript is being referenced on each ballad.

It has taken over a hundred years for Katherine Jackson's music manuscript to see print. It has been my great honor to oversee that task.

Here at last is *English-Scottish Ballads from the Hills of Kentucky*.

8

Introduction by Katherine Jackson French

To the Singing Mothers of Colonial America

This little volume has a modest, though distinctly unique, purpose—the securing of these quaint renditions of the old English and Scottish ballads for future generations; these, journeying across the seas to Virginia and the Carolinas, were later hidden away in the Kentucky hills for 150 years. They are peculiarly Anglo-American, most characteristic of the traditional history and spirit of their composers of the fourteenth, fifteenth, and sixteenth centuries, and likewise, after generations of contact, made to be a part of the blood, bone, and sinew of the settlers in the remote land. Though told in their own homely household speech and illustrative of their own crude life, withal they are poems of the highest art—because they are not artful. They have lived because they were loved, and, with this excuse for existence, they have played for ages on free, generous, and impulsive minds. This, then, becomes an immemorial record of sentiment, loyalty, principle—a conserver of their love for poetry of song. Ballads are then an immemorial record of the pure ancestry of the singer and an undoubted proof of the sturdiness and truth of song in having been sufficient for another period of long yesterdays.

In this isolated section, far removed from all activities of modern civilization, life is lived in the open mid all that is fresh and green—glorious mountains, trees of baronial proportions, rapid creeks, and narrow passes. The inhabitants are strikingly homogeneous, breathing one unlettered atmosphere, one habit of thought, one measure of defense and sympathy. Things are real, without ornamentation and gloss, without sentimentality and romance. The traditional pioneer life of the eighteenth century continues. Rarely are children told modern stories or given recent books of fiction; however, not a few of them will tell the guest of men who have been frightened by the headless horseman or of men who have been visited by the white-footed deer in which is the spirit of the frightened man's ancestor and that can be killed only by an enchanted bullet! Likewise, the paucity of modern song and social entertainment has caused the mother to endeavor to teach her daughter these songs of the ancients. Oral transmission has retained ballads of the purest type, although the singer is unconscious of the antiquity or the possibility of finding them in print. To her, a ballad (ballet) is what it was to her Elizabethan forebears, a "written-down" copy or a broadside of anything sung.

To the women of the community is the credit of the preservation due. When the older men sing, they rarely go beyond eighteenth-century hymns or such songs of the fatherland as "Annie Laurie," "Ben Bolt," "Blue Bells of Scotland," or "The Maid of Dundee"; the younger men will most often sing a banjo or fiddle tune, perhaps of English origin or influence, as the Jacobite songs of Prince Charlie or "The Swapping Song of Jack Straw," airs thought frivolous and unbecoming for any mother. The women in their constant intercourse with the children come nearer to the heart of the stories of the ballads and are keener in picturing the tragic situation and in sympathizing with the crying out of the soul of the woman in the ancient song. The mother's environment and condition of life make the narrative seem both natural and true. In addition, there is the loyalty to her own mother and grandmother in continuing this unbroken line of singers and in giving pleasure to the family and neighbors. Singing thus has a distinctly social connection; companies are invited and asked to join in the refrains, which, however unintelligible and meaningless, are none the less emotional, expressive, and communal. In such a gathering the original intent of the word *ballad*, the *huc et illud inclinare, vacillare*, impresses one as the leader sways backward and forward in her low, straight chair, her face expressive at the thought of the stanzas sung.

The ballads most popular are the romantic and domestic tragedies, with an occasional fondness for such themes as the return of the dead, the union in death, using forever the rose and briar symbol; the original "goodnights" are apparently forgotten, for new outlaws sing on the gallows, in true McPherson or Maxwell fashion,[1] their confession, break the fiddle, if no one cares for it as a memorial, and are hanged! Constant repetition has brought about many amusing changes, omissions of seemingly less important lines and stanzas, verbal inaccuracies, confusion, and substitution of familiar phrases and titles for such as are not generally known to her; the attempt to retain the original word, if there be no exchange possible, even when it conveys no thought, is often pathetically ludicrous. From all of these, we see that ballads have once again demonstrated the fact that they spring up in a special place, in the heart of a silent people, whose soul breathes in their burdens. The words flit from age to age, from lip to lip, of a class of the times long dead that continues nearest the state of natural man. On the whole, they are admirably localized and thus understood; for example, in the familiar "Barbara Allen's Cruelty," those prosaic people with much of the drudgery and little of the idealistic feeling have no reason for singing of the "master dear," bed curtains, towers, bowers, chancels, or the traditional "merry month of May"; and, further, while the first singers may have filled their glasses with "blude red wine" and "make the healths gae round and round," these sturdy Saxons of 1911, away from grapes and trunk lines, drink only moonshine whiskey or brandy. "A-drinkin'" is therefore most expressive. They may well forget the towers and bowers, the gay knights and ladies, but the mother has a ribbon for Margaret's tresses, and the youth of chivalry, who had never heard of a bridal veil, will never dream of kissing the rose petals on the bride's knee; but there is surely free liberty and independence in the fight of the one valiant son instead of the usual seven! The daring, as seen in land feuds, the sympathy of man for man, the slow picturesque energy, never lifeless, never strenuous, the generous, impulsive, open mind—all are similar to the native characteristics of the first writers of ballads.

In spite of discrepancies, the old landmarks are ever in evidence: dramatic narrative, told in leaps and bounds from dialogue to narrative and back again, naturalness almost to barbarity, emotion, direct vision, spontaneity, simplicity, unschooled diction with a sense and feeling for harmony. There is much alliteration, constant overflow, impure rhyme and assonance, and many recurring phrases and epithets. The thought is never indistinct, always looming forth with emphasis that comes from the need to express some deep passion in a few words. The variation is slight from one community to another, for all the hill country is unified in spirit, belief, interest, and customs.

The keeping alive of such verse shows a wholeness and sane effort to meet the demand of the popular taste. It is the result of a distinctly poetic gift, applied to all subjects and all sorts of spirits, and made most appealing when some passionate mind is aroused to expression.

As such, these songs stir one in a strangely intimate fashion to a height that artistic verse can rarely attain. This speaking soul, this poetry, should be an effective possession and increase our respect for the pioneers, their love for liberty, endurance, restraint, and manliness—all typical of the spirit and sap of the stock. These songs should touch the heart, not as an individual call, but as an outcry from a great community of lonely men and women.

9
"English-Scottish Ballads from the Hills of Kentucky"

1a. Lady Isabel and the Elf Knight: Pretty Polly
Informant: Mrs. Jennie Combs, Berea, Kentucky

(Child, No. 4, edition uncertain) *"May Colvin" (first published in Herd's* Collection, vol. I, *p. 153, 1769) introduces some popular tragedies of a false lover who has outwitted his fiancè as a speaking bird appears, conscious of the evil performed and reproving the heroine. The following is called "Pretty Polly."*

1. "Make ready, make ready, pretty Polly,"
    says he,
"And go along with me;
We will go to the Scotia,
There for to marry thee."

2. She worried herself in her father's gold,
As much as it could be;
And two fine horses she carried away,
To ride to the bank of the sea.

3. "Light down, light down, pretty Polly,"
    he said,
"Your bridal bed you see;
For I have drowned six kings' daughters,
And the seventh one you shall be.

4. "Lay off, lay off, your clothes so fine,
And lay them on a stone;
For they are too fine and costly,
To rot in the salt sea foam."

5. She lit down in trembling and fear,
"Young man, turn your back on me;
For it never became a gentleman,
A naked woman to see."

6. He immediately turned his back to her,
His face toward the tree;
And with her little slender arms,
She heaved him into the sea.

7. "Lay there, lay there, you false-hearted
    man,
Lay there in place of me;
For if you have drowned six kings'
    daughters,
The seventh one you shall be."

8. She lit upon the bonny brown,
And led the dappled gray;
She came back to her father's house,
Three hours before it was day.

9. "Oh, what is the matter, pretty Polly?"
The little parrot did say,
"I thought you went to Nova Scotia,
For there to marry and stay."

10. "Hush up, hush up, my sweet little
    parrot,
And tell no tales on me;
Your cage shall be of pure, beaten gold,
And hang on the willow tree."

11. Her father, hearing the speaking, says,
In the chamber, where he lay;
"What's the matter, my pretty parrot,
You're hollering so long before day?"

12. "The cats are here at my cage door,
Layin' violent hands on me;
And I was callin' pretty Polly
To come, run them away from me."

(Lyrics: KJF v. 1, 2, 3, 4)

"English-Scottish Ballads from the Hills of Kentucky"   147

1b. Lady Isabel and the Elf Knight: Pretty Polly
(Child, No. 4, edition uncertain)

Informant: Unknown

(KJF's manuscript in Jameson. KJF's surviving lyrics to "Pretty Polly" do not match this melody as the scansion is entirely off; this must have been a different version whose lyrics have since disappeared.)

1c. Lady Isabel and the Elf Knight: Six Pretty, Fair Maids
Informant: Unknown
(Child, No. 4, edition uncertain) *Similar versions are very numerous.*

1. There was a proper, tall young man,
And William was his name;
He came away o'er the ragin' sea,
He came a-courtin' me, O me,
He came a-courtin' me.

2. He followed me up, he followed me down,
He followed me in my room;
I had no wings for to fly away,
No tongue to say him nay, O nay,
No tongue to say him nay.

3. He took part of my father's gold,
One-half of my mother's fee;
He took two of my father's stable steeds,
For there stood thirty and three, O three,
For there stood thirty and three.

4. The lady rode the milk-white steed,
The gentleman rode the gray;
They rode all down by the north green-land,
All on a summer's day, O day,
All on a summer's day.

5. "Light off, light off, my pretty miss,
I tell you now my mind;
Six pretty, fair maids I've drowned here,
And the seventh you shall be, O be,
And the seventh you shall be."

6. "Hush up, hush up, you old vilyun,
That haint what you promised;
You promised to carry me o'er the ragin' sea,
And there for to marry me, O me,
And there for to marry me.

7. "Turn your back and trim them nettles,
That grow so near the brim."
The young lady with her skillfulness,
She tripped her false lover in, O in,
She tripped her false lover in.

8. "Lie there, lie there, you old vilyun,
Lie there in the place of me;
You have nothin' so fine nor costly
But to rot in the salt-water sea, O sea,
But to rot in the salt-water sea."

9. First, she rode the milk-white steed,
And then she rode the gray;
She returned back home, to her father's house,
Three long hours before it was day, O day,
Three long hours before it was day.

(Lyrics: KJF v. 1, 3, 4)

2. Earl Brand: Fair Ellender

Informant: Miss Bettie Combs, Perry County, Kentucky

(Child, No. 7, edition uncertain) *"The Douglas Tragedy," known in Denmark and other European countries, has been localized by the Scots as having occurred at Blackhouse on the Douglas Burn, a tributary of the Yarrow. This is sung in many counties of Kentucky with slight variation as "Fair Ellender."*

1. He rode up to the old man's gate,
So boldly did he say,
"Your youngest daughter you may keep,
For the oldest I'll take away."

2. "Rise up, rise up, you seven brotherin,
Go bring your sister down;
For it never shall be said that the steward's son
Shall take your sister to town."

3. He put her on the milk-white steed,
And he rode the dapple bay;
He threw his horn-bugle around his neck
And his sword, and they went riding away.

4. As he rode out, about three miles from town,
When he cast his eye around,
He saw her old father and seven brothers all
Come tripling over the plain.

5. "O Ellender, sweet Ellender, you sit down,
And hold the steed up to the rein;
Whilst I play your old dear father,
And your seven brotherin."

6. Fair Ellender, she sat down
And she never changed a note;
Until she saw her old, dear father's head
Come tumbling to her feet.

7. "O sweet William, slack your hand,
For a father have I no more;
If you ain't satisfied with this,
I wish you were in your mother's chamber
And I, in some house or room."

8. He put her on the milk-white steed,
And he rode the dapple bay;
He threw the horn-bugle 'round his neck,
And he went bleeding away.

(Lyrics: KJF v. 1, 2, 3, 4; KJF in Raine as "The Fate of Lovers.")

3a. The Twa Sisters: The Lord of the Old Country

(Child A, vol. I, No. 10, *p. 118*) *It is rarely heard, but by perusing the two variants, the reader will recognize the original. The refrain "Bow down" is probably an outgrowth of "Binorie," rather than Edinburgh; the introduction of the harp and messages of the heroine have been forgotten.*

Informant: Unknown

There was a lord lived in the Old Country, bow down, There was a lord lived in the Old Country, these vows were given to me; There was a lord lived in the Old Country, and he had daughters, one, two, three; I'll be true, true to my love, If my love will be true to me.

2. "Sister, oh sister, let's us walk out
Bow down,
Sister, oh sister, let's us walk out
These vows were given to me;
Sister, oh sister, let's us walk out,
And see the boats a-sailin' about;"
I'll be true, true to my love,
If my love will be true to me.

3. They walked down to the water's brim,
Bow down,
They walked down to the water's brim,
These vows were given to me;
They walked down to the water's brim,
And the oldest plunged the youngest in;
I'll be true, true to my love,
If my love will be true to me.

4. Down she sank, and off she swum,
Bow down;
Down she sank, and off she swum,
These vows were given to me;
Down she sank, and off she swum,
Until she came to the miller's pond;
I'll be true, true to my love,
If my love will be true to me.

5. The miller was hung upon Fish-gate,
Bow down;
The miller was hung upon Fish-gate,
These vows were given to me;
The miller was hung upon Fish-gate,
For drownin' of my sister Kate;
I'll be true, true to my love,
If my love will be true to me.

(Lyrics: KJF v. 1, 3, 4; KJF in Raine. Melody: KJF v2, 3; KJF in Raine; KJF in Jameson.)

3b. The Twa Sisters: The Lord of the Old Country
Informant: Mrs. Jennie Combs, Berea, Kentucky
(Child A, vol. I, No. 10, *p. 118*)

1. There was a lord in the Old Country,
Bow down,
There was a lord in the Old Country,
These vows were made to me;
There was a lord in the Old Country,
And he had daughters one and two;
You be true to your own love,
And I'll be true to you.

2. Johnnie bought the youngest a gay gold ring,
Bow down,
Johnnie bought the youngest a gay gold ring,
These vows were made to me;
Johnnie bought the youngest a gay gold ring,
Johnnie never bought the old one nary a thing;
You be true to your own love,
And I'll be true to you.

3. He bought the youngest a beaver hat,
Bow down,
He bought the youngest a beaver hat,
These vows were made to me;
He bought the youngest a beaver hat,
And the oldest sister didn't like that;
You be true to your own love,
And I'll be true to you.

4. The sisters were walking around the sea bend,
Bow down,
The sisters were walking around the sea bend,
These vows were made to me;
The sisters were walking around the sea bend,
The oldest pushed the youngest in;
You be true to your own love,
And I'll be true to you.

5. She floated down to the miller's dam,
Bow down,
She floated down to the miller's dam,
These vows were made to me;
She floated down to the miller's dam,
The miller drew her safe to land;
You be true to your own love,
And I'll be true to you.

6. The miller robbed her of her gold,
Bow down,
The miller robbed her of her gold,
These vows were made to me;
The miller robbed her of her gold,
And plunged her back into the hole;
You be true to your own love,
And I'll be true to you.

7. The miller was hung upon Fishgate,
Bow down,
The miller was hung upon Fishgate,
These vows were made to me;
The miller was hung upon Fishgate,
For drownin' of my sister Kate;
You be true to your own love,
And I'll be true to you.

8. Long come a harper, fine and fair,
Bow down,
Long come a harper, fine and fair,
These vows were made to me;
Long come a harper, fine and fair,
Who strung a harp of her golden hair;
You be true to your own love,
And I'll be true to you.

9. The only tune that it played then,
Bow down,
The only tune that it played then,
These vows were made to me;
The only tune that it played then
Was "Woe to my sister, who pushed me in!"
You be true to your own love,
And I'll be true to you.

(Lyrics: KJF v. 1, 3, and 4 are verses 1-6 only. Version 2 includes verses 7 and 8.)

4. Lord Randal: Lord Randall

(Child B, vol. I, No. 12, *p. 15, and from Kinloch's* Ancient Scottish Ballads, *p. 110. The title was changed by Scott in* Minstrelsy of the Scottish Border, vol. 3, *p. 4.*) *The ballad is common to the Gothic nations.*

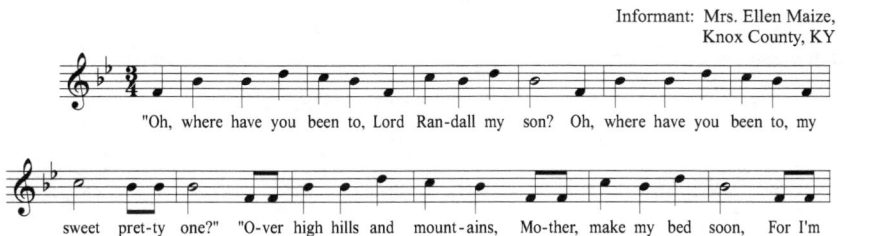

Informant: Mrs. Ellen Maize,
Knox County, KY

"Oh, where have you been to, Lord Ran-dall my son? Oh, where have you been to, my sweet pret-ty one?" "O-ver high hills and mount-ains, Mo-ther, make my bed soon, For I'm sick to the heart and I want to lie down."

2. "What did you eat for your supper,
Lord Randall, my son?
What did you eat for your supper,
My sweet, pretty one?"
"Fried eel and fresh butter,
Mother make my bed soon,
For I'm sick to the heart,
And I want to lie down."

3. "What do you will to your father,
Lord Randall, my son?
What do you will to your father,
My sweet, pretty one?"
"Nothing but a dead son to bury,
Mother, make my bed soon,
For I'm sick to the heart,
And I want to lie down."

4. "What do you will to your mother,
Lord Randall, my son?
What do you will to your mother,
My sweet, pretty one?"
"My land and fine houses,
Mother, make my bed soon,
For I'm sick to the heart,
And I want to lie down."

5. "What do you will to your sister,
Lord Randall, my son?
What do you will to your sister,
My sweet, pretty one?"
"My trunk full of money,
Mother, make my bed soon,
For I'm sick to the heart,
And I want to lie down."

6. "What do you will to your sweetheart,
Lord Randall, my son?
What do you will to your sweetheart,
My sweet, pretty one?"
"A rope to the gallows,
Mother, make my bed soon,
For I'm sick to the heart,
And I want to lie down."

(Lyrics KJF v. 1, 2, 3, 4. Melody KJF v. 2, 3.)

5. Edward

Informant: Mrs. James Baker, Madison County, KY

(Child, No. 13, edition uncertain) *The great praise accorded "Edward," by Herder (*Works XXV, No. 19*) might be continued here, although the ballad is altered – the wife being taken away, and the brother instead of the father being killed. The "old yeller hound" and the "little gray nag" and the "two sycamore sprouts" add interesting local color. Many popular songs, as "The Waxford Girl" and "The Miller Boy" are written from that.*

1. "How comes that blood on your shirt sleeve?
My son, come tell unto me."
"It is the blood of the little guinea gay
That flew away from me, me, me,
That flew away from me."

2. "It is too red for your little guinea gay,
My son, come tell unto me."
"It is the blood of the old yeller hound
That trailed a deer for me, me, me,
That trailed a deer for me."

3. "It is too red for the old yeller hound,
My son, come tell unto me."
"It is the blood of the little gray nag
That ploughed a furrow for me, me, me,
That ploughed a furrow for me."

4. "What did you fall out about?
My son, come tell unto me."
"We fell out about two sycamore sprouts
That grew by the roots of the tree, tree, tree,
That grew by the roots of the tree."

5. "What will you do when your father comes home?
My son, come tell unto me."
"I'll put my foot on yonder ship,
And sail across the sea, sea, sea,
And sail across the sea."

6. "What will you do with your dear little wife?
My son, come tell unto me."
"I'll put her foot on yonder ship,
And take her across with me, me me,
And take her across with me."

7. "What will you do with your dear little babes?
My son, come tell unto me."
"I'll leave them here with my old mother dear,
To keep her company, ny, ny
To keep her company."

8. "What will you do with your house and land?
My son, come tell unto me."
"I will leave it here with my old mother dear,
For to raise my children free, free, free,
For to raise my children free."

9. "When will you come back again?
My son, come tell unto me."
"When the sun and the moon shall rise in the west,
And that will never be, be, be,
And that will never be."

(Lyrics KJF v. 1, 2, 3, 4)

"English-Scottish Ballads from the Hills of Kentucky" 155

6. The Cruel Mother: The Greenwood Side
(Child No. 20, edition uncertain)

Informant: Miss Jane Cornett
of Knox County, KY

Christmas times is a-rollin' on, When the nights are long and cool; When three little babes come runnin' down, And run in their mother's room.

2. As she was going to her father's hall,
All down by the greenwood side;
She saw three little babes a-playin' ball,
All down by the greenwood side.

3. One was Peter and the other was Paul,
All down by the greenwood side;
And the other was naked as the hour it was born,
All down by the greenwood side.

4. "Oh babes, oh babes, if you were mine,"
All down by the greenwood side;
"I would dress you in silks so fine,"
All down by the greenwood side.

5. "Oh mother, oh mother, when we were young,"
All down by the greenwood side;
"You neither dressed us coarse nor fine,"
All down by the greenwood side.

6. "You took your pen-knife out of your pocket,"
All down by the greenwood side;
"And you pierced it through our tender heart,"
All down by the greenwood side.

7. "You wiped your pen-knife on your sleeve,"
All down by the greenwood side;
"And the more you wiped it, the bloodier it grew,"
All down by the greenwood side.

8. "You buried it under a stone,"
All down by the greenwood side;
"You buried it under a marble stone,"
All down by the greenwood side.

9. "The hill* gates are open, and you must go through,"
All down by the greenwood side;
"The hill gates are open and you must go through,"
All down by the greenwood side.

*It's likely that the word here was "Hell," and was either misheard or changed, as per Jackson's aversion to profanity.
(Lyrics KJF v. 2. Music KJF manuscript; also v. 2 in Jameson.)

156   KATHERINE JACKSON FRENCH

7. The Three Ravens: The Three Crows
(Child, No. 26, edition uncertain)

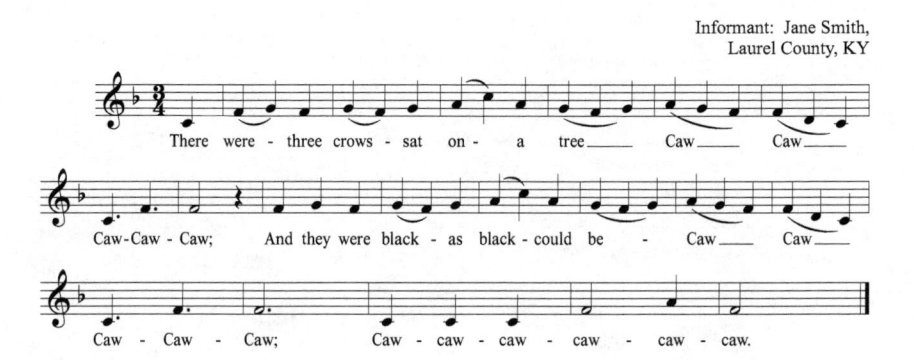

Informant: Jane Smith,
Laurel County, KY

[Musical notation with lyrics:]
There were three crows sat on a tree___ Caw___ Caw___ Caw-Caw-Caw; And they were black as black could be Caw___ Caw___ Caw - Caw - Caw; Caw - caw - caw - caw - caw - caw.

2. One of them spake to his mate
Caw, caw, caw-caw-caw;
"Where shall we now our breakfast take?"
Caw, caw, cawcaw-caw;
Caw, caw, caw caw-caw-caw.

3. "There lies a horse upon a plain."
Caw, caw, caw caw caw;
"It was by a cruel butcher slain,"
Caw, caw, cawcaw-caw;
Caw, caw, caw caw-caw-caw.

(Lyrics and music: KJF v. 2. Editor's note: This melody is of course best known as "Bonny Doon" by Robert Burns, which exemplifies the practice of borrowing melodies when the usual tunes cannot be recalled.)

8. The Twa Brothers: Little Willie
Informant: Mrs. Olivia Huff, Berea, KY

(Child, B, vol. I, No. 49, *p. 444*) *A ballad of child-life with excessive mourning over the dead is seen in "Little Willie, The Twa Brothers." Here, the interest in the story is not so much in the discussion of the murder, accidental or committed in passion, as in the grief-stricken mother.*

1. Two little brothers goin' to school,
The oldest to the youngest called;
"Come, go with me to the green, shady grove,
And I'll wrestle you a fall."

2. They went on to the green, shady grove,
Where they wrestled up and down;
The oldest to the youngest said,
"You've given me a deadly wound."

3. "Rip my shirt from off my back,
Rip it from gore to gore;
And then tie up these bleeding wounds,
So they will bleed no more.

4. "When you go home, tell mother dear,
If she isn't quarrelin' about me then;
That I'm buried in the new churchyard,
Let be what church it may be then."

5. She mourned and she mourned,
She mourned for Little Willie;
She nearly mourned him out of his grave
To come home and be with her.

(Lyrics KJF v. 1, 2, 3, 4)

9a. Young Beichan and Susie Pye: Lord Bateman

(Child B, vol. I., No. 53, *p. 454*) *The original is "Young Beichan and Susie Pye" or "The Turkish Lady," also spoken of popularly in England as "Lord Bateman," supposed to be Gilbert Beckett, father of St. Thomas a Beckett of Canterbury. See Percy* Society Collection 17, 85; *Jamieson's* Popular Ballads.

Informant: Nathan Ambrose, *Berea, KY

Lord Bateman was in England born. He thought himself of high degree; He could not rest nor be contented Until he had voyaged across the sea.

2. He had gold and he had silver,
And he had houses of high degree;
But he could never be contented,
Until he journeyed across the sea.

3. He sailed east and he sailed west,
Until he reached the Turkish shore;
And there he was taken and put in prison,
He lived in hopes of freedom no more.

4. Through his left shoulder they bored a hole,
And in that hole they tied a rope;
They made him pull coal carts of iron,
Till he became sick and sore and tired.

5. For seven long months he was lamenting,
For seven long months in prison chains;
Then he happened to see a Turkish lady,
Who set him free from his prison chains.

6. As she walked across the floor,
She chanced Lord Bateman once to see;
She stole the key from her father's dwelling,
Saying, "I will go, set Lord Bateman free.

7. "Have you got houses, have you got lands,
Or do you live at high degree?
Will you give it all to the Turkish lady
If she from prison will set you free?"

8. "I've got houses and I've got lands, love,
And I do live at a high degree;
And I'll give it all to the Turkish lady,
If she from prison will set me free."

9. She went down to the lowest cellar,
And drew him a glass of the strongest wine;
And every health she drank to him,
"What would I give if you were mine?"

10. "Let us make a vow, and make a strong one,
For seven long years we will make it stand;
I vow I will marry no other woman,
You vow you will marry no other man."

11. Seven long years are past and gone,
Seven long years are at an end;
She gathers all her finest clothing,
Saying, "I go to seek my friend."

12. She sailed east and she sailed west, love,
Until she reached the English shore;
She rode up to the gay, fine houses,
Whose they were, she did not know.

13. She inquired after Lord Bateman's palace,
At every corner of the street;
She inquired after Lord Bateman's palace,
Of every person she chanced to meet.

14. "Are these Lord Bateman's fine houses,
Or, is Lord Bateman not at home?"
"Oh, yes, he is here with all his company,
This day he has his bride brought home."

15. She wrung, she wrung her lily white hands,
Crying, "Alas, I am undone;
I wish I were in my native country,
Across the seas to remain.

16. "Go, ask him for a loaf of bread, sir,
And draw me a glass of the strongest wine;
And ask him if he has forgotten,
Who set him free, when close confined."

17. The porter went in to his master,
Bowing low upon his knees;
"Arise, arise, you brisk young porter,
And tell me what the matter is."

18. "Oh, come and see the prettiest woman,
That ever your two eyes did see;
She has more gold about her clothing,
Than would buy your bride and company."

19. He stamped his foot upon the floor,
He broke his table in pieces three;
Saying, "If she is the Turkish lady,
With her, love, I'm bound to be."

20. Now spoke the young bride's mother,
Who never was known to speak so free;
Saying, "Would you leave your little darling,
For the Turkish lady, across the sea?"

21. "You can take your little darling,
She's none the better nor the worse for me;
Your daughter came here on a horse and saddle,
And she may return in a chariot free.

22. "Your daughter came here on a horse and saddle,
And she may return in a chariot free;
And I'll go marry the Turkish lady,
Who has crossed the roaring sea for me."

*Berea College student,
(Lyrics: KJF v. 1, 2, 3, 4. Melody: KJF v. 2, 3; KJF in Raines; KJF in Jameson.)

9b. Young Beichan and Susie Pye: Lord Bateman
Informant: Unknown

(Child B, vol. I, No. 53, *p. 454*) *A second ballad of happy climax with scenes and stories, dating from a 12th century Crusade, is "Lord Bateman," or "The Turkish Lady" (illustrated by Cruikshank, 1839), from the favorite Young Beichan and Susie Pye; for the connection of this here with Gilbert Becktet, father of the Canterbury saint, see Child, vol. II, p. 454. In one copy, Northumberland is twice used as the location of the hero's home and property. Very many variants exist, but the following is as true to the soil, and as untainted, though not as full or as eloquent, as any one known.*

1. Lord Bateman was a noble lord,
A noble lord of high degree;
He sailed himself on board a ship,
Some foreign country he would see.

2. He sailed east, he sailed west,
Until he came unto Turkey;
Where he was taken and put in prison,
Until his life was quite weary.

3. In this prison, there grew a tree,
And it grew so stout and strong;
And he was chained by the middle,
Until his life was almost gone.

4. The Turk, he had only one daughter,
The fairest creature eyes ever did see;
She stole the keys of her father's prison,
Said she'd set Lord Bateman free.

5. "Have you got land, or have you got houses,
Or do you live at high degree?"
"And I'd give it all to the fair young lady,
Who out of prison would set me free."

6. Then she took him to her father's palace,
And gave to him the best of wine;
And every health that she drank to him,
Was, "I wish Lord Bateman you was mine.

7. "For seven long years, I'll make a vow,
And seven long years I'll keep it strong;
If you wed no other woman,
I will wed no other man."

8. The she took him to her father's harbor,
And gave to him a ship of fame;
"Farewell, farewell to you, Lord Bateman,
I fear I never shall see you again."

9. When seven long years was come and gone,
And fourteen days well known to me;
She packed her gay gold and clothing,
And said, "Lord Bateman I will see."

10. When she came to Lord Bateman's castle,
So boldly there she rang the bell;
"Who's there? Who's?" cried the proud young porter,
"Who's there? Unto me tell."

11. "Oh, is this Lord Bateman's castle,
And is his lordship here within?"
"Oh, yes, oh, yes," cried the proud young porter,
"He has just taken his young bride in."

12. "Tell him to send me a slice of cake,
And a bottle of the best of wine;
And not to forget the fair young lady,
That did release him, when close confined."

13. Away, away, went this proud young porter,
Away, away, away went he;
Until he came unto Lord Bateman,
When on his bended knee fell he.

14. "What news, what news, my proud
   young porter?
What news, what news have you brought to
   me?"
"Oh, there is the fairest of all young ladies,
That ever my two eyes did see.

15. "She has got rings on every finger,
And on one of them she has got three;
And she has as much gold around her middle
As would buy all of high degree.

16. "She tells you to send her a slice of cake,
And a bottle of the best of wine;
And not to forget the fair young lady
That did release you when close confined."

17. Lord Bateman in a passion flew,
He broke his sword in splinters three;
"I'll give all my father's wealth and riches,
Now if Sophia has crossed the sea."

18. Then up spoke his young bride's mother,
Who never was heard to speak so free;
"Don't forget my only daughter,
Altho' Sophia has crossed the sea."

19. "I own I've made a bride of your daughter,
She's none the better or worse for me;
She came to me on a horse and saddle,
And she may go back in a carriage and three."

20. Then another marriage was prepared
With both their hearts so full of glee;
"I'll range no more to foreign countries,
Since Sophia has crossed the sea."

(Lyrics KJF v. 1, 3, 4)

10a. Young Hunting: Loving Henry
Informant: Unknown

(Child B, vol. I, No. 68, *p. 142*) *A further use of the bird, which after revealing his knowledge of the secret, is promised a cage of silver and gold is in "Lovin' Henry" and a less pure variant, "William and Ellender."*

1. "Get down, get down, loving Henry," she said,
"And stay all night with me;
And every golden cord that's around my bed
Shall be applied to thee,
Shall be applied to thee."

2. "I can't get down nor I won't get down
Nor stay all night with you;
For there's a little girl in Eden land*
That I love better than you,
That I love better than you."

3. As she stooped over his saddle girt,
To kiss her snowy white cheek;
All in her right hand, she held a keen knife,
And in him, she stabbed it deep,
And in him, she stabbed it deep.

4. "O, live, oh, live, loving Henry," she said,
"Oh, live ere one, two, three;
Oh, don't you see my own heart's blood,
Come flowing down so free?
Come flowing down so free?"

5. "Oh, must I ride east, or must I ride west,
Or anyways under the sun;
To get a doctor, that is good and kind,
To cure this wounded one,
To cure this wounded one?"

6. "You need not ride east or you need not ride west,
Nor anyways under the sun;
For there's no other doctor, but God above
Who can cure this wounded one,
Who can cure this wounded one."

7. She picked him up by his curly brown hair,
The other, by his feet;
She carried him down to the deep stone,
Where the water was cold and deep,
Where the water was cold and deep.

8. "Lie there, lie there, loving Henry," she said,
"Till the dewdrops on your urn;
For there's another girl in the Eden land*
That will mourn for your return,
That will mourn for your return."

9. As she turned round to go back home,
A bird sat on a limb;
"Go home, go home, you cruel girl,
And there lay and mourn for him."

10. "Fly down, fly down, little bird," she said,
"And sit on my right knee;
Your cage must be made of silver and gold,
And hung on a willow tree,
And hung on a willow tree."

11. "I can't fly down nor I won't fly down,
Nor sit on your right knee;
For you have murdered your own true love,
And I'm sure you would murder me,
And I'm sure you would murder me."

12. "Oh, if I had my cedar bow,
And arrow tied with a string;
I would shoot a diamond through your head
So you could no longer sing,
So you could no longer sing."

13. "Oh, if you had your cedar bow,
And arrow tied with a string;
I would fly to the top of the highest tree,
And there I would sit and sing,
And there I would sit and sing."

*Jackson notes that "Eden Land" means "virgin."
(Lyrics: KJF v. 1, 3, 4)

10b. Young Hunting: William and Ellender

Informant: Mrs. Lucy Banks, Madison County, KY
(Child B, vol. I, No. 68, *p. 142*)

1. Sweet William rode till he came to the gate,
And tingled to get in;
None was so ready as fair Ellender
To rise and let him come in.

2. "Get down, get down, sweet William," she said,
"And with me stay all night;
And you shall have a fire to set by,
And a candle burnin' bright."

3. "I won't get down or I can't get down,
Nor I won't get down at all;
For I have a fair beauty bride,
Waitin' in Immanuel's Hall."

4. As he stood off from her saddle-skirts
To kiss her lily-white cheeks;
She had a sharp, keen knife in her hand
And in him plunged it deep.

5. "Can I ride to the east, can I ride to the west,
Or anywhere under the sun?
Can I find a kind doctor
Who can cure a wounded man?"

6. "You men to ride to the east, you men to ride to the west,
Or anywhere under the sun;
For there's none but God alone
Can cure this wounded man."

7. Some took him by the lily-white hand,
Some took him by the feet;
They plunged him into a dark, deep well
Some fifty favors deep.

8. As she rode home, along the road,
She heard some little bird say,
"Go home, go home, you cruel girl,
Relent and mourn for thee."

9. "I wish I had my little bow-bend,
And arrow fixed with a string;
That I might shoot that pretty little bird,
That sits on the briar and sings."

10. "I wish you had your little bow-bend,
And an arrow fixed with a string;
That I might fly from briar to briar,
And you might hear me sing."

(KJF v. 1, 2, 3, 4)

11a. Lord Thomas and Fair Annet

(Child A, vol. I, book II, No. 12, *p. 121;* also Richard Whittington, A Collection of Old Ballads, vol. 1, *p. 249 [London: J. Roberts, 1725].*)

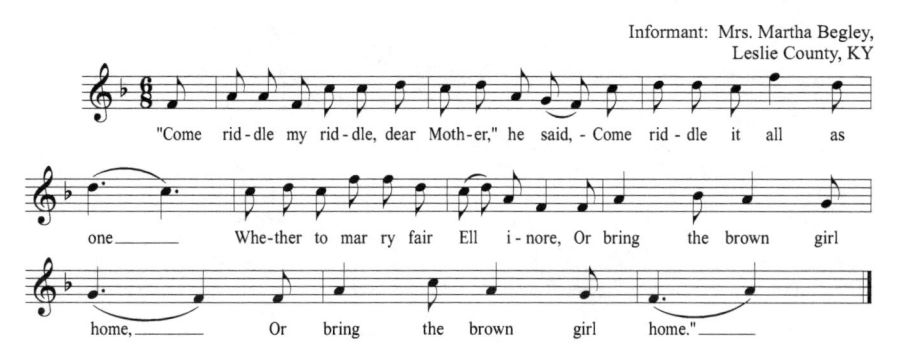

Informant: Mrs. Martha Begley, Leslie County, KY

"Come rid-dle my rid-dle, dear Moth-er," he said, - Come rid-dle it all as one____ Whe-ther to mar ry fair Ell i-nore, Or bring the brown girl home,____ Or bring the brown girl home."____

2. "The brown girl, she's got house and land,
Fair Ellinor, she has none;
But let this blessing be on you, my son,
Go, bring the brown girl home." (Repeat)

3. He dressed himself in scarlet red,
His waiters all in green;
Through many a city that he rode through,
They took him to be a king. (Repeat)

4. He rode up to fair Ellinor's gate,
And knocked upon her ring;
There's none no readier than fair Ellinor
To go let Lord Thomas come in. (Repeat)

5. "What news, what news, Lord Thomas,"
   [she says,]*
"What news do you bring to me?"
"I'm come to invite you to my wedding,
The brown girl, the bride to be." (Repeat)

6. "Bad news, bad news, Lord Thomas,"
   she says,
"Bad news you've brought to me;
I was hoping to be that bride myself,
And you the groom for to be." (Repeat)

7. "Come read my riddle, dear mother," she says,
"Come riddle it all in one;
Whether I go to Lord Thomas's wedding,
Or tarry this day at home?" (Repeat)

8. "Ten thousand may be there, your friends,
Ten times as many your foes;
Therefore, dear child, under my consent,
It's tarry with me at home." (Repeat)

9. "Ten thousand may be there, my friends,
Ten times as many my foes;
It's tarry my life, or tarry my death,
It's to Lord Thomas's wedding I'll go." (Repeat)

10. She dressed herself in satin so white
Her waiters all in green;
Through every village that she rode through,
They took her to be some queen. (Repeat)

11. She rode up to Lord Thomas's gate,
And knocked upon the ring;
There's none no readier than Lord Thomas himself,
To let fair Ellinor in. (Repeat)

12. He took her by the lily white hand
And led her through the hall;
He lifted up her beautiful veil,
And kissed her before them all. (Repeat)

13. "Lord Thomas, Lord Thomas, is this your bride?
If it is, she looks very brown;
When you might have married as fair a lady
As ever the sun shined on." (Repeat)

14. "Despise her not, fair Ellinor," he said,
"Despise her not unto me;
For I think more of your little finger,
Than I do of her whole body." (Repeat)

15. The brown girl had a little penknife,
It was both long and sharp;
Between the long rib and the short,
She probed Fair Ellinor's heart. (Repeat)

16. "What's the matter, fair Ellinor?" he says,
"You look so pale and wan;
You once did bear as good a colour
As ever the sun shined on." (Repeat)

17. "Oh, are you blind, Lord Thomas?" she said,
"Or can't you so very well see?
Can you not see my own heart's blood,
Come trickling down my knee?" (Repeat)

18. Lord Thomas had a broad sword,
It was keen and small;
He cut his own bride's head right off,
And throwed it against the wall. (Repeat)

19. He put the butt against the floor,
The point against his heart;
Was there ever three true lovers met so soon,
And soon they had to part? (Repeat)

20. "Go dig my grave both long and large,
And dig it wide and deep;
And bury fair Ellinor in my arms,
And the brown girl at my feet." (Repeat)

*Editor's note: Jackson left "She says" out of all four copies of this verse. It does not scan without it, however, and the next verse, which mirrors it, includes it, so I have inserted it here.

(Lyrics: KJF v. 1, 2, 3, 4. Melody: KJF v. 2, 3; KJF in Raines; KJF in Jameson.)

"English-Scottish Ballads from the Hills of Kentucky"   167

11b. Lord Thomas and Fair Anet: Lord Thomas
(Child A, vol. I, book. II, No. 12, *p. 121; Richard Whittington,* A Collection of Old Ballads volume 1, *p. 249 [London: J. Roberts, 1725]*.)

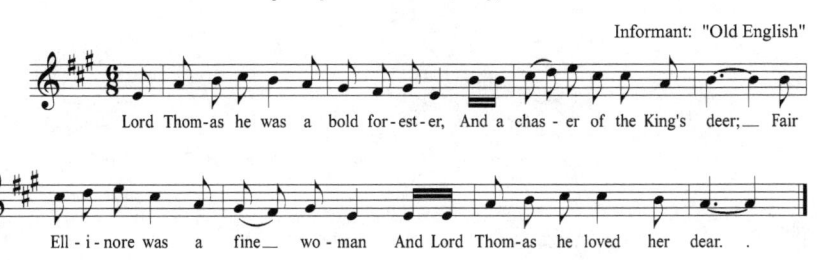

Informant: "Old English"

Lord Thom-as he was a bold for-est-er, And a chas-er of the King's deer;— Fair Ell-i-nore was a fine— wo-man And Lord Thom-as he loved her dear.

Likely copied from Whittington and included for comparison.
(KJF v. 3)

12. Fair Margaret and Sweet William

(Child A, vol. II, book 2, No. 12, *p. 140, or* Percy's Reliques, volume 3, *p. 164*) *This ballad is referred to in Fletcher's Knight of the Burning Pestle (by Francis Beaumont, edited by John Fletcher, London: Walter Barre, 1613), 2 and 3. It is also known in German and Dutch versions.*

Informants: Mrs. Malvina Begley
and Mrs. Lizane Napier, Leslie County, KY

Sweet William a-rose one May morning, And dressed himself in blue; "Oh tell unto me that long long love, That's between Lady Marg-ret and you."

2. "I know nothing about Lady Margaret's love
I know that she don't love me;
Tomorrow morning at eight o'clock,
Lady Margaret my bride shall see."

3. Lady Margaret was standing in her own hall door,
A-combing back her hair;
Whom should she spy but sweet William and bride
As they to the church drew nigh?

4. She threw away her ivory comb,
In silk bound up her hair;
She stepped out of her own hall door,
And never returned there.

5. The day being gone, the night coming on,
When most all men were asleep;
Sweet William espied Lady Margaret's ghost,
Standing at his bride's feet.

6. "Oh, how do you like your bed?" she said,
"Oh, how do you like your sheet?
Oh, how do you like that pretty fair girl
That's lying in your arms asleep?"

7. "Very well, very well, I like my bed,
Much better I like my sheet;
The best of all is that pretty fair girl
That's standing at my bed feet."

8. The night being passed, and day coming on,
When most men were awake;
Sweet William said he was pestered in his head
With a dream he dreamt last night.

9. "Such dreams, such dreams I do not like,
Such dreams they are not good;
I dreamed that my hall was filled with wild swine,
And my bride was a-swimming in blood."

10. He called before him his merry men all,
He counted them one, two, three;
He asked the leave of his own dear wife
If Lady Margaret he might go see and see.

11. "Go and see Lady Margret now,
Go and welcome her for me;
For I know you love Lady Margaret much better
Than ever you did love me."

12. Sweet William rode up to Lady Margaret's gate,
And tingled loud at the ring;
None was so ready as Margaret's seventh brother
To rise and bid him come in.

13. "Is Lady Margaret in her kitchen?" said he,
"Or is she in her hall;
Or is she in her own dwelling room,
Among the ladies all?"

14. "She's neither in her kitchen," said he,
"Nor is she in her hall;
Yonder she lies in her cold coffins,
That sits by the side of the wall."

15. "Unfold, unfold those Holland sheets,
That are made of linen so fine;
Let me kiss once more those cold, clay lips
That oft have kissed mine."

16. "Unfold, unfold those Holland sheets,
That are made of linen so fine;
Today, they shall hang over Lady Margaret's corpse,
And tomorrow shall hang over mine."

17. Three times he kissed those cherry, cherry lips,
Three times he kissed her chin;
And then he kissed her cold, clay lips,
Which pierced his heart within.

18. "Lady Margaret, she died on yesterday,
And I shall die tomorrow;
Lady Margaret she died for pure love's sake,
And I shall die for sorrow."

19. Lady Margaret was buried in the new church yard,
Sweet William was placed close by her;
Out of her grave sprung a blood-red rose,
And out of his, a green briar.

20. They grew and they grew to the high church tower,
They could not grow any higher;
There they tangled and tied into a bow-knot,
For all true lovers to admire.

(Lyrics KJF v. 1, 2, 3, 4. Melody KJF v. 3, and v. 2, which migrated to Jameson.)

13. Lord Lovel: Lord Lovely

Informant: Mrs. Margaret Green, Perry County, KY

(Child, vol. II, No. 105, *p. 426*) *Another familiar instance of unhappy youths only united in death is found in that splendid old ballad, "Lord Lovely."*

1. Lord Lovely, he stood at his castle gate,
A-combing his milk-white steed;
When along came Lady Nancy Belle,
A-wishing her lover good speed, speed, speed,
A-wishing her lover good speed.

2. "Oh, where are you going, Lord Lovely?" she says,
"Oh, where are you going?" says she;
"I'm going, my dear Lady Nancy Belle,
Strange countries for to see, see, see,
Strange countries for to see."

3. "Oh, when will you be back?" she says,
"Oh, when will you be back?" says she;
"In a year or two, at the most," he said,
"I'll return to you, fair Nancy, oy, oy,
I'll return to you, fair Nancy."

4. He had not been gone but a year and a day,
Strange countries for to see;
When languishing thoughts came into his head,
Lady Nancy Belle he would see, see, see,
Lady Nancy Belle he would see.

5. He rode, he rode upon his white steed,
Till he came to London town;
And there he heard St. Pancras' ball,
And the people all mourning, round, round, round
And the people all mourning round

6. "What's the matter?" Lord Lovely, he said,
"What is the matter?" says he;
"A lord's daughter's dead," a lady replied,
"And some call her Lady Nancy, oy, oy,
And some call her Lady Nancy."

7. He ordered the grave to be opened forthwith,
And the shroud to be folded down;
And there he kissed her cold, clay lips,
Till the tears come trickling down, down, down,
Till the tears come trickling down.

8. Lady Nancy died, as it might be today,
Lord Lovely, he died tomorrow;
And out of her bosom, there grew a red rose,
And out of Lord Lovely's, a briar, briar, briar,
And out of Lord Lovely's, a briar.

9. They grew and they grew, till they reached the church top,
And there, they couldn't grow any higher;
And there they entwined in a true lover's knot,
Which all true lovers admire, mire, mire,
Which all true lovers admire.

(Lyrics KJF v. 1, 2, 3, 4; KJF in Raines.)

14. The Lass of Roch Royal: The Lovers' Farewell
Informant: Mrs. Lizane Napier, Leslie County, KY
(Child vol. II, No. 76, *p. 213*)

1. "The time draws near, my dearest dear,
When you and I must part;
But little do you know the grief
Of my poor broken heart.

2. "Lord send that I could go with you,
Or you could tarry here;
Your company is so charming, love,
So charming is to me.

3. "It will make me think when you are away
That a day is three and an hour is ten;
It makes me weep when I might sleep,
And say I've lost a friend."

4. "Your eyes are of the sparkling blue,
Like diamonds they do shine;
Your body waves with modesty,
You've won this heart of mine.

5. "Your cheeks are of the rosy red,
Your lips of ruby be;
There's not a fault in you, my love,
That mortal eyes can see.

6. "The crow is black, although, you know,
That she may turn to white;
If ever I prove false to you,
Bright days shall turn to night.

7. "Bright days shall turn to night, my love,
The elements shall whirl;
The fire shall freeze like ice, my love,
The raging sea shall burn.

8. "So farewell my own true love,
So farewell for awhile;
For I'm going away, but I'll come back again,
Although it be ten thousand mile.

9. "Ten thousand miles, my own true love,
Through London, Scotia and Spain;
My poor heart will never be at rest
Till I see your face again.

10. "Oh who will glove your hands, my love?
Or who will shoe your feet?
Or who will kiss your rosy red cheeks,
When I'm in a foreign land?"

11. "My father he will shoe my feet,
My mother will glove my hands;
And you can kiss my red, rosy cheeks,
When you return from a foreign land."

12. "Oh, don't you see that little turtle dove,
A-flying from vine to vine?"
It's mourning for the loss of its mate,
As I will mourn for mine.

Editor's Note: Jackson points out in "A Fortnight of Balladry" that this is descended in part from "The Lass of Roch Royal." I have thus listed it as such, though it clearly strays far from the older texts. In truth, it combines verses from "Lass of Roch Royal," "My Love is Like a Red, Red Rose" by Robert Burns, and "True Lover's Farewell." A number of later songs likewise descend from these prototypes including "Fare You Well, My Own True Love," "The Storms Are on the Ocean," and "The Blackest Crow."

(Lyrics: KJF v. 2)

15. The Wife of Usher's Well: A Lady and a Lady Gay

(Child vol. II, No. 79, p. 238) *Another, very appealing to mothers, is the somewhat corrupt "Lady Gay," grown out of "The Wife of Usher's Well.". Here are two traits, very common in folklore, the excessive grief of the mothers, with a hint of reproof from the children, and the warnings of the chickens/cock, significant not of extravagant or erring spirits but a ghostly signal of recall.*

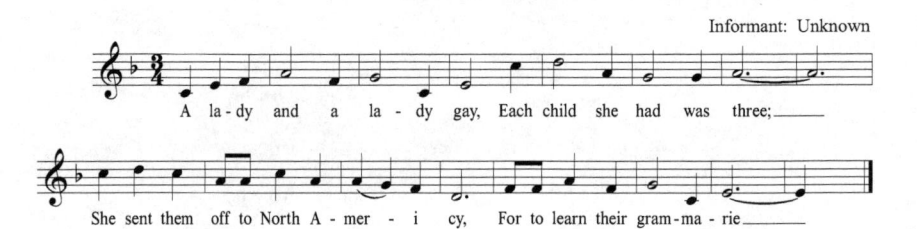

Informant: Unknown

A la-dy and a la-dy gay, Each child she had was three;
She sent them off to North A-mer-i-cy, For to learn their gram-ma-rie

2. They had been gone but a little time,
Three months, perhaps and a day;
Till sickness swept all over that land,
And swept those babes away.

3. Mother, asleep in an upper room,
Saw in her dream that night
Her three little babes in a coffin cold,
And the moon was shinin' bright.

4. She prayed if there was a king in Heaven,
Who chose to wear a crown
That He would send them home that night,
Or in the mornin' soon.

5. 'Twas twelve long months, about Christmas time,
The night being long and cold;
The three little ones came runnin' home,
And into their mother's arms.

6. She set a table before them soon,
On it spread bread and wine;
"Now, come along, my little babes,
Come eat and drink of mine.

7. "Go, spread a bed in the backward room,
And on it put a white sheet;
On top of that, a golden spread,
For to make a sweeter sleep."

8. "Take it off, take it off," said the eldest one,
"Take it off, take it off," said he;
"Woe, woe, woe to this wide, wicked world
Since pride has been in view."

9. "Awake, awake," said the next eldest one,
"The chickens are crowing for day;
And yonder stands our Saviour dear,
And with Him we must stay.

10. "Cold clods of clay lie over our heads
Green grass grows at our feet;
You've shed tears enough for me, mother,
For to wet a winding sheet."

(Lyrics KJF v. 1, 2, 3; KJF in Raine. Music KJF v. 2, 3; KJF in Raine; KJF in Jameson.)

16a. Little Musgrave and Lord Barnard's Wife: Lord Vanner's Wife

(Child, vol II, No. 81, p. 24) "Lord Vanner's Wife," from "Little Musgrave and Lady Barnard," also telling of a false wife is not often heard. The less pure "Lord Daniels' Wife" has been less localized.

"Gracefully" Informant: Unknown

The first came-in were lil-ly - white, the next were-pink and-blue; The next - came - in, Lord - Van - ner's wife, the - flow - er of the view.

2. This Magrove, a-being there,
Fair as the morning sun;
She looked at him and he looked at her,
The likes was never known.

3. She stept up to him and says "Kind sir,
Won't you take a ride with me?"
…..
…..

4. Says, "I dare not to, I dare not to
I dare not to for my life;
For the ring that you wear on your finger,
You are Lord Vanner's wife."

5. "Well, if I am Lord Vanner's wife,
Lord Vanner is not at home;
Lord Vanner is to Redemption gone,
Takin' McHenry's throne."

6. This little foot page a-bein' by,
Hearin' every word they said;
He swore Lord Vanner should hear the news
Before the risin' sun.

7. He run until he came to the river-side
And he jumped in and swam;
He swam and he swam to the other side,
And he arose and run.

8. He run till he came to McHenry's throne,
He dingled so loud with the ring;
There's none so ready as Lord Vanner himself
To arise and let him in.

9. "What news, what news, my little foot-page,
What news have you brought to me?
Has any of Casten walls fell down,
Or any of my men false be?"

10. "There's none of your Casten walls fell down,
Nor none of your man false be;
This young Magrove is in faire Scotland,
In bed with your lady."

11. "If this be lie you bring to me,
And a lie I believe it be,
I'll build a gallows just for you
And hangeth you shall be."

12. "If this be lie I bring to thee,
As you believe it to be,
You needn't build any gallows for me,
Just hang me on a tree."

13. Lord Vanner callin' up his best men,
By one, by two, by three;
Sayin', "Let's take a trip to fair Scotland,
This happy couple for to see."

14. It's "How do you like my blanket, sir?"
It's "How do you like my sheet?
How do you like that fair lady
Lies in your arms asleep?"

15. "Very well I like your blanket, sir,
Very well I like your sheet;
Ten-thousand times I like this fair lady
Lies in my arms asleep."

16. "Git up, git up, put on your clothes,
And fight me like a man;
Never should have been said in fair Scotland,
I killed a naked man."

*Editor's Note: This first verse and the melody as noted in the above manuscript are the same as Chappell's 1871 *Popular Music of the Olden Time*. Jackson does not however notate this as "Old English" as she does with some of the other tunes. She may have written this out for comparison, or it may have been heard in the field but coincides with Chappell's version. Her performance note, "gracefully," leads me to conclude the latter.

(Lyrics KJF 1, 2, 3, 4. Music KJF v. 2. Verse 3 is missing the third and fourth lines in all versions. Katherine's first verse on music manuscript did not coincide with her either of her full set of lyrics. The music manuscript verse read:

"As it fell out on a high holiday
As many there be in the year
When young milk maids hither do go
Then masses matins to hear.")

16b. Little Musgrave and Lady Barnard: Lord Daniel's Wife
Informant unknown
(Child A, vol II, No. 81, *p. 242*)

1. The first came down all dressed in red,
The next came down in green;
The next came down, Lord Daniel's wife,
She's fine as any queen, queen,
She's fine as any queen.

2. "Come and go home with me, little Gayly," she said,
"Come and go home with me tonight;"
"For I know by the rings on your fingers,
You are Lord Daniel's wife, wife,
You are Lord Daniel's wife."

3. He had sixteen miles to go,
And ten of them he run;
He run till he came to the broken-down bridge,
He held his breath and swum, swum,
He held his breath and swum.

4. He swum till he came where the grass grows green,
He turned to his heels and run;
He run till he came to Lord Daniel's gate,
He rattled those bells and rung, rung,
He rattled those bells and rung.

5. He travelled over hills and valleys,
Till he came to his staff, stand still;
He placed his bugle to his mouth,
And blew most loud and shrill, shrill,
He blew most loud and shrill.

6. He took little Gayly by the hand,
And led her through the hall;
He took off her sword and cut her head right off,
And kicked it against the wall, wall,
And kicked it against the wall.

(Lyrics KJF v. 1, 3, 4)

17a. Barbara Allen: Barbara Allen's Cruelty

(Child vol. 2, No. 84, p. 276) There are two versions extant and kept distinct. "Bonny Barbara Allen" was first printed in Allen Ransay's Tea-Table Miscellany No. 2 (Edinburgh: Thomas Ruddimen, 1724), p. 171. It was alluded to by Samuel Pepys, 2 Jan, 1666; this concludes with the adieu of the young man. The second, "Barbara Allen's Cruelty" or "The Young Man's Tragedy" will be found in Percy's Reliques, vol. III, p. 169, and in Child (cited above).

Informant: Mrs. James Baker, Berea, KY

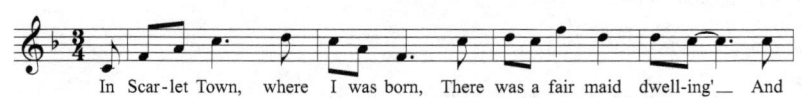

In Scar-let Town, where I was born, There was a fair maid dwell-ing' And ev'ry youth cried, "Well-a-day," - Her - name was Barb' ra Al-len

2. All in the merry month of May,
When green buds they were swellin';
Young Jemmy Grove on his death-bed lay,
For love of Barbara Allen.

3. And death is painted on his face,
And o'er his heart is stealin';
Then haste away to comfort him,
Oh lovely Barbara Allen.

4. So slowly, slowly she came up,
And slowly she came nigh him;
And all she said when there she came,
"Young man I think you're dying."

5. He turned his face unto her straight,
With deadly sorrow sighing;
"Oh, pretty maid, come pity me,
I'm on my death-bed lying."

6. "If on your death-bed you do lie,
What needs the tale you're telling?
I cannot keep you from your death,
Farewell," said Barbara Allen.

7. He turned his face unto the wall,
And death was with him dealin';
"Adieu, adieu, my friends all,
Adieu to Barbara Allen."

8. As she was walking o'er the fields,
She heard the bells a knellin';
And every stroke did seem to say,
"Unworthy Barbara Allen."

9. She turned her body round about,*
And spied the corpse a comin';
"Lay down, lay down the corpse," she said,
"That I may look upon him."

10. With scornful eyes she looked down,
Her cheeks with laughter swellin';
Whilst all her friends cried out anain,
"Unworthy Barbara Allen."

11. The more she looked, the worse she felt,
She fell to the ground a cryin';
Sayin', "If I'd done my duty today,
I'd a saved this young man from dyin'."

12. (Incomplete verse:
"She got in one mile o' town…")**

13. When he was dead and in his grave,
Her heart was struck with sorrow;
"Oh, mother, mother, make may bed,
For I shall die tomorrow.

14. "Hard-hearted creature, him to slight,
Who loved me so dearly;
Oh, that I'd been more kind to him,
When he was alive and near me."

15. She on her death-bed as she lay,
Begged to be buried by him;
And soon repented of the day,
That she did e'er deny him.

16. "Farewell," she said, "Ye virgins all,
And shun the fault I fell in;
Henceforth take warning by the fall,
Of cruel Barbara Allen."

17. Sweet William*** died on Saturday night,
And Barbara died on Sunday;
Their parents died for the loss of the two,
And were buried on Easter Monday.

18. They buried him on one side of the church,
And he was buried nigh her;
And on his grave they planted a rosie bush,
And on hers a green briar.

19. They grew and they grew, till they grew so high
That they could grow no higher;
They lapped and tied in a true love knot,
The red rose and the briar. ****

*Alternative start of verse 9: "She looked to the east, she looked to the west."

**Verse 12 is incomplete in all versions.

*** "Jemmy Grove" does not carry throughout the lyric, but switches here to "Sweet William." I have not corrected it here but duplicated it just as she wrote it.

**** *Alternative ending:*
18. She was buried in the old church yard,
And he was buried a nigh her;
On Sweet William's grave there grew a red rose,
On Barbara's a green briar.

19. They grew and they grew, till they grew so high
They could not grow any higher
They lapped and tied in a true love knot,
For all true lovers to admire.

(Lyrics: KJF v. 1, 2, 3, 4. Melody: v. 2; KJF's musical manuscript, lyrics, and melody also found in Jameson.)

17b. Barbara Allen: Bonny Barbara Allen
Informant: Miss Ollie Huff

(Child vol. 2, No. 84, p. 279) *Other variants place the time in autumn when "yellow leaves were fallin'." The hero's name is often changed to "Sir James Graham from the West Countree," or to "Sweet William," "Johnnie," or "William Green." A comparison of the ancient and modern tunes (Chappell's* Popular Music of the Olden Times, *No. 2, p. 538) will show the deep-seated feeling for music in the remarkable likeness. This genuine love is shown not only by the manual laborers, men and women, who chant and sing as a solace and ease in the wearisomeness of the work, but also by the pleased content of the horses and oxen.*

1. As I was a-crossin' the London's bridge,
The hick'ry buds were swellin';
Poor William on his death bed laid,
For the love of Barbara Ellen.

2. In come his sister's little son,
Says, "Uncle, I b'lieve you're dyin';
I'll run away to younders town,
And I'll fetch you Barbara Ellen."

3. He run and he run, till he got there,
And the sweat was on him a-streamin';
He made his bow and his hat fell off,
"Adieu to Barara Ellen."

4. "Oh, what's the matter with my little son?
Me thinks you have been runnin';"
"Oh, yes, uncle's sick, has sent for you,
If your name be Barbara Ellen."

5. "Oh don't you remember the t'other day,
When you were murty drinkin';
You drank a glass to the ladies all round,
And you slighted Barbara Ellen?"

6. "Oh yes, I remember the t'other day,
When I was murty drinkin';
I drank a glass to the ladies all round,
And my love to Barbara Ellen."

7. He turned his pale face to the wall,
And death was on him, atonin';
"Adieu, adieu, to my friends all round,
Farewell to Barbara Ellen."

8. So slowly, slowly, she got up,
And slowly she moved from him;
She hadn't gone three miles out of town,
Till she heard three death bells tollin'.

9. She looked east, she looked west,
When she saw his cold corpse comin';
"Pray, set you here, you cold, cold corpse,
And let me gaze upon you."

10. The more she looked, the more she mourned,
Till she burst out in a'cryin;
She laid her hands all upon his breast,
And the blood came streaming down 'em.

11. "Go, fix my bed for me, mother dear,
And make it soft and narrow;
This young man has died for the love of me,
And I will die of sorrow.

Editor's Note: It is worth noting that nearly all the different names for the hero in versions cited by Jackson – William Young, Jemmy Grove, William Green – evoke youth, nature, fertility, and verdancy.

(Lyrics: KJF v. 1, 2, 3, 4)

17c. Barbara Allen: Barbara Allen
(Child vol. 2, No. 84, *p. 276*)

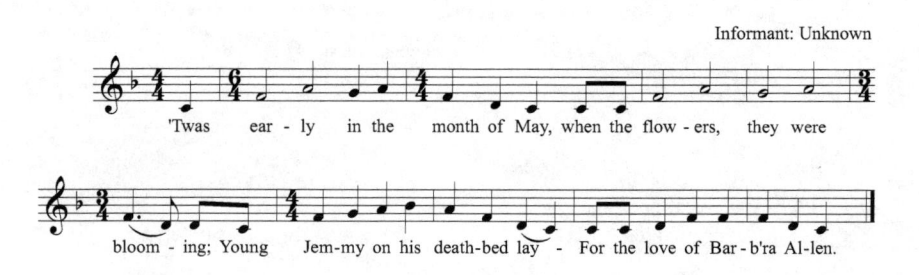

Informant: Unknown

'Twas ear-ly in the month of May, when the flow-ers, they were bloom-ing; Young Jem-my on his death-bed lay - For the love of Bar-b'ra Al-len.

The displacement of the downbeat in the last three measures is as Jackson notated it.
(Lyrics and melody: KJF v 2)

17d. Barbara Allen: Barbara Allen
(Child vol. 2, No. 84, *p. 276*)

Informant: "Old English"

In Scar-lett Town where I was born, There lived a fair maid dwell-in'; And ev'-ry youth cried - "Well-a-day!" Her name was Barb - 'ra Al-len.

It is unclear what "Old English" refers to. Jackson gives no source. She could be referring to a version from a collection, or it may simply be the version Jackson considered to be in common usage at the time, assuming the source to be "Old English." It is likely included for comparison.

(Lyrics and music: KJF, v. 3)

18. The Bailiff's Daughter of Islington: The Beggar Girl
Informant: Unknown

(Child, vol. II, No. 105, *p. 426*) *"The Bailiff's Daughter of Islington" introduces the Romantic ballads with a happy ending. The following is, perhaps, the nearest approach to the original of any extant ballad, only one stanza being lost, and the simplest wording changed.*

1. There was a youth, a well-loved youth,
And he was a squire's son;
He loved the Bailiff's daughter,
That lived in Islington.

2. But she was shy and would not believe
That he did love her so;
No, nor at any time, would she
Any favorance to him show.

3. But when her friends did take it in,
His fond and foolish mind;
They sent him up to fair London,
A 'prentice for to bind.

4. And when he had been seven long years,
And never his love could see;
"Many a tear have I shed for her
When she little thought of me."

5. Then all the maids of Islington,
Went for to sport and play;
All but the Bailiff's daughter,
She secretly stole away.

6. And as she went along the high road,
The weather bein' hot and dry;
She set down upon a green bank,
The true-love came riding by.

7. She started up with color so red,
Catchin' holt of his bridle rein;
"One penny, one penny, kind sir," she said,
"Will ease me of much pain."

8. "Before I give you a penny, sweetheart,
Pray tell me where you were born;"
"At Islington, kind sir," she said,
"Where I've had many a scorn."

9. "I beg you sweetheart, tell to me,
Oh, tell me whether you know
The Bailiff's daughter of Islington?"
"She is dead, sir, long ago."

10. "If she is dead, then take my horse,
My saddle and bridle also;
For I will go to some far-off country,
There no man will me know."

11. "Oh, stay, you goodly youth,
She's standing by your side;
She is here alive, she is not dead,
And ready to be your bride."

12. "Oh, farewell, grief, and welcome joy,
The thousand times therefore;
For I have found my own true love,
Whom I thought I'd never see more."

(Lyrics KJF v. 1, 3, 4)

19a. Sir Hugh: The Jew's Daughter (Little Hugh)
Informant: Miss Ruth Hackney, Letcher County

(Child, vol. III, No. 155, *p. 233*, or *Percy's* Reliques, vol. I, No. 40). *This is a very old ballad, based on an alleged murder which took place in 1265. The story is told in Chaucer's "Prioress's Tale"* (Canterbury Tales, *ca. 1400*).

1. The hallowdays had just come on,
The dewdrops they did fall;
And every scholar of the school,
Went out to playing ball, ball, ball,
Went out to playing ball.

2. Up stept a lady in the door,
With some apples in her hand;
Saying, "Come, come, my little son Hugh,
And one of these you shall have, have, have,
And one of these you shall have."

3. "I won't, nor I can't, nor I will not go,
To thee I will not come;
For if my mother knew of it,
She would make my blood run, run, run
She would make my red blood run."

4. She took him by the lily white hand
And took him from porch to hall;
She locked him up in a little tight room,
Where no one could hear him call, call, call,
Where no one could hear him call.

5. She took him by the lily white hand,
And led him to yonder gate;
Where they were all lying asleep,
And none of them were awake, awake, awake,
And none of them were awake.

6. She took out a little penknife,
And sticked him like a swine;
And then she took a basin in her hand
To catch his life's blood in, in, in,
To catch his life's blood in.

7. She locked him up in a little tin trunk,
And bade him lie still and sleep;
And then went out to the cold, deep well,
Where it was so cold and deep, deep, deep,
Where it was so cold and deep.

8. She threw him in, saying "Sink, sink, sink,
To never rise again;
For it will be a scandal to me,
And to all of my kin, kin, kin...
And to all of my kin.

9. The day passed off and the night came on,
And the scholars all went home;
And all the mothers had little sons,
But Hugh's, and she had none, none, none,
But Hugh's, and she had none.

10. She picked her up a little bark switch,
Went walking down the road;
Saying, "If I find my little son, Hugh,
I'll surely whip him home, home, home,
I'll surely whip him home."

11. She went on to yonder gate,
Where they were lying asleep;
Then went on to the deep, cold well,
Where it was so cold and deep, deep, deep,
Where it was so cold and deep.

12. Saying, "If you're in here, speak, speak, speak,
While I'm in hearing of thee."
"Here I am in the cold, deep well
With a penknife run through me, me, me,
With a penknife run through me."

13. "Go tell all my little school mates,
Not to forget the bark and the birch;
And bury me in yonder church, church, church,
And bury me in yonder church
Where it was so cold and deep, deep, deep,
Where it was so cold and deep."

In verse 8, "kind" rather than" kin" is used in versions 1, 3, and 4. Version 2 ends after verse 12.
(Lyrics KJF v. 1, 2, 3, 4)

19b. Sir Hugh: It Rains a Mist

(Child B, vol. III, No. 155, *p. 233*)

Informant: Mrs. Lucy Banks, Madison County, KY

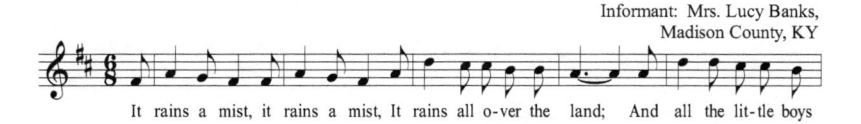

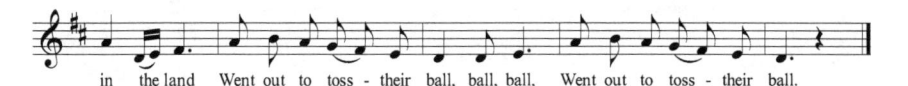

It rains a mist, it rains a mist, It rains all o-ver the land; And all the lit-tle boys in the land Went out to toss-their ball, ball, ball, Went out to toss-their ball.

2. They tossed one up, they tossed one high,
They tossed one over the wall;
Into a Jew's garden they tossed one ball,
Where no one dare go nigh, nigh, nigh,
Where no one dare go nigh.

3. Out came the Jew's daughter, all dressed, all dressed,
To call the little boy in;
"If you'll come in, my little boy,
Then you shall have your ball, ball, ball,
Then you shall have your ball."

4. "I won't go in, I won't go in,"
This little boy did cry;
"For they that go in can never come out,
Can never come out again, again, again
Can never come out again."

5. She took him by the lily white hand,
And led him through the hall;
Into a cellar, so dark and damp,
Where no one could hear him call, call, call,
Where no one could hear him call.

6. "Oh, spare me, o spare me,"
This little boy did cry;
"And when I am grown to be a man,
My treasure shall be thine, thine, thine,
My treasure shall be thine."

7. She placed him on a table wide,
Beneath a silver knife;
She called for a basin as bright as gold
To catch his heart's blood in, in, in,
To catch his life's blood in.

8. "Oh, place my Bible at my head,
My prayer-book at my feet;
And if my playmates ask for me,
Tell them that I'm asleep, sleep, sleep,
Tell them that I'm asleep.

9. "Oh, place my prayer-book at my feet,
My Bible at my head;
And if my parents ask for me,
Tell them that I am dead, dead, dead,
Tell them that I am dead."

(Lyrics: KJF v. 2. Melody: KJF v. 2; KJF in Raine; KJF in Jameson.)

20a. The Daemon Lover: The House Carpenter

(Child B, as "James Harris," vol. IV, No. 243, p. 360; and Child A, as "The Daemon Lover," book II, vol IV, No. 82, p. 158. Also from "The Demon Lover" of Scott's Minstrelsy from the Scottish Border, vol. 3, p. 194 [Edinburgh: Robert Cadell, 1849.] This ballad illustrates the type of the false wife leaving her home and family to go away with an old love.

Mrs. James Baker, Berea, KY *

"We're met, we're met, my own true love, We're met, we're met once more; I've just re-turned from the salt salt sea, and it's all for the sake of thee, And it's all for the sake of thee."

2. "O, hold your tongue of your former vows,
For they'll bring bitter strife;
O, hold your tongue of your former vows,
For I have become a wife. (Repeat)

3. "I might have had a king's daughter,
Far, far beyond the sea;
I might have had a king's daughter,
Had it not been for love of thee." (Repeat)

4. "If you had married a king's daughter,
I'm sure you are to blame;
For I have married a house carpenter,
And I think he's a nice young man." (Repeat)

5. "Just leave your house carpenter,
And go along with me;
I'll take you where the grass grows green,
On the banks of the sweet Willie." (Repeat)

6. She turned herself three times around,
She looked at her babies three;
"Stay at home, stay at home, my sweet young babe
Keep your father company." (Repeat)

7. She dressed herself in scarlet dress,
She dressed her waiter in green;
And every city that she rode through,
They took her to be some queen. (Repeat)

8. She sailed, she sailed, one week or two,
I know it was not three;
And this fair lady began to weep,
And she wept bitterly. (Repeat)

9. "Now is it for my lands you weep,
Or is it for my store;
Or is it for your house carpenter
That you will never see anymore?" (Repeat)

10. "It's neither for your lands I weep,
Nor is it for your store;
It's all for the love of my sweet little babes
That I never will see anymore. (Repeat)

11. "What hills, what hills, now do I see,
What hills, so black and blue?"
"The hills are hills of Hell, you see,
Awaitin' both me and you." (Repeat)

12. "What hills, what hills now do I see,
What hills as white as snow?"
"The hills are hills of Heaven, you see,
Where you and I will go." (Repeat)

13. She sailed, she sailed two weeks or three,
I know it was not four;
Till the ship sprung a leak
And she sank to rise no more. (Repeat)

Verse 10 only occurs in version 2 and in KJF in Raine.
(Lyrics: KJF v. 1, 2, 3, 4; KJF in Raines; KJF in Perrow. Melody: KJF v. 2, 3; KJF in Jameson; KJF in Raine; KJF in Perrow.)

20b. The Daemon Lover: The House Carpenter, The Salt Salt Sea

(Child B, *as "James Harris,"* vol IV, No. 243, *p. 360*; Child A, *as "The Daemon Lover,"* book II, vol IV, No. 82, *p. 158*.)

Informant: "from Laurel" (County)

"So fare you well my own true love, So, fare you well for a-while; I'm go-ing a-way, but I'm coming back a-gain if I go ten-thou-sand miles, If I go ten-thou-sand miles."

2. "Who will shoe my two little feet?
Who will glove my hands?
And who will kiss my red rosy cheeks,
While you are in some foreign land,
While you are in some foreign land?"

3. "Your father will shoe your two little feet,
Your mother will glove your hand;
And I will kiss your red, rosy cheeks,
When I return again,
When I return again.

4. "We're met, we're met, my own true love,
We're met, we're met," said he;
"I'm just returning from the salt, salt sea,
And it's all for the sake of thee,
And it's all for the sake of thee.

5. "I once could a married the King's daughter, dear,
I'm sure she would a married me;
But a crown of gold I did refuse,
And it's all for the sake of thee,
And it's all for the sake of thee."

6. "If you could a married the King's daughter, dear,
I'm sure you are to blame;
For I have married a house carpenter,
And I think he's a nice young man,
And I think he's a nice young man."

7. "If you will leave your house carpenter,
And go along with me;
I'll take you away where the grass grows green,
On the banks of the sweet Willie,
On the banks of the sweet Willie."

8. "If I were to leave my house carpenter,
And go along with thee;
What would be there to maintain me,
Or to keep me from slavery,
Or to keep me from slavery?"

9. "I have seven ships sailing the ocean,
And have seven hundred slaves;
And all may be at your command,
If you will go with me,
If you will go with me."

10. She picked up her tender little babe,
And kisses gave it three;
Says, "Stay at home with your father, my dear,
For to keep him company,
For to keep himm company."

11. They had not been on ship two days,
I'm sure it was not three;
Till she began to weep and mourn,
And she wept most bitterly,
And whe wept most bitterly.

12. "Oh is it for my gold you weep,
Or is it for my store;
Or is it about your house carpenter,
That you never will see any more,
That you never will see any more?"

13. "It's neither for your gold I weep
Or neither for your store;
It's all about my tender little babe,
That I never will see any more,
That I never will see any more."

14. They had not been on ship three days,
I'm sure it was not four;
Till in that ship there sprang a leak
When it sunk to rise no more,
When it sunk to rise no more.

(Melody and lyrics: KFJ in Perrow/Wilgus. A note says, "Sent to Mrs. Ewing Marshall, Louisville, by Katherine Jackson French, April 16, 1912. Collected in eastern Kentucky, probably in Leslie or Perry County." Perrow states that the melody was "notated by memory." Jackson states in the accompanying letter that this version is from Laurel County. She also cites the melody as matching Scott's *Minstrelsy*. The "Who will shoe your pretty little foot" are wandering verses from "The Lass of Roch Royal.")

21. The Golden Vanitee: The Green Willow Tree
Informant: Mrs. James Baker, Berea, KY
(Child B, vol. V, No. 286, *p. 135*)

1. There was a ship sailed for the North Amerikee,
From down in the lonesome Lowlands low;
There was a ship sailed for the North Amerikee,
And she went by the name of the Green Willow Tree,
And she sailed from the Lowlands low.

2. She'd only been a sailing for two weeks or three,
O ho, the lonesome Lowlands low;
She'd only been a-sailing for two weeks or three,
Till she was overtaken by the Turkish Revele,
As she sailed from the Lowlands low.

3. Then said the captain, "What shall we do?"
Crying, "O the lonesome Lowlands low;"
Then said the captain, "What shall we do?
The Turkish Revele will surely cut us in two,
As we sail from the Lowlands low."

4. Up spake a sailor boy, "What will you give to me?"
Crying, "O the lonesome Lowlands low;"
Up spake a sailor boy, "What will you give to me?
If I will go and sink for you the Turkish Revele,
As we sail from the Lowlands low."

5. "I'll give you gold, I'll give you fee,"
Crying, "O the lonesome Lowlands low;"
"I'll give you gold, I'll give you fee,
And my only daughter for your wedded wife to be,
As we sailed from the Lowlands low."

6. The lad leapt down and away swam he,
Crying, "O the lonesome Lowlands low;"
He fell upon his breast, and away swam he,
And he swam till he came to the Turkish Revele,
As we sailed from the Lowland low.

7. There were some playing cards and some playing checks,
As we sailed from the lonesome Lowlands low;
There were some playing cards and some playing checks,
And before they cleared the boards, they were in water to their necks,
As they sailed from the Lowlands low.

8. Then the lad turned back and away swam he,
Crying "O, the lonesome Lowlands low;"
Then he fell upon his breast and away swam he,
And he swam till he came to the Green Willow Tree,
And we sailed from the Lowland low.

9. Cried he, "Kind Captain, I have done your decree,"
Crying, "O, the lonesome Lowlands low;"
Cried he, "Kind Captain, I have done your Decree,
Now take me on board ere I perish in the sea."
And we sailed from the Lowlands low.

10. "Nay, nay, Sailor-boy, I'll never take you on board,"
O ho, the lonesome Lowlands low;
"Nay, nay, Sailor-boy, I'll never take you on board,
Never will I be to you as good as my word,"

And we sailed from the Lowland low.

11. "T'is only the respect that I have for your crew,
O ho, the lonesome Lowlands low;
'Tis only the respect that I have for your Crew,
Or I'd sink your ship and you with it too,"

And we sailed from the Lowland low.

12. Then he fell upon his breast and away swam he,
Crying, "O, the lonesome Lowlands low;
He fell upon his breast and away swam he,
"Adieu, adieu to the Green Willow Tree,
Adieu the Lowland low."

(Lyrics: KJF v. 2; Raine's *Mountain Ballads* has an identical version though not attributed to KJF.)

22. The Trooper and the Maid: Pretty Peggy, O
Informant: Mrs. Margaret Combs Green, Knott County, KY
(Child B, vol. V, No. 299, *p. 172*)

1. As we walked down to Fernario,
As we walked down to Fernario,
Our captain fell in love with a lady like a dove,
And they called her by name, pretty Peggy, O.

2. "What would your mother think, pretty Peggy, O,
What would your mother think, pretty Peggy, O,
What would your mother think, for to hear the guineas chink,
And the soldiers a-marchin' before ye, O?

3. "You shall ride in your coach, pretty Peggy, O,
You shall ride in your coach, pretty Peggy, O,
You shall ride in your coach, and your true love by your side,
Just as grand as any lady in the Ario."

4. Come steppin' down the stairs, pretty Peggy, O
Come steppin' down the stairs, pretty Peggy, O,
Come steppin' down the stairs, combin' back your yellow hair,
Take the last farewell of your sweet William, O.

5. "If ever I return, pretty Peggy, O,
If ever I return, pretty Peggy O,
If ever I return, this city I'll burn,
And destroy all the ladies in the Ario."

6. "Our captain he is dead, pretty Peggy, O,
Our captain he is dead, pretty Peggy, O,
Our captain he is dead, and he died for a maid,
And's buried in the Louisiana Country, O."

(Lyrics: KJF v. 2)

23a. The Merchant's Daughter of Bristow: The Wealthy Merchant of London, or Jackaro

Informant: Unknown

(Child A, book 2, vol. IV, *appendices, p. 328*) *A happy ballad with a nice, unintelligible, meaningless refrain, is seen in "The Wealthy Merchant of London," from "The Merchant's Daughter of Bristow" A different variant reveals the hero is in Germany, wounded on the battlefield.*

1. I'll tell you of a wealthy merchant,
In London he did dwell;
He had only one daughter,
The truth to you I'll tell,
Refrain: And sing lay the lilly-low,
      And sing lay the lilly-low.

2. She was sitting in her parlor,
Singing a true love song;
Her father said unto her,
"O, daughter, you are wrong." (Refrain)

3. "Oh, father, cruel father,
This heart you can't incline;
There's none but Jack, the sailor
Can win this heart of mine." (Refrain)

4. She went into the tailor's shop,
She dressed in men's array;
She went to some big Captain
To carry her away. (Refrain)

5. "Your name I'd like to know it
Before you go on board."
She, smiling in her countenance,
Says, "Call me Jack Munfro." (Refrain)

6. "Your waist is long and slender,
Your fingers, they're too small;
Your cheeks are too red and rosy
To face the cannonball." (Refrain)

7. "My waist, it's long and slender,
My fingers they are small;
But little does it daunt me
To see ten thousand fall." (Refrain)

8. All among the officers,
And all among the crew;
A-seeking for young Jackie,
And she found him too. (Refrain)

9. She pulled out a kerchief,
A private mark to show;
Sayin', "Jackie, do you know me,
And will you marry me now?" (Refrain)

10. The squire he was sent for,
And the knot it was tied;
And all the young officers
Agreed to Jackie's bride. (Refrain)

Another stanza is frequently added with personal appeal:
"This kipple they are suited
And oft times did agree;
And also they got married,
And why not you and me?"

(Lyrics: KJF v. 1, 3, 4)

23b. The Merchant's Daughter of Bristow: The Wealthy Merchant of London, or Jackaro

Informant: Margaret Combs Green, Knott County, KY
(Child A, book 2, vol. IV, *appendices*, p. 328)

1. Once there was a silk merchant,
In London he did dwell;
He had one lovely daughter,
The truth to you I'll tell,
Oh, the truth to you I'll tell.

2. She had sweethearts a-plenty,
She courted day and night;
Upon little Jack, the sailor,
She pressed her heart's delight,
Oh, she pressed her heart's delight.

3. Her father heard the callin',
So quickly he come in;
"Good morning, Mrs. Frasier,
Is that your sweetheart name?
Oh, is that your sweetheart's name?"

4. They locked him in his dungeon,
His body to confine;
"There's none but Jack, the sailor
Will ever suit my mind,
Oh, will ever suit my mind."

5. "Oh, daughter, daughter, daughter,
If you'll quit that boy today;
I'll pay him forty shillings
To bear him faraway
Oh, to bear him far away."

6. She answered, "Quickly, quickly,
I'll quit that boy today;"
But yet all in her heart,
She loved her darling still,
Oh, she loved her darling still.

7. He sailed all o'er the ocean
He sailed all o'er the sea;
So safely he had landed
In the wars of Germany,
Oh, in the wars of Germany.

8. This girl bein' a girl of honor
With money in her hand;
She set her resolution
To visit some foreign land,
Oh, to visit some foreign land.

9. She went down to the tailor's shop,
She dressed all in men's gray;
She labored for the captain
For to bear her far away,
Oh, for to bear her far away.

10. "Your waist, it is too slender,
Your fingers, they too small;
Your cheeks too red and rosy
To face the cannon ball,
Oh, to face the cannon ball."

11. "I know my waist is slender,
My fingers, they are small;
But little does it daunt me
To see ten thousand fall,
Oh, to see ten thousand fall."

12. "Young man," says he, "Hire your name
Before on board you go."
She smiled all in her countenance,
"They call me Jack-a-Ro,
Oh, they call me Jack-a-Ro."

13. She sailed all o'er the ocean
She sailed all o'er the sea;
So safely she has landed
In the wars of Germany,
In the wars of Germany.

14. She went down to the battlefield,
She viewed them up and down;
Amongst the dead and wounded,
Her darling boy she found,
Oh, her darling boy she found.

15. She picked him up all in her arms,
She carried him up to the town;
Inquiring for a doctor,
To heal his bloody wound,
Oh, to heal his bloody wound.

16. This kipple they are married,
And oftimes did agree;
And also they got married,
And's why not you and me?
Oh, and's why not you and me?

(Lyrics: KJF v. 2)

24a. The Golden Glove: A Wealthy Young Farmer
Informants: Mrs. Begley of Leslie Co, KY and Mrs. J.L. Combs of Berea, KY

The original is "The Golden Glove" or "The Squire of Tamworth," in Robert Bell's Ballads of Peasantry, *p. 70 (West Strand: John W. Parker and Sons, 1857) which has become "The Wealthy Young Farmer." It is yet enjoying great popularity, perhaps because of its simple story and the clever ruse of the bride in obtaining her choice.*

1. There was a young squire, from London he came,
He courted a nobleman's daughter in vain;
All for to marry her was his intent,
And at last this young squire did gain their consent.

2. The day was appointed, the knot to be tied,
A farmer was chosen to give way the bride;
In the room of being married, she turned to her bed,
For the thoughts of the farmer run so in her head.

3. This thought of the farmer run so in her mind,
A way for to gain him, she quickly did find;
Coat, wescot and breeches, this lady put on,
And away she went huntin', with her dog and her gun.

4. She hunted all round where the farmer did dwell,
Because in her heart she loved him so well;
'Twas often she fired but nothin' did she kill,
At length the farmer come out onto the field.

5. "Why didn't you go to the weddin'?" she cried,
"To wait on the squire and give him his bride?"
"Kind miss," he says, "If the truth I must tell,
I cannot give her away, I love her too well."

6. It pleased the damsel to see him so bold,
She pulled out a glove that was flowered with gold;
"This I've picked up, as I come along,
Since I've been huntin', with my dog and gun."

7. Then away she went home with her heart full of love,
She put out an oration, that she'd lost her a glove;
"And the man that will find it and bring it to me,
I vow and declare his sweet bride will be."

8. As soon as the farmer this news he did hear,
Straightway to the damsel a courtin' did steer;
"Honored lady, I've picked up your glove,
Will you be so kind as to grant me your love?"

9. "It's already granted," this damsel replied,
"I love the sweet breath of the farmer," she cried;
"I'll be mistress of your dairy and milker of your cows,
While my jolly young farmer goes whistlin' to his plow."

10. And when they got married, she told of
 her fun,
How she hunted the farmer with her dog and
 her gun;
But now I've got him so fast in the snare,
"I'll enjoy him forever, I'll vow and declare."

(Lyrics: KJF v. 1, 2, 3, 4)

"English-Scottish Ballads from the Hills of Kentucky"   197

24b. The Golden Glove: A Wealthy Young Farmer
(Robert Bell, Ancient Poems, Ballads and Songs of the Peasantry of England, *West Strand: John W. Parker and Sons, 1857, p. 70)*

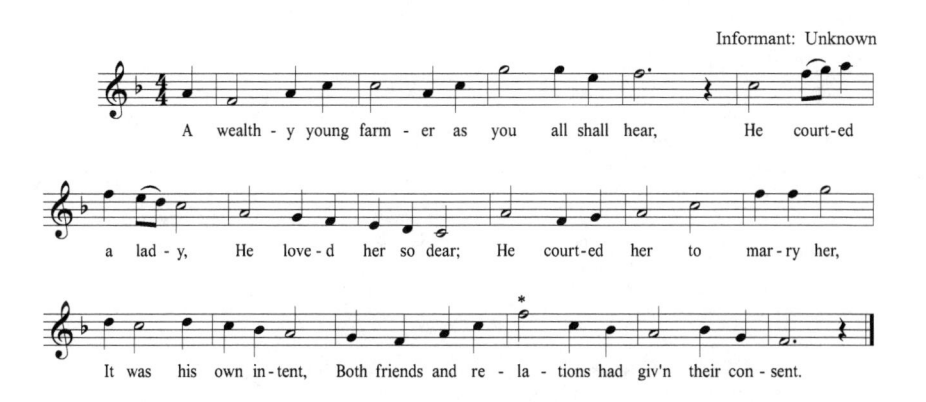

Informant: Unknown

A wealth-y young farm-er as you all shall hear, He court-ed a lad-y, He lov-ed her so dear; He court-ed her to mar-ry her, It was his own in-tent, Both friends and re-la-tions had giv'n their con-sent.

*Versions 3, and KJF in Raines and Jameson, put this ending
a third higher from this point on, which I believe to be a mistake. I have taken the ending from version 2. The odd rhythmic setting could be Jackson's attempt to notate irreglar elongations of notes on the part of the singer, or could siply be an error.

(Lyrics and melody: KJF v. 2, 3; KJF in Raines; KJF in Jameson.)

25. William Hall

Informant: Unknown

The foregoing has helped to give rise to a large cycle of recognition ballads, in which identity is established between separate couples, by some previous gift – usually a ring. "John Reilly" refers to colonial settlements in Pennsylvania; "William Hall" will serve as a typical illustration of the genre.

1. There once was a gay and handsome farmer
He was a credit to any land;
He courted a fair and loving lady
Whom he left in a far and distant land.

2. And his parents came for to know this,
They grew angry and this did say:
"We'll send him away and over the ocean
Where her face he'll no more see."

3. He sailed the ocean over and over
Till the length of the day;
Sayin', "If Mollie is alive and I can find her,
It's, it's married we will be."

4. Cold drops of rain fell as it happened,
He chanced his true love for to meet;
Sayin' "You are a gay and handsome lady,
How do you think you can fancy me?"

5. "You are intrudin' on a gay, fair damsel,
And me, your bride not fittin' to be;
I have a sweetheart that sails the ocean,
Been gone seven long year from me.

6. "Seven long year make no alteration,
And seven more'll make none with me."
"Oh, describe him, describe that man to me
Perhaps I knew just such a fellow
As I've lately come from sea."

7. "Oh, he was handsome, and he was pretty,
Oh he was witty and he was tall;
Had black hair, and wore it curly,
Oh, them pretty black eyes were all."

8. "Yes, I knew just such a fellow
By the name of William Hall;
A shinin' sword I saw pierce through him
Over dead this man did fall."

9. Such screams, such screams by any fair lady,
Enough to make any man prove true;
"Since we have parted, all broken-hearted,
Oh, good Lord, what shall we do?"

10. "Cheer up, cheer up, my pretty fair lady,
Hence perlikely, I am he,
And to convince you of the story,
Here is the ring you gave to me."

11. Oh they joined hands and hearts together
Away they went to the old church yard
And they got married to one another
Whether their parents say yes or no.

Editor's Note: This is not a Child ballad. This "broken token" ballad was collected in England in 1904 by Frank Kidson and Ralph Vaughn-Williams.

(KJF v. 4)

"English-Scottish Ballads from the Hills of Kentucky"   199

26. The Serving Maid

"The Serving Maid" is added, not so much for the wording as for the interesting air, quaint, weird, and typical, which is often used for other ballads and hymns, to which the regular tune is forgotten.

Informant: Unknown

Betsy was a beauty fair, From eastern shores Betsy came here; A serving maid 'Twas for to be, Her father bound her to a gay lady.

2. A gay lady, who had but one son,
Who Betsy's beauty favored on;
Late in the day, as I've heard tell,
He said to Betsy, "I love you well." *

3. His mother bein' in the room,
Chanced to hear what they did say;
And resolved all in her mind,
To break them of their heart's design.

4. Early next mornin', she arose,
And said to Betsy, "Put on your clothes;
It's out of town that you must go,
And wait on me a day or so."

5. A short time after, she returned,
Leavin' Betsy far behind;
"You're welcome home, dear mother,
But what keeps Betsy that I claim as mine?

6. "I love her as I do my life,
And am determined to make her my wife."
"Oh, son, oh, son, your love's in vain,
For Betsy's sailin' across the main."

7. A short time after, her son took sad,
Nothin' in the world would make him glad;
She sends for doctors, far and wide,
She sends for doctors, skilled and tried.

8. She wrung her hands and tore her hair,
Like a woman in despair;
Sayin', "If my son were alive again,
I'd send for Betsy across the main."

*All three versions of the melody have the lyrics for verse one as above. All versions of the lyrics have the third and fourth lines of that verse switched. I have opted to go with the order in the musical manuscript.

(Lyrics: KJF v. 1, 3, 4; KJF in Jameson; KJF filed in the biography file of the KJF collection. Melody KJF v. 3; KJF in Jameson; KJF in Raine; also filed in the biography file of the KJF collection.)

27. McAfee's Confession
Informant: Unknown

(Child vol. IV, no. 195, p. 34) *A popular example of the old Goodnights, modelled, perhaps unconsciously, after "McPherson's Farewell" or "Lord Maxwell's Goodnight." The event occurred in 1847.*

1. Draw nigh, young friends, and learn from me
A sad and mournful history;
Oh, may you not forgetful be,
Of all this day, I'll tell to thee.

2. Before I arrived at my fifth year,
My father and my mother, dear
Were both laid in their silent grave
By Him, who them their being gave.

3. No more a father's voice I hear,
No more a mother's love I share;
I was no more a father's toy,
I am a helpless orphan boy.

4. Oh, when my uncle bid me chide,
I turned from him dissatisfied;
I began again in wickedness,
And Satan served with eagerness.

5. Oh, well I mind the very day,
When from my home I ran away;
And to my sorrow since in life,
I took unto myself a wife.

6. She was as good and kind to me
As any woman need to be;
And here alive would be, no doubt,
Had I not seen Miss Betty Stout.

7. Ah, well I mind the very night
When all was still, the stars shone bright;
My wife was lying on her bed,
When I went up to her and said:

8. "Here is some medicine for you I bought
And which for you this day I bought;
Ah, take it dear, it will cure you
Of these wild fits, pray take it, do."

9. She gave to me one tender look,
And in her mouth the poison took;
And laid again down on her bed,
And to her last long sleep she laid.

10. I, fearing that she was not dead,
Upon her throat, my hand I laid;
And there such deep impression took,
Her soul soon from her body fled.

11. Ah, then my soul was filled with woe,
I cried out, "Whither shall I go?
How can I quit this mournful place,
This world again, how can I face?"

12. I'd freely give up all my store,
Had I ten thousand worlds or more;
If I could bring again to life
My dear, my darling murdered wife.

13. Her body lies beneath the sod,
Her soul, I trust, has gone to God;
While I am doomed to endless pain,
Destruction surely, I must obtain.

14. Young men, young men, be warned by me,
And shun all evil company;
Walk in the way of righteousness,
And God, your soul will surely bless.

15. The minute now is drawing nigh,
When from this earth my soul shall fly;
And meet my God there at his bar,
And hear my final sentence there.

16. Adieu, adieu, my friends, adieu,
No more on earth shall I see you;
In Heaven's bright and shining plain,
I hope I'll meet you all again.

"Goodnight" ballads come from a long line of British Isle ballads which invariably contain a rebel (usually Scottish or Irish) outlaw hero who is caught and hanged, but before hanging, he plays a tune of his homeland and defiantly snaps his fiddle bow in two so his oppressors may not steal his music. Jackson cites this when she discusses "Callahan's Confession" in "A Fortnight of Balladry." The condemned in the above story is not nearly so noble, and is condemned for the murder of his wife. As with many traditional songs, numerous places claim this as their own. John Harrington Cox lists several versions of this in *Folk Songs of the South*. It was also collected in the Ozarks by Vance Randolph, and by Alan Lomax in Ohio.

(Lyrics: KJF v. 1, 2, 4)

28. Confession of Edward W. Hawkins

Informant: Unknown

Composed in the jail of Estill County, KY, while under sentence of death, May, 1857. Another gallows ballad in the manner of "Lord Maxwell's Goodnight."

1. Young men, young men, come learn of me
A sad and mournful history;
And may you not forgetful be
Of the story I'll relate to thee.

2. For murder I am now arraigned,
In the dark dungeon bound and chained;
Where I am yet compelled to stay
Until the twenty-ninth of May.

3. And then I'll leave my dungeon home,
And be consigned to the cold tomb;
And there, I must forgotten lie,
Then come, young men, and see me die.

4. Come, see me meet a youthful grave,
To trouble, then, no more a slave;
My friends, I do not fear to die,
Or meet my Maker in the sky.

5. My sins are great, I do admit,
My Saviour's power is greater yet;
Then on His mercy I rely,
For pardon when I come to die.

6. O, welcome, death, how sweet a sound
When I shall no longer be bound;
I've twenty-eight days yet to mourn,
Bound in my gloomy dungeon home.

7. And then my soul must fly away
To darkest night or brightest day;
And there it must forever be,
Through fearful, vast eternity.

8. Come, stand around me, young and old,
And see me welcome death so bold;
My youthful heart, it is so brave,
I do not fear to meet the grave.

9. Young men, young men, be warned by me,
And always shun bad company;
Now I must bid you all adieu,
Remember, my advice is true.

(Lyrics KJF v. 1, 3, 4)

29. Summer is A-Cumin in

Informant: Unknown

Sum-mer is a-cum-in in____ Merr-ly sing Cuck-oo Grow-eth seed and blow-eth med and springth the wood a new____ Sing Cuck-oo A-we-ble-teth af-ter lomb Louth af-ter clal-ue cu Bul-luc stert-eth, buck-e vert-eth Mu-rie sing Cuck-oo-oo-Cuck-oo, Cuck-oo____ Well sing-es thu Cuck-oo ne swik thu

(The fragment ends here.)

Editor's Note: This song is not a ballad, but was in Jackson's collection of ballads. It dates back to the 13th century, and is a good example of how early the Ionian (major) 7-note scale was in common usage.

(Lyrics and music: KJF v. 2.)

30. Sourwood Mountain

Editor's Note: Melody attrirbuted to KJF in James Watt Raine Collection. Katherine cites this as a tune she heard on her first trip into the mountains. It was played by the sons of "Sister Marthy," and Katherine comments on their playing style as exhibiting "force and decision expanding into rough jollity."

Appendix A
A Note on the Ballads

I use the same names Francis Child did for these most of these ballads since Jackson modeled her collection on his and cited the numbers of the songs as they appeared in his collection. The names/numbers of the twenty-eight ballads and forty-three variants (and one tune) in the extant collection and synopses of their plotlines are followed by Jackson's titles for the variants of each song and a brief synopsis (my own) for ease of reference.

British Survivals

1. *"Lady Isabel and the Elfin Knight" (Child no. 4)*. A man attempts to murder Polly, who would have been his seventh victim. She outsmarts him and kills him.
   a) "Pretty Polly."
   b) "Pretty Polly."
   c) "Six Pretty Fair Maids."
2. *"Earl Brand" (Child no. 7)*. A lover kills a girl's family. He rides away bleeding.
   a) "Fair Ellender."
3. *"The Twa Sisters" (Child no. 10)*. A jealous sister kills her younger sister.
   a) "The Lord of the Old Country."
   b) "The Lord of the Old Country."
4. *"Lord Randal" (Child no. 12)*. An evil woman poisons her love. He tells his mother in a riddle song.
   a) "Lord Randall."
5. *"Edward" (Child no. 13)*. A young man is dying. Like Lord Randall, he tells his mother, but he is murdered by his brother.
   a) "Edward."

6. *"The Cruel Mother" (Child no. 20).* A mother kills her children. Their ghosts visit her and say she is going to hell.

   a) "The Greenwood Side."

7. *"The Three Ravens" (Child no. 26).* Crows are ready to feast on a dead knight.

   a) "The Three Crows."

8. *"The Twa Brothers" (Child no. 49).* One brother kills the other. The mother mourns.

   a) "Little Willie."

9. *"Young Beichan and Susie Pye" (Child no. 53).* A Turkish lady saves a lord from prison and then waits seven years until he leaves his bride at the altar for her.

   a) "Lord Bateman."

   b) "Lord Bateman."

10. *"Young Hunting" (Child no. 68).* A spurned woman murders her love interest and throws his body in a well.

    a) "Loving Henry."

    b) "William and Ellender."

11. *"Lord Thomas and Fair Annet" (Child no. 73).* Brown Girl is rejected by Lord Thomas, goes to his wedding, and stabs his wife. He kills her and cuts off her head. This is a twist as the murder is usually that of Brown Girl by Fair Ellender.

    a) "Lord Thomas and Fair Annet."

    b) "Lord Thomas."

12. *"Fair Marge't and Sweet William" (Child no. 74).* William leaves his wife because he is in love with Margaret. Margaret dies and visits him as a ghost, and William too dies of grief.

    a) "Fair Marge't and Sweet William."

13. *"Lord Lovel" (Child no. 75).* Lord Lovel goes away, and, when he comes back, his love is dead. He too dies of grief.

    a) "Lord Lovely."

14. *"The Lass of Roch Royal" (Child no. 76).* A husband goes away. His wife is left alone.

    a) "The Lovers' Farewell."

15. *"The Wife of Usher's Well" (Child no. 79).* A mother sends her three children to school in America. They die, and their ghosts visit her.

    a) "A Lady Gay."

16. *"Little Musgrave and Lady Barnard" (Child no. 81).* A woman seduces a boy. Her husband is told by a servant and cuts off her head.

    a) "Lord Vanner's Wife."

    b) "Lord Daniel's Wife."

17. *"Barbara Allen" (Child no. 84).* A young woman spurns a young man. He dies, and she dies of grief for him.

    a) "Barbara Allen's Cruelty."

    b) "Bonny Barbara Allen."

    c) "Barbara Allen."

    d) "Barbara Allen."

18. *"The Bailiff's Daughter of Islington" (Child no. 105).* Lovers are parted. When he returns, she does not recognize him. He tests her love, and they are reunited.

    a) "The Beggar Girl."

    b) "William Hall."

19. *"Sir Hugh" (Child no. 155).* A Jewish woman murders a child.

    a) " Little Hugh."

    b) " It Rains a Mist."

20. *"The House Carpenter"/"The Daemon Lover" (Child no. 243).* A woman's lover's ghost returns to her and takes her away from her husband to hell.

    a) "The House Carpenter."

    b) "The Salt, Salt Sea."

21. *"The Golden Vanitee" (Child no. 286).* A cabin boy saves a ship in war but drowns because his captain abandons him.

    a) "The Green Willow Tree."

22. *"The Trooper and the Maid" (Child no. 299).* Peggy falls in love with the captain, but he is killed, and she is left alone.

    a) "Pretty Peggy, O."

23. *"Merchant's Daughter of Bristow" (Child no. 228).* A woman follows her love on board a ship, dressed as sailor. They marry.

    a) "The Wealthy Merchant of London" ("Jackaro").

    b) "The Wealthy Merchant of London" ("Jackaro").

24. *"The Golden Glove" (Ballads of Peasantree P.S. 17:106).* A woman tricks a man into marrying her by dressing like a farmer and pretending to lose her glove.

    a) "A Wealthy Young Farmer."

    b) "A Wealthy Young Farmer."

25. *"William Hall" (Kidson, Vaughan-Williams, collected as "John Reilly").* This is a variant on the "broken token" theme. A man gives half a token to his love before going away and shows it to her on his return.

Additional Ballads, Songs, and Tunes

26. *"The Serving Maid."* A mother finds out her son is in love with Betsy and sends her across the sea. The son dies of grief.
27. *"McAfee's Confession" (Child no. 195).* A man is condemned to death for murdering his love.
28. *"Confession of Edward W. Hawkins."* A self-confessed murderer expresses remorse before execution.
29. *"Summer Is a-Cumin In."* The very old English round.
30. *"Sourwood Mountain."* A joyful mountain tune.

Appendix B

Informants for the Ballads of Katherine Jackson

Ambrose, Nathan; Berea, KY
Baker, Mrs. James; Madison County, KY
Banks, Lucy; Madison County, KY
Begley, Malvina, Leslie County, KY
Begley, Martha; Leslie County, KY
Combs, Bettie; Berea, KY
Combs, Jennie; Berea, KY
Cornett, Jane; Knox County, KY
Green, Margaret; Perry County, KY
Green, Margaret Combs; Knott County, KY
Hackney, Ruth; Letcher County, KY
Honicutt, Eliza; Laurel County, KY
Huff, Olive; Berea, KY
Huff, Mrs. Ollie; Berea, KY
Maize, Ellen; Knox County, KY
Napier, Lizane; Leslie County, KY
Smith, Jane; Laurel County, KY

Appendix C
Time Line of the Ballad Wars

1851

Francis Child becomes professor of rhetoric at Harvard College.

1876

Frances Child is given the title professor of English at Harvard College and devotes himself to the study of English balladry.

1880

Francis Child publishes *The English and Scottish Popular Ballads*.

1888

George Lyman Kittredge begins teaching at Harvard.

1893

Lila Edmunds publishes "Songs from the Mountains of North Carolina" in the *Journal of American Folklore* (two songs and one ballad, lyrics only).[1]

1896–

Francis Gummere is friend to Kittredge, who reigns as America's chief ballad expert and the heir to Child.

1898

Kittredge writes an introduction to and publishes the last volume of Child's *The English and Scottish Popular Ballads.*

1902

The Hindman Settlement School, started by Katherine Pettit and May Stone, opens its doors.

1902–1905

Katherine Jackson attends Columbia University. While she is there, her friends tell her of hearing a speaker from Berea College lecture on uncollected ballads in the Kentucky mountains.

1905

Emma Bell Miles publishes *The Spirit of the Mountains,* which contains a chapter on Appalachian culture and music, including five songs with lyrics and music and one ballad.

Josiah Combs becomes the first graduate of the Hindman Settlement School.

1905–1911

Josiah Combs becomes Hubert Shearin's protégé at Transylvania University.

1907

The lyrics of ballads Katherine Pettit has collected at the Hindman Settlement School, particularly from young Josiah Combs, are published in the *Journal of American Folklore* by George Lyman Kittredge, who takes the byline.

Campbell visits the Hindman Settlement School. Ada Smith sings "Barbara Allen" for her.

1908

Olive and John Campbell go on a fact-finding mission into Appalachia. Along the way, Olive begins to collect ballads.

The Frosts meet the Campbells at Berea.

1909

Katherine Jackson goes ballad collecting in the hills of Kentucky.

Louise Rand Bascom publishes lyrics in "Ballads and Songs of Western North Carolina" in the *Journal of American Folklore.*

1910

Olive Campbell's first set of ballads (both lyrics and music) is sent to Kittredge by John Glenn of the Sage Foundation. The request for aid in publication is turned down.

Katherine Jackson comes to Berea and asks for help publishing her collection of lyrics of and music for Kentucky ballads.

William Goodell Frost and John C. Campbell get together in New York.

1911

Katherine Jackson comes to Berea again. William Goodell Frost meets her. He promises help in publication.

Jackson contacts Hubert Shearin and shares her ballads.

Katherine Pettit takes Campbell's side in the matter of Jackson and her apparently imminent publication.

Frost holds onto Jackson's ballads.

Shearin and Combs publish the *Syllabus of Kentucky Folk-Songs.*

Shearin publishes the article "Kentucky Folk-Songs," in which he apparently used some of Jackson's work. He corresponds with Kittredge and flatters him in print.

Combs does not want Campbell using the ballads she had collected from him in his student days. She uses at least one of them anyway. Once again, Combs goes uncredited.

1912

Balis Ritchie self-publishes the collection *Lover's Melodies: A Choice Collection of Old Sentimental Songs Our Grandmothers Sang and Other Popular Airs*. This was printed on Ritchie's own printing press and was not widely distributed. It contained seventeen songs, of which three are Old World ballads.

Frost holds onto Jackson's ballads.

William A. Bradley comes to Kentucky, makes the acquaintance of Frost, Jackson, Shearin, Combs, and Pettit.

1912–

Bradley publishes articles in *Harper's* about Kentucky that include Jackson, Shearin, and Combs, then moves to France, where he translates Combs's manuscript and begins to ascend the ladder of the publishing world.

1913

Jackson asks Frost to ask Bradley for help regarding the publication of her collection.

Alphonso Smith begins collecting ballads.

Frost holds onto Jackson's ballads.

1914

Combs publishes "Sympathetic Magic in the Kentucky Mountains" in the *Journal of American Folklore* and is edited by Kittredge.

Jackson asks Frost to send her ballads to Alphonso Smith for inclusion in his upcoming volume. She also asks that he send them to Francis Gummere to obtain an endorsement. Frost does neither, continuing to hold them.

Enlisted by Jackson, Gummere writes Frost and supports the idea of Jackson's book.

1915

Jackson asks for her ballads back. They are not returned. Frost, one final time, sits on Jackson's ballads. For reasons unknown, by now he has placed them on a shelf in the Mountain Room with a note that says: "K. Jackson. Hold."

Jackson gives up on her ballad collection and goes on with the rest of her life.

1916

Publication of Loraine Wyman and Howard A. Brockway's *Lonesome Tunes.* Cecil Sharp and Maud Karpeles begin collecting ballads in the Southern Appalachians.

1917

Cecil Sharp and Olive Dame Campbell publish *English Folk Songs from the Southern Appalachians,* and Sharp becomes the authority on southern balladry. That collection is the basis for a lasting perception of Appalachian ballads and music. After that, Olive goes on and does great work for the people of Appalachia.

Josephine McGill puts together a collection of twenty Kentucky songs (including thirteen ballads) at the request of May Stone and publishes *Folk-Songs of the Kentucky Mountains.*

1918

William A. Bradley writes "The Women on Troublesome" for *Scribner's,* about Katherine Pettit, May Stone, and the Hindman School.

1921

William A. Bradley moves to Paris.

1922

Louise Pound publishes *American Ballads and Songs,* which includes ballads and other songs from across America, some gleaned from other people's collections.[2]

1923

James Watt Raine publishes *Mountain Ballads for Social Singing,* songs collected from the singing of Berea College students, an in-house book intended to be used on the campus by students.

1924

James Watt Raine publishes *Land of the Saddlebags,* which includes words and music to a half dozen Kentucky ballads.

1925

John Harrington Cox publishes *Folk-Songs of the South,* which includes many kinds of songs, not just ballads.

1926

William A. Bradley translates Josiah Combs' dissertation as *Folksongs of the Southern United States.* It appears in Paris in *Vient de paraitre,* a venue for publishing doctoral theses.

Susannah Wetmore and Marshall Bartholomew's *Mountain Songs of North Carolina* appears.[3]

1927–

The Bristol Sessions, the Big Bang of country music, take place, and the Radio Age begins. Ballads are now part of popular entertainment presented by Bradley Kincaid and others in ways designed to please large audiences.

1928

Kincaid puts out his first songbook, *My Favorite Mountain Ballads and Old-Time Songs.*[4]

1929

Arthur Kyle Davis, a Kittredge student, edits and publishes *Traditional Ballads of Virginia* after Alphonse Smith's death.

John Jacob Niles publishes *Seven Kentucky Mountain Songs.*

1932

Maud Karpeles publishes an expanded second edition of *English Folk Songs from the Southern Appalachians,* leaving Olive Dame Campbell's name off the cover (it appeared only in the front matter). Kentucky is much better represented in this reissue. Scholarship by this time moves into the audio age and is geared toward recording rather than book publication, as exemplified by the Lomaxes. The artifact is now becoming a combination of the performer and the recording, not merely the song itself. The collectors who follow, including Dorothy Scarborough and the Lomaxes, cease to be focused only on ballads. The Ballad Wars are over.

Notes

Introduction

1. Olive Dame Campbell and Cecil J. Sharp, *English Folk Songs from the Southern Appalachians* (New York and London: G. P. Putnam's Sons, 1917).

2. I am defining *large* as fifty-plus ballads (Jackson claimed to have collected over sixty by 1910) and *scholarly* as including analysis and citations linking collected songs to other, older British Isle versions like those found in the collections of Francis Child, Thomas Percy, William Chappell, James Johnson, William Motherwell, etc.

1. "The Spirit and Sap of the Stock"

Epigraph: Katherine Jackson French, "A Fortnight in Ballad Country," BCA RG 4, ser. 3, box 1, folder 1-7, Katherine Jackson French Ballad Collection, Berea College Special Collections and Archives, Berea, KY.

1. Katherine Jackson French, "History of the Founders and the Founding of London," quoted in "Mayor Dedicates Jackson Memorial," *Sentinel Echo* (London, KY), August 00, 1940.

2. *Sentinal Echo* (London, KY), August 22, 1940; Jarvis Jackson to Nephew, July 25, 1882, Jackson File C, "John and Jarvis Jackson," Jackson Family Folder, MSS, Laurel County Historical Society, London, KY; Eleanor Jackson Pennington, Genealogical Chart, Jackson Family Notebook, Laurel County Historical Society; William Harvey Jackson Tombstone, Russell Dyche Cemetery, London, KY; "William Harvey Jackson" (obituary), *Mountain Echo,* January 6, 1899; Russell Dyche, *History of Laurel County* (London, KY: Laurel County Historical Society, 1954), 67; McKee Family Notebook, McKee Family Folder, Notebook FMH, Laurel County Historical Society.

3. Indicative of this is the fact that Jackson was a member of the National Society of the Colonial Dames of America, whose mission statement reads: "The National Society of The Colonial Dames of America actively promotes our national heritage through historic preservation, patriotic service and educational projects. The Corpo-

rate Societies shall be composed entirely of women who are lineal bloodline descendants from an ancestor of worthy life who, residing in an American colony, rendered efficient service to our country during the Colonial period." "About the NSCDA," n.d., National Society of the Colonial Dames of America, http://nscda.org/about-us/membership-inquiries.

4. *Mountain Echo,* January 6, 1899, in *Mountain Echo, 1873–1879: Excerpts from the Mountain Echo,* transcribed by Geri Sutton (London, KY: Laurel County Historical Society, 2001), 1; Dyche, *History of Laurel County,* 242; Jackson Family Tombstones, Russell Dyche Cemetery; Carol F. Hopper and Daniel Hopper, *1880 Laurel County Census with Vital Statistics* (Lily, KY, 1989); Family Tree, Jackson Family Notebook, "John-Mary-Jarvis," Jackson Family Folder, MSS, Laurel County Historical Society.

5. Dyche, *History of Laurel County,* 67.

6. I refer to Katherine Jackson French as "Katherine Jackson" or "Jackson" before her marriage in 1911 and as "Katherine French" or "French" after.

7. Dyche, *History of Laurel County,* 67; Katherine Jackson French Tombstone, Russell Dyche Cemetery; Family Tree, Jackson Family Notebook; Hopper and Hopper, *1880 Laurel County Census.*

8. Mary Katherine (Kay) Tolbert Buckland, telephone interview with the author, March 6, 2014; "Katherine Jackson French, Long a Leader in Education" (obituary), clipping from an unidentified newspaper, BCA RG 4, ser. 4, box 1, folder 1-8, Katherine Jackson French Ballad Collection, Berea College Special Collections and Archives, Berea, KY.

9. C. B. Faris, John Pitman, and W. T. Moren, *Laurel Seminary: Brief Sketch of Its History* (London, KY: Mountain Echo, 1891), 3–6, Laurel Seminary Folder, "Schools" Files, Laurel County Historical Society; Kitty Jackson Report Card, *Early Report Cards of the Laurel Seminary,* "Bottom Report by Mrs. W. F. (Kittie Jackson) French," April 15, 1881, and Annie Jackson Report Card, February 19, 1892, Laurel Seminary Folder, "Schools" Files, Laurel County Historical Society. Like many eastern Kentucky mountain towns, London was mostly pro-Union during the Civil War and found itself on the doorstep of several battles, including the Battle of Wildcat Mountain in 1861. The Laurel Seminary was occupied by both armies at various times. After the war, the building was put back in order, and the school reopened its doors.

10. Jarvis Jackson Tombstone, Russell Dyche Seminary, London, KY.

11. *Mountain Echo,* June 22, 1877, quoted in Dyche, *History of Laurel County,* 67; *Mountain Echo,* August 3, 1877, in *Excerpts from the Mountain Echo,* 77.

12. *Mountain Echo,* July 13, 1877, in *Excerpts from the Mountain Echo,* 73.

13. Dyche, *History of Laurel County,* 67–68. It is likely that the London Cornet Band and the London Brass Band were the same entity as the terms *cornet band* and *brass band* were used interchangeably by the general population.

14. Faris, Pitman, and Moren, *Laurel Seminary.*

15. Erica Rumbley, "From Piano Girl to Professional: The Changing Form of

Music Instruction at the Nashville Female Academy, Ward's Seminary for Young Ladies, and the Ward-Belmont School, 1816–1920" (PhD diss., University of Kentucky, 2014).

16. Katherine Jackson Diary, February 12, March 24, April 9, and April 10, 1900, private collection.

17. Katherine Jackson Student Record Card, and Roster, both Science Hill Female Academy, "Pupils Science Hill Female Academy 1879–1900," MC 608, B1 5416, box 13, folder 76, Science Hill Female Academy Collection, Filson Historical Society.

18. Joan Marie Johnson, *Southern Women at the Seven Sister Colleges* (Atlanta: University of Georgia Press, 2008), 2.

19. Barbara Welter, "The Cult of True Womanhood: 1820–1860," *American Quarterly* 18, no. 2, pt. 1 (summer 1966): 151–74, 152, quoted in Linda K. Kerber, *Toward an Intellectual History of Women* (Chapel Hill: University of North Carolina Press, 1997), 162.

20. "Science Hill Female Academy," in *The Kentucky Encyclopedia*, ed. John E. Kleber (Lexington: University Press of Kentucky, 1992), 817.

21. Julia Tevis, *Sixty Years in a School Room* (Cincinnati: Western Methodist Book Concern, 1878), 463.

22. Julia Tevis quoted in Joanne Passet, *Sex Variant Woman: The Life of Jeannette Howard Foster* (Cambridge, MA: Da Capo, 2008), 55. See also "Science Hill Female Academy."

23. *Science Hill Female Academy School Catalog, 1887–1888*, MC 608, S 416, box 6, folder 33, "Catalogs from the Poynter Years," 1879–1890, Filson Historical Society.

24. "History of Science Hill," 2014, Wakefield-Scearce Galleries, http://www.wakefieldscearce.com/science-hill.

25. *Science Hill: An English Classical School for Girls and a Wellesley Preparatory, 1888–1889*, MC 608, BI S 416, box 6, folder 33, Science Hill Female Academy Collection.

26. Ledger, MS B1 5416, box 13, folder 81, Day Book, September 1891, 152, MC 608, Science Hill Female Academy Collection; Faculty List, *Science Hill: An English Classical School for Girls and a Wellesley Preparatory, 1890–1891*, MC 608, BI S 416, box 6, folder 34, Science Hill Female Academy Collection; Ledger, MS BI S 416, box 6, folder 34, Day Book, 1892–1893, MC 608, Science Hill Female Academy Collection; Program from Science Hill Centennial Commencement, May 30–June 2, 1892, private collection; Attendance Book, "Report for Year Ending June 6, 1893," MC 608, B1 5416, folder 120, Science Hill Female Academy Collection.

2. Young Lady From London

1. French Student Record Card, Science Hill Female Academy.
2. *Mountain Echo*, August 9, 1895, in *Excerpts from the Mountain Echo*, 85.

3. *Mountain Echo,* March 1, 1895, June 14, 1895, in *Excerpts from the Mountain Echo,* 58; Katherine Jackson French Student Record Card, Ohio Wesleyan University, Ohio Wesleyan University Archives, Delaware, Ohio.

4. Steven Mintz, "Statistics: Education in America, 1860–1950," 2017, History Now, Guilder Lehrman Institute of American History, https://www.gilderlehrman.org/content/statistics-education-america-1860-1950.

5. Quoted in Johnson, *Southern Women,* 4.

6. Peter Temin, "The Post-Bellum Recovery of the South and the Cost of the Civil War," *Journal of Economic History* 36 no. 4 (1976): 487–92; Agnes Scott College, http://georgia.teach-us.org/203-agnes_scott_college.htm.

7. Rebecca Montgomery, *The Politics of Education in the New South: Women and Reform in Georgia, 1890–1930* (Baton Rouge: Louisiana State University Press, 2006), cited in Johnson, *Southern Women,* 4.

8. Johnson, *Southern Women,* 3.

9. *Fifty-Fourth Catalogue of Ohio Wesleyan University, 1898* (Delaware: Ohio Wesleyan University, 1898), 13–14.

10. Roger Geiger, *The History of American Higher Education: Learning and Culture from the Founding to World War II* (Princeton, NJ: Princeton University Press, 2015); Pamela Roby, "Women and American Higher Education," *Annals of the American Academy of Political and Social Science* 404, no. 1 (November 1972): 118–39.

11. *The College Transcript* (Ohio Wesleyan University), March 6, 1897; French Student Record Card, Ohio Wesleyan University. Ohio Wesleyan operated on a trimester schedule. Emily Gattozzi (Ohio Wesleyan Archives curator), email to the author, February 18, 2014.

12. *Fifty-Fourth Catalogue of Ohio Wesleyan University,* 11–12, 43, 85; Emily Gattozzi, email to the author, February 18, 2014. It is not clear whether these were performance, music theory, or music history courses as they are listed simply as *music* on her transcript.

13. "Exchange," *The College Transcript,* March 12, 1898.

14. *The College Transcript,* March 6, 1897.

15. *The College Transcript,* June 20, 1898.

16. Katherine Jackson French Student Record Card, Ohio Wesleyan University.

17. French Student Record Card, Ohio Wesleyan University; *The College Transcript,* March 6, 1897. The music program at Ohio Wesleyan at about the time Jackson attended was described as "well-organized" with "a large and competent corps of instructors, both gentlemen and ladies." W. G. Williams, *Fifty Years of History of the Ohio Wesleyan University* (Cleveland: Cleveland Printing and Publishing Co., 1895).

18. "Pencil Points," *The College Transcript,* March 12, 1898; *The College Transcript,* June 20, 1898. Jackson's committee later planted an oak at the senior class's pregraduation ceremony.

19. *The College Transcript,* June 20, 1898.

20. *The College Transcript,* June 20, 1898.

21. "Monnett Hall: What We Gather Passing Up and Down the Corridors,"

The College Transcript, April 16, 1898; "Pencil Points: Gathered from Everywhere and about Everybody," *The College Transcript,* March 12, 1898; "Field Day at Monett Hall Last Thursday Evening," *The College Transcript,* June 11, 1898; "Fraternity Picnics," *The College Transcript,* June 11, 1898.

22. *The College Transcript,* November 18, 1899; Dyche, *History of Laurel County,* 68.

23. *Mountain Echo,* January 13, 1899, in *Excerpts from the Mountain Echo,* 3.

24. *Fifty-Sixth Catalogue of Ohio Wesleyan University, 1900* (Delaware: Ohio Wesleyan University, 1900), 105.

25. Emily Gattozzi, email to the author, February 18, 2014.

26. *Mountain Echo,* July 21, 1899, October 27, 1899, in *Excerpts from the Mountain Echo*; "Epworth League," n.d., *Encyclopedia of Cleveland History,* Case Western Reserve University, https://case.edu/ech/articles/e/epworth-league. The Epworth League was a group for young Methodist adults. During the time referenced, the national organization boasted over 1.75 million members.

27. "List of Graduates," in *Fifty-Seventh Catalogue of Ohio Wesleyan University, 1900* (Delaware: Ohio Wesleyan University, 1900).

28. *The College Transcript,* June 14, 1900.

29. Jocelyn K. Wilk, email to the author, February 3, 2014.

30. "Alumni," *The College Transcript,* February 23, 1901; French Student Record Card, Science Hill Female Academy; Mary Katherine (Kay) Tolbert Buckland, interview with the author, November 22, 2014. Kay Buckland, Jackson's granddaughter, says that Jackson initially taught mathematics but then decided: "'If I'm going to teach all my life, I'm not going to teach this boring stuff!'" "And that," Buckland concluded, "was when she decided to study English literature." Notice, National Bureau of Education to Katherine Jackson French, May 7, 1900, private collection.

31. Katherine Jackson, "Outline of the Literary History of Colonial Pennsylvania" (PhD diss., New York: Columbia University, 1906); Andrew W. Phillips to Katherine Jackson, May 21, 1900, private collection.

32. "Women at Columbia," March 2004, Columbia 250, Columbia University, http://c250.columbia.edu/c250_events/symposia/history_women_timeline.html; Jackson, "Outline of the Literary History of Colonial Pennsylvania," n.p.; Jocelyn K. Wilk, email to the author, February 3, 2014. Serendipitously, Jackson's fellow female ballad collector Dorothy Scarborough was to teach at Columbia about fifteen years later. Both Loyal Jones and Ron Pen suggested I look for a link between Scarborough and Katherine. I did and found none. Scarborough attended Columbia twelve to fourteen years after Katherine did and did not embark on the collecting trip that led to her *A Song Catcher in Southern Mountains* (New York: Columbia University Press, 1937) until 1930, twenty-one years after Katherine's trip into the Kentucky mountains. Jackson was well ensconced at Centenary College in Louisiana by then, living the life of an English professor and leader of women in the Shreveport community.

33. Johnson, *Southern Women,* 8.

34. Mary Jean Wall, *How Kentucky Became Southern: A Tale of Outlaws, Horse*

Thieves, Gamblers, and Breeders (Lexington: University Press of Kentucky, 2010), 204; Recommendation for Southern Fellowship, Laura McGill, Dean of Barnard College, to Dr. Lilian Welsh, the Woman's College, Baltimore, March 14, 1904, private collection; Johnson, *Southern Women*, 7.

35. "Lynching in America," n.d., American Experience, PBS.org, https://www.pbs.org/wgbh/americanexperience/features/emmett-lynching-america.

36. Melissa Stein, "Measuring Manhood" (lecture delivered at Berea College, September 25, 2018). There is no evidence as to whether Jackson was familiar with these theories.

37. Johnson, *Southern Women*, 95–108. In truth, northerners also harbored prejudices. The northern version tended to be a velvet racism, however, and customarily reared its head in the form of segregated neighborhoods, economic ostracism, and the occasional "race war" (meaning black people fought back) rather than outright lynchings.

38. "Black Milestones in Education: Columbia Lions Edition," April 18, 2008, Twilight and Reason, https://twilightandreason.wordpress.com/tag/columbia-university. In 1908, Pixley ka Isaka Seme became the first black student to graduate from Columbia. He was from South Africa, not the United States, and later founded the African National Congress.

39. Sam Roberts, "No Longer Majority Black, Harlem Is in Transition," *New York Times*, January 5, 2010; Robert A. Gibson, "The Negro Holocaust: Lynching and Race Riots in the United States, 1880–1950," n.d., Yale–New Haven Teachers Institute, http://teachersinstitute.yale.edu/curriculum/units/1979/2/79.02.04.x.html; "From the Courier Journal," in *Excerpts from the Mountain Echo*, 41; *Mountain Echo*, June 29, 1877, July 6, 1877, in ibid., 71, 72–73.

40. "Women at Columbia."

41. Recommendation for Southern Fellowship.

42. French, "Outline of the Literary History of Colonial Pennsylvania," v.

43. French, "Outline of the Literary History of Colonial Pennsylvania," 4, 41, 119.

44. Jocelyn K. Wilk, email to the author, February 3, 2014.

45. "Katherine Jackson, Long a Leader in Education." This article claims that Jackson was the first woman from Kentucky to earn a PhD from any "standard university," but that is incorrect. She was preceded by at least one other woman. See Geiger, *The History of American Higher Education*, 403; "US Population from 1900," 2001, Demographia, http://www.demographia.com/db-uspop1900.htm.

46. "Local Items," *Mountain Echo*, May 25, 1905, September 20, 1901, in *Excerpts from the Mountain Echo*.

47. Katherine Jackson, "Seminar C" notebook from Columbia University, 1903–1904, private collection. The viewpoint that ballads were a group creation was pioneered by Francis Gummere, from whom Jackson would later seek endorsement for her ballad collection. See Francis Gummere, *Old English Ballads* (Boston: Ginn & Co., 1897), and *The Popular Ballad* (New York: Dover, 1907).

48. *Mountain Echo,* March 24, 1882, in *Excerpts from the Mountain Echo,* 20; Katherine Jackson French, Handwritten Autobiography, Katherine Jackson French Collection, BCA RG 4, ser. l, box 1, Berea College Special Collections and Archives. It is likely that one of the lecturers was William Goodell Frost, who gave a speech at Barnard College in 1903 on "mountain whites" and their culture. Jackson's friends probably reported it to her later. See "Address by Dr. Frost," *Barnard Bulletin,* January 19, 1903; and Jackson, "Seminar C" notebook from Columbia University, 1903–1904.

49. *Mountain Echo,* July 4, 1907, in *Excerpts from the Mountain Echo,* 12; *Mountain Echo,* August 17, 1905, in ibid., 196; Unsigned, Undated Letter (probably to Katherine Jackson French?), private collection; "List of Post-Graduate Students," in *Yale University Catalogue, 1907–1908* (New Haven, CT: Tuttle, Morehouse, & Taylor Co., 1907), 622.

50. Isma Dooley, "The Social Whirl: Visiting Women," *Atlanta Constitution,* April 9, 1916; French, Handwritten Autobiography.

3. Act Two

1. Family Register of Wm. Franklin French and Minerva Katherine Jackson, Katherine Jackson French Bible, private collection; Photographs, private collection; Mary Katherine (Kay) Tolbert Buckland, interview with the author, November 22, 2014; "W. F. French Succumbs at Age of 78," newspaper article, [1955], private collection; William Franklin French, Mason's Card, 1911, private collection; Jackson Family Genealogical Chart, private collection.

2. Dyche, *History of Laurel County,* 115; Lou Eberlein, "Reminiscences of Mrs. Eberlein" (typescript, June 1943, private collection); Jackson Diary, n.d. [1900?].

3. Eberlein, "Reminiscences of Mrs. Eberlein."

4. Anne Firor Scott, *Natural Allies: Women's Associations in American History* (Urbana: University of Illinois Press, 1991), 91.

5. Dyche, *History of Laurel County,* 115; Katherine Jackson French and F. H. E. Ross, *The Story of the Years in Mountain Work* (Nashville: Woman's Missionary Council, [1918?]); Eberlein, "Reminiscences of Mrs. Eberlein." It is worth noting that the founding of the Sue Bennett School had input from both Poynters of the Science Hill Academy.

6. Isma Dooley, "The Social Whirl."

7. Family Register of Wm. Franklin French and Minerva Katherine Jackson; Mary Katherine (Kay) Tolbert Buckland, telephone interview with the author, March 6, 2014.

8. Katherine French Tolbert, Note on Music Books, private collection.

9. Emily J. Arendt, "'Ladies Going about for Money': Female Voluntary Associations and Civic Consciousness in the American Revolution," *Journal of the Early Republic* 34, no. 2 (Summer 2014): 157–86, 168, 171, 172.

10. Scott, *Natural Allies,* 13; Robert W. Ikard, "The Cultivation of Higher Ideals:

The Centennial Club of Nashville," *Tennessee Historical Quarterly* 65, no. 4 (Winter 2006–2007): 342–69, 343.

11. Scott, *Natural Allies,* 96, 102. Not surprisingly, black women's clubs had an even harder time of it than did white clubs. They began in 1895 as "nothing less than the organized anxiety of women who have become intelligent enough to recognize their own low social condition and strong enough to initiate the forces of reform." Fannie Barrier Williams, "The Club Movement among Colored Women of America," in *The New Woman of Color: The Collected Writings of Fannie Barrier Williams,* ed. Mary Jo Deegan (DeKalb: Northern Illinois University Press, 2002), 54–58, 55. Some of them invited white guest speakers, with the ulterior motive of breaking down barriers between black women and the white society that excluded them. Women in these clubs sometimes studied music and art, but their main concern was to improve the conditions of African Americans in their communities and in the country in general. Needless to say, their efforts were not universally welcomed, and neither were the efforts of the white clubs that worked with them.

12. Barbara Smith Corrales, "Parlors, Politics, and Privilege: Clubwomen and the Failure of Woman Suffrage in Lafayette, Louisiana, 1897–1922," *Louisiana History: The Journal of the Louisiana Historical Association* 38, no. 4 (Autumn 1997): 453–71.

13. Betty Brandon, "Women in Southern Politics," in *The New Encyclopedia of Southern Culture,* vol. 10, *Law and Politics,* ed. Charles Reagan Wilson (Chapel Hill: University of North Carolina Press, 2008), 456. It should be noted that, though Katherine Jackson French scarcely saw a club she did not like or want to join, she never joined the United Daughters of the Confederacy, and, as a resident of Louisiana for a quarter century, she certainly had many opportunities to do so.

14. "The Woman's Department Club, Written for the State Federation Report, 1922," box 10, folder 372, Woman's Department Club Records, 1919–2007, Louisiana State University, Shreveport; "Lynching in America: Confronting the Legacy of Racial Terror," n.d., Equal Justice Initiative, https://eji.org/reports/lynching-in-america. The founding documents of the Woman's Department Club do not mention race. While they make a point of noting that residents of Caddo Parish would be allowed, they do not designate whether that includes people of color. Caddo Parish had the second highest rate of black lynchings in the country in those years, according to the Equal Justice Initiative. It is unclear whether the Woman's Department Club was extending an invitation to black and mixed-race people or inviting violent white supremacists to join its ranks. It was for the times quite progressive on a number of issues, but race was never explicitly mentioned in any of its motions.

15. "Woman's Department Club Elects Officers and Department Heads; Pays Tribute to Late Dr. French," *Shreveport Times,* January 18, 1959.

16. "General Meetings, November 5, 1919 through May 4, 1926," board #1, box 1A, Collection 372, Woman's Department Club Records.

17. "Membership Minutes, 1919–1926," February 28, 1920, box 1A, Collection 372, Woman's Department Club Records; "General Meetings, November 5, 1919 through May 4, 1926."

18. "Original Cost of Woman's Department Club," box 10, folder 372, Woman's Department Club Records; CP Inflation Calculator, http://www.in2013dollars.com/1919-dollars-in-2018?amount=15.

19. Scott, *Natural Allies,* 80.

20. "Membership Minutes, 1919–1926"; "General Meetings, November 5, 1919 through May 4, 1926."

21. "A Brief History of the Club," in *The Woman's Department Club, 25th Anniversary Yearbook, 1919–1944* (Shreveport, LA: Woman's Department Club, 1944).

22. "Woman's Department Club Elects Officers"; "Membership Minutes, 1919–1926."

23. Katherine Jackson French, Woman's Department Club Lecture Notes, private collection.

24. Application for National Register of Historic Places, Shreveport, Woman's Department Club Records.

25. Mamie B. Helper to Katherine Jackson French, April 29, 1921, private collection.

26. Pearl Matthews to Katherine Jackson French, n.d., private collection; Clarissa H. to Katherine Jackson French, May 6, 1922, private collection.

27. Poem by Martha Hardy Trimble, n.d., private collection.

28. Shirley Kelley, interview with the author, March 8, 2017; Jackson Diary, 1930s; Mrs. Henry S. Hinton, "Social Calendar," *Shreveport Times,* October 10, 1920; "New State President," *The Magnolia* (Louisiana Division of the AAUW), Bulletin no. 15, April 1941, 1. As Kay Buckland told me: "They never had any money; all the nice things they had were given to them." Mary Katherine (Kay) Tolbert Buckland, interview with the author, November 23, 2014. Some of the gifts are still in the family today.

29. Cecelia Ellerbe, "Tribute to Katherine Jackson French," n.d., private collection; "Woman's Department Club Elects Officers"; "A Brief History of the Club."

30. Jackson Diary, 1920s. *Heart of the City: A History of the Shreveport First United Methodist Church* (Shreveport, LA: First United Methodist Church, 1995), 27–28.

31. Jackson Diary, 1920s; *Yoncopin* (Shreveport, LA: Centenary College, 1924); "Centenary College of Louisiana Opens Its 100th Session," *Shreveport Times,* August 20, 1924. This view of egalitarian access to education stemmed from her deeply held Christian faith and perhaps from her experiences with Berea College and William Goodell Frost as well.

32. Charles Brown, telephone interview with the author, March 7, 2017.

33. Dr. Betty McKnight Spears, telephone interview with the author, March 7, 2017; "New Endowed Scholarship Honors Long-Time Centenary Professor," *Centenary College of Louisiana News,* 2017, https://www.centenary.edu/news-media/story/new-endowed-scholarship-honors-long-time-centenary-professor. Spears went on to a distinguished career herself at Centenary. She became deeply involved in the lives of her students and was a noted inspirational and (according to Centenary president David Rowe) iconic figure.

34. Dr. Lee Morgan, telephone interview with the author, March 7, 2017.

35. Faculty Minutes, Centenary College, September 20, 1932, May 22, 1941, and April 24, 1942, Centenary College Archives and Special Collections, Shreveport, LA.

36. Mary Katherine (Kay) Tolbert Buckland, telephone interview with the author, March 6, 2014, and interviews with the author, November 21, 2014, and November 22, 2014; "W. F. French Succumbs at Age of 78."

37. Mary Katherine (Kay) Tolbert Buckland, interviews with the author, November 21, 2014, and November 23, 2014.

38. "Centennial Held at Science Hall," unidentified newspaper, 1925, private collection; Science Hill Graduation Program, 1931, private collection.

39. Hinton, "Social Calendar."

40. "What Music Means to Me," *Shreveport Times,* May 8, 1930.

41. "Noted Southern English Scholar Is Member of Centenary Faculty," *Shreveport Times,* July 23, 1933.

42. Mary Katherine (Kay) Tolbert Buckland, interview with the author, November 22, 2014.

43. "Dr. Katherine French Elected to Head AAUW," unidentified newspaper article, private collection; "Dr. French, Mrs. Moody Attend AAUW Biennial Convention in Cincinnati," unidentified newspaper article, 1941, private collection; Program, American Association of University Women Convention, May 5–9, 1941, and May 5–9, 1947, private collection.

44. "Dr. French, Mrs. Moody Attend AAUW Biennial Convention."

45. *There Shall Be No Night* was a 1940 Pulitzer Prize–winning play by Robert E. Sherwood about the German invasion of Poland and the decision of residents to fight against it. French must have traveled to New York to see it, perhaps visiting her daughter, who was in graduate school at Columbia University at the time. She is quoting the passage from memory.

46. "AAUW to Meet This Week," *Shreveport Times,* March 1, 1942.

47. Unidentified newspaper article photograph, private collection.

48. Katherine Jackson French to His Excellency Lord Halifax, n.d., private collection.

49. "President's Report," *The Magnolia* (Louisiana Division of the AAUW), Bulletin no. 17, April 1942, 1.

50. Mary Katherine (Kay) Tolbert Buckland, interview with the author, November 22, 2014; Lucy Lamb to Katherine Jackson French, February 11, 1942, private collection; "President's Report"; Certificate, State of Louisiana to Katherine Jackson French, March 18, 1942, private collection.

51. Katherine Jackson French to Membership of the Louisiana AAUW, February 10, 1943, private collection.

52. "Convention of University Women to Be Held in Natchitoches," undated newspaper article, private collection.

53. "Past Presidents of the Louisiana Division," n.d., private collection; "Dr.

French to Address Alexandria Branch AAUW," unidentified newspaper article, private collection.

54. Sarah Clapp to Katherine Jackson French, March 31, 1943, private collection.

55. Agnes Ellen Harris to Katherine Jackson French, March 29, 1943, private collection.

56. AAUW Conference Booklet, 1949–1950, private collection; International Study Grant Biographies, AAUW Booklet, 1952, private collection.

57. "Death Claims Retired Teacher," unidentified newspaper article, private collection; Mary Katherine (Kay) Tolbert Buckland, telephone interview with the author, March 6, 2014.

58. Undated newspaper article, private collection.

59. Annie Jackson Pollard to Katherine Jackson French, July 27, 1932, private collection.

60. Mary Katherine (Kay) Tolbert Buckland, interview with the author, November 23, 2014.

61. *Yoncopin* (Shreveport, LA: Centenary College, 1931).

62. She means Arthur Kyle Davis Jr., ed., *Traditional Ballads of Virginia* (Cambridge, MA: Harvard University Press, 1929).

63. Katherine Jackson French to Katherine French, April 29, 1932, private collection.

64. Katherine Jackson French to Katherine French, April 29, 1932.

65. Katherine Jackson French to Katherine French, undated letter, private collection. Ultimately, Katherine French Tolbert became the supervisor of art for the Shreveport City School District. Her husband, Carl Tolbert, a professional clarinetist, was the supervisor of music for the same system. "We always used to laugh about the artists getting together," says their daughter Kay. Mary Katherine (Kay) Tolbert Buckland, email to the author, February 12, 2016. Katherine and Carl's marriage lasted until Katherine's death in April 2014. Carl followed her a year later.

66. Jeanette Marks to Katherine Jackson French, June 10, 1932, private collection.

67. Mary Katherine (Kay) Tolbert Buckland, interview with the author, November 22, 2014.

68. Jackson Diary, 1920s–1930s.

69. *Sentinel Echo* (London, KY), August 22, 1940 ("A History of London"); Mary Katherine (Kay) Tolbert Buckland, interview with the author, November 21 and 22, 2014; "Noted Southern English Scholar Is Member of Centenary Faculty."

70. Mary Katherine (Kay) Tolbert Buckland, interviews with the author, November 21, 2014, and November 22, 2014; "W. F. French Dies in Louisiana; Rites Here Saturday," unidentified newspaper article, 1955, private collection.

71. "Noted Southern English Scholar Is Member of Centenary Faculty."

72. Mary Katherine (Kay) Tolbert Buckland, interview with the author, November 22, 2014.

73. Katherine Jackson French Diaries, 1920–1924, 1930s, private collection; "W. F. French Succumbs at Age of 78."

74. AAUW LA Conference Booklet, April 2–3, 1948, private collection; "Dr. French Retires," *This Is Centenary*, vol. 2, no. 4 (August 1948).

75. Proclamation, Centenary College President and Board of Trustees, May 29, 1949, private collection.

76. *Yoncopin* (Shreveport, LA: Centenary College, 1948), dedication.

77. *Yoncopin* (Shreveport, LA: Centenary College, 1930), 3.

78. *Yoncopin* (1934), 162, 159, 144, 117; *Yoncopin* (Shreveport, LA: Centenary College, 1934), 2.

79. Photograph, *This Is Centenary*, vol. 2, no. 4 (August 1948).

80. Poems on Scrap of Paper, private collection.

81. Lela S. Mason to Katherine Jackson French, July 3, 1953, private collection.

82. Katherine Jackson French to Katherine French, n.d., private collection.

83. Funeral Ceremony Book for W. F. French, December 27, 1955, private collection; "W. F. French Dies in Louisiana"; Mary Katherine (Kay) Tolbert Buckland, interview with the author, November 21, 2014. It is interesting to note that most of the obituaries mention that Frank was the husband of Katherine and then go on to list *her* accomplishments. "W. F. French Dies in Louisiana" is the exception.

84. Mary Katherine (Kay) Tolbert Buckland, telephone interview with the author, March 6, 2014; Woman's Department Club Proclamation, private collection.

85. Mary Katherine (Kay) Tolbert Buckland, interview with the author, November 22, 2014, and telephone interview with the author, March 6, 2014.

86. "The rose still grows beyond the wall" from card sent on the death of Katherine Jackson French from Mrs. Norman Preston, Woman's Society of Christians First Methodist Church of Shreveport, to Katherine French Tolbert, 1958, private collection; Mary Katherine (Kay) Tolbert Buckland, interview with the author, November 22, 2014; Bertie Shreve Jackson (and Bob Jackson) to Katherine French Tolbert, January (1958?), private collection.

87. Mary Katherine (Kay) Tolbert Buckland, interview with the author, November 23, 2014, and telephone interview with the author, March 6, 2014. There is no further information on who R.Z. was or what happened to her.

88. "Death Claims Retired Teacher"; Mary Katherine (Kay) Tolbert Buckland, telephone interview with the author, March 6, 2016.

89. Mary Katherine (Kay) Tolbert Buckland, interview with the author, November 23, 2014.

90. "Treasured Memories," Service Book, November 13, 1958, private collection.

91. Mary Katherine (Kay) Tolbert Buckland, interview with the author, November 23, 2014.

92. Edith Porter to Katherine French Tolbert, November 17, 1958, private collection; C. J. Tooke Jr. to Katherine French Tolbert, n.d., private collection.

93. "Women's Department Club Elects Officers."

94. Treasured Memories."

95. Not to be confused with the famed writer Wallace Stegner but another English teacher who started there the same year French did and left four years sooner.

4. "A Fortnight of Balladry"

Epigraph: Katherine Jackson, "English-Scottish Ballads from the Hills of Kentucky," Katherine Jackson, "English-Scottish Ballads from the Hills of Kentucky" (version 3), BCA RG 4, ser. 2, box 1, folder 1-3, Katherine Jackson French Ballad Collection.

1. For this discussion, I use "Jackson," not "French," because it was Katherine Jackson French's surname at the time.
2. Francis James Child, *The English and Scottish Popular Ballads,* 10 bks. in 5 vols. (Boston: Riverside Press/Houghton/Osgood & Co., 1880; reprint, New York: Dover, 1882–1898).
3. Ron Pen, personal communication, April 2018.
4. Josiah Combs, *Folk-Songs of the Southern United States* (Austin: University of Texas Press, 1967), 80.
5. Cecil Sharp Diary, July 31, 1917, quoted in Mike Yates, "Cecil Sharp in America: Collecting in the Appalachians," January 15, 1999, https://www.mustrad.org.uk/articles/sharp.htm.
6. Bradley Kincaid, *Favorite Old-Time Songs: Volume 2,* OCHS-155 (Brighton, MI: Old Homestead Records, 1984), RG 13, ser. 8, box 14, folder 9, Bradley Kincaid Collection, Berea College Special Collections and Archives. Interestingly, Kincaid claimed Scottish, not Anglo-Saxon, ancestry.
7. William Goodell Frost, "Our Southern Highlanders," *The Independent* 72 (January–June 1912): 708–14, and "God's Plan for the Southern Mountains," *Biblical Review,* July 1921, 405, 412.
8. Those other musics of the mountain were certainly in existence. While ballads were being used as cultural evidence of Anglo superiority by some early collectors, not all had that focus. Shearin did; Combs mostly did (though he did not publish his dissertation on Kentucky folk songs until the 1920s and, then, only in France); Kittredge did. But others did not. Emma Bell Miles's *The Spirit of the Mountains* (New York: James Pott & Co., 1905), a description of mountain life, included thirty-two examples of lyric fragments, seven complete lyrics to songs, six tunes, and a handful of complete lyrics with music, one of which was a ballad; the rest were native songs. Louise Rand Bascom's "Ballads and Songs of Western North Carolina (*Journal of American Folklore* 2, no. 84 [April–June 1909]: 238–50) included lyrics from both Old and New World songs. John Lomax's *Cowboy Songs and Other Frontier Ballads* (New York: Sturgis & Walton, 1911) contained many New World creations. At Berea College, Old World ballads had been collected from the 1890s on by C. Raymond Rexford, who was followed by both James Watt Raine and John F. Smith. Smith's collection was much broader in scope than were those of the other Bereans and included not only old ballads but also popular songs, spirituals, and camp meeting songs. (In fact, the collections of both Raine and Smith were broad enough to be dismissed as "modern stuff, quite worthless," by Cecil Sharp when he visited Berea in 1917, though he judged Raine's as a bit better than Smith's. Cecil Sharp's Appala-

chian Diaries, https://www.vwml.org/topics/sharp-diaries/sharpdiary1917.) All these collections were initially intended for use by students at Berea. Raine later went on to include some of those songs in his *Land of the Saddlebags* (New York: Council of Women for Home Missions and Missionary Education Movement of the United States and Canada, 1924). John Jacob Niles began transcribing traditional songs as early as 1910 and transcribed songs of African American soldiers during World War I. In the 1920s, Carl Sandburg traversed the country in search of all kinds of American music, to be followed in short order by Alan Lomax, whose broad scope of collecting and crossing of cultural and racial lines put the Ballad Wars and their Anglo focus to bed forever.

9. Katherine Jackson French, "A Fortnight in Ballad Country," *Mountain Life and Work* 31, no. 3 (1955): 30–40, 30.

10. Katherine Jackson French, "A Fortnight of Balladry," n.d., 2, BCA RG 4, ser. 3, box 1, folder 1-7, Katherine Jackson French Ballad Collection.

11. French, "A Fortnight of Balladry," 1.

12. French, "A Fortnight of Balladry," 1.

13. French, "A Fortnight in Ballad Country," 30–32.

14. French, "A Fortnight of Balladry," 3.

15. Katherine Jackson, "English-Scottish Ballads from the Hills of Kentucky," BCA RG 4, ser. 2, box 1, folder 1-3, Katherine Jackson French Ballad Collection. "English-Scottish Ballads" went through several versions. The first has no extant title. The second was called "English-Scottish Ballads from the Hills of Kentucky." It was subtitled "Old World Ballads, Collected in the Hills of Kentucky." The third was called "Mountain Ballads." The fourth has no extant title. I use the title of the second version when referencing the collection as this was the version French told Frost to publish. It is also the title used in Carolyn A. Carter, "Guide to the Katherine Jackson French Ballad Collection," BCA RG 4, ser. 2, Berea College Special Collections and Archives. Jackson made no note of meter in some of her transcriptions. Her one nod to rhythm was to use bar lines. She credited Lizane Napier in the notated version of "The Lover's Farewell" included in the full ballad collection.

16. French, "A Fortnight of Balladry," 4. See also French, "A Fortnight in Ballad Country," 32.

17. French, "A Fortnight of Balladry," 5.

18. French, "A Fortnight in Ballad Country," 32.

19. Jackson, "English-Scottish Ballads from the Hills of Kentucky." Stephen Wade notes that, five years later, the song appeared in the tune lists of John. F. Smith (which Smith compiled from information his students brought him about the songs their families sang and constitutes a broad picture of music made in the hills of Kentucky in the early twentieth century) and was played in competition at Berea in the 1920s. He also claims that a report in the *Berea Citizen* regarding the playing of "The Last of Callahan" by Bev Baker at a 1919 fiddle contest was the first mention of the tune in print. (Katherine's notation came ten years earlier.) See Stephen Wade, *The Beautiful Music All around Us* (Urbana: University of Illinois Press, 2015), 275–77.

On Smith, see Steve Green, "The Berea Tune Lists: An Archival Resource for the Study of Social Music in Eastern Kentucky and East Tennessee in 1915" (Berea, KY: Berea College, n.d.), https://libraryguides.berea.edu/ld.php?content_id=8500910.

20. French, "A Fortnight of Balladry," 6.
21. French, "A Fortnight in Ballad Country," 33.
22. French, "A Fortnight in Ballad Country," 33.
23. French, "A Fortnight in Ballad Country," 35.
24. French, "A Fortnight in Ballad Country," 34–35.
25. French, "A Fortnight in Ballad Country," 35.
26. French, "A Fortnight in Ballad Country," 35.
27. French, "A Fortnight of Balladry," 5.
28. French, "A Fortnight in Ballad Country," 37–40.
29. French, "A Fortnight of Balladry," 10–11.
30. French, "A Fortnight of Balladry," 15. (The melody of "The House Carpenter" is notated in Jackson, "English-Scottish Ballads from the Hills of Kentucky.") The view that "the ballad is not dead" was heresy against what Jackson had been taught at Columbia and followed a line of reasoning opposite to that championed by Gummere: that balladry was dead and there was nothing left to do but collect the artifacts.
31. French, "A Fortnight of Balladry," 13–14.
32. Mary Taylor Brewer, *Rugged Trail to Appalachia: A History of Leslie County, Kentucky and Its People, Celebrating Its Centennial Year, 1878–1978* (Wooten, KY, 1978). Brewer mentions Lizane Napier in this book about families of Leslie County and claims that she sang and danced even as an old woman.
33. Scarborough, *A Song Catcher in Southern Mountains*, 15–17: "Folk songs are shy, elusive things. If you wish to capture them, you have to steal up behind them, unbeknownst, and sprinkle salt on their tails." Elizabeth McCutcheon Williams, ed., *Appalachian Travels: The Diary of Olive Dame Campbell* (Lexington: University Press of Kentucky, 2012), 85.
34. French, "A Fortnight of Balladry," 14. See also Jackson, "English-Scottish Ballads from the Hills of Kentucky."
35. French, "A Fortnight of Balladry," 6.
36. French, "A Fortnight in Ballad Country," 32.
37. French, "A Fortnight of Balladry," 10–11.
38. French, "A Fortnight of Balladry," 14; Dooley, "The Social Whirl."
39. Jackson, "English-Scottish Ballads from the Hills of Kentucky," dedication.
40. Dooley, "The Social Whirl."
41. Deborah Thompson questions the dominance of women ballad singers, pondering "whether this is an assumption based on the imposition of contemporary gender roles." She cites Lomax and Malone as sources for this train of thought. She presents this idea as a precursor to the other side of the stereotype, that of Appalachian instrumentalists as predominantly male, which she then counters. See Deborah J. Thompson, "Searching for Silenced Voices in Appalachian Music," in "Geography

and Music," special issue, *Geo/Journal* 65, nos. 1–2 (2006): 67–78. The early experiences of Campbell, Sharp, Jackson, and McGill would contest Thompson's first claim and remain neutral on the second.

5. Berea Beloved

1. See "Guide to the Katherine Jackson French Ballad Collection"; Eleanor Marsh Frost to William Goodell Frost, December 6, 1910, BCA RG 4, ser. 7, folder 1-1, Katherine Jackson French Ballad Collection.

2. Sidney Saylor Farr, "Appalachian Ballad Collectors: James Watt Raine, John F. Smith, Katherine Jackson French, and Gladys V. Jameson" (undergraduate paper, Berea College, May 1980), box 23, folder 1, RG 09/9.0, Faculty and Staff Records, Berea College Special Collections and Archives.

3. "Mountain Songs." *Berea Quarterly* 14, no. 3 (October 1910): 25–29; Harry Rice, "A Perfect Wild Flower and the Straightjacket of Lines and Spaces: Berea's Two Spheres of Music," 2014, Berea College Special Collections and Archives, Berea College, http://libraryguides.berea.edu/musicspheresessay.

4. Rice, "A Perfect Wild Flower."

5. Rice, "A Perfect Wild Flower." The Berea College music program now proudly boasts a diverse selection of music groups. In addition to the Concert Choir/Chamber Choir and the Wind Ensemble, the college also offers the Black Music Ensemble, the Folk-Roots Ensemble, the Bluegrass Ensemble, the Afro-Latin Ensemble, the Fusion Ensemble, the Mariachi Band, and the Jazz Ensemble. These groups are open to all students regardless of major. In addition, the college offers courses in Appalachian music, world music, and African American music and an occasional songwriting class. The Berea College Celebration of Traditional Music, begun by Loyal Jones in 1974 and run by an ad hoc committee, is still in full swing as well. Appalachian dance is also a strong part of Berea's heritage, as represented by the Country Dancers. Two major folk dance festivals occur yearly, the Mountain Folk Festival for high school students in the fall and the Christmas Country Dance School.

6. Katherine Jackson to William Goodell Frost, October 24, 1910, BCA RG 4, ser. 1, folder 1-1, item 16, Katherine Jackson French Ballad Collection.

7. Eleanor Marsh Frost to William Goodell Frost, November 21, 1910, BCA RG 03/3.03, ser. 7, box 30, folder 18, W. G. Frost Papers, Berea College Special Collections and Archives.

8. "Eleanor Marsh Frost," *Register of the Kentucky Historical Society* 94, no. 3 (Summer 1996): 225–47; Marsh Family Genealogy, BCA RG 03/3.03, ser. 7, box 30, folder 30-1, Frost Papers; "Alexander Marsh," BCA RG 03/3.03, ser. 7, box 30, folder 33-1, Frost Papers.

9. Eleanor Marsh Frost Diary, October 21, 1918, BCA RG 03/3.03, ser. 7, box 34, folder 37-1, Frost Papers; Eva Crocker to Elisabeth Peck, June 20, 1951, BCA RG 03/3.03, ser. 6, box 30, folder 30-3, Frost Papers; "Eleanor Marsh Frost," 238; Frost Diary, January 3, 1910, BCA RG 03/3.03, ser. 7, box 33, folder 36-7, Frost Papers.

10. Frost Diary, March 26, 1910, BCA RG 03/3.03, ser. 7, box 33, folder 36-7, Frost Papers; Frost Diary, May 27, 1909, BCA RG 3.30, ser. 7, box 33, folder 36-6, Frost Papers.

11. Eleanor Marsh Frost to William Goodell Frost, November 21, 1910.

12. William Goodell Frost to Eleanor Marsh Frost, November 25, 1910, Correspondence, Peck Note, BCA RG 4, ser. 4, box 1, Katherine Jackson French Ballad Collection. Sidney Saylor Farr thought that Frost wrote this after Jackson's visit. See Farr, "Appalachian Ballad Collectors," 9. Clearly, however, it was written before since Jackson came to Berea on the twenty-eighth and the letter was written three days earlier. This letter, then, reflects Frost's mind-set before Jackson's visit, not after.

13. Eleanor Marsh Frost to William Goodell Frost, December 6, 1910; *Berea College Catalog for 1904–1905* (Berea, KY: Berea College Printing Department, 1904).

14. Eleanor Marsh Frost, Fragment, December 6, 1910, Peck Note, BCA RG 4, ser. 4, Katherine Jackson French Ballad Collection.

15. Esther Close Reminiscence, BCA RG 03/3.03, ser. 7, box 30, folder 30-3, Frost Papers.

16. The Berea Model School program stressed basic preparation in academics, music, "hand-work," and drawing, as distinguished from the Academic Department, the Collegiate Department, and the Normal School. *Bulletin of Berea College and Allied Schools* (Berea, KY: Berea College, 1909), 29.

17. Eleanor Marsh Frost to William Goodell Frost, December 6, 1910.

18. Elijah F. Dizney was a particularly important force in traditional music in Berea. He was soon (in 1915) to help organize the first of a series of fiddle contests, along with John F. Smith and Alson Baker. This series ran for over ten years. "Berea Fiddle Contests, 1919–1928," n.d., Traildriver, http://traildriver.com/web%20content/projects/appalachia/berea%20contests/nberea%20contests%20page.html.

19. "Lord Bateman," Music Manuscript, RG 09/9.28, box 1, folder 4, Gladys Jameson Papers, Berea College Special Collections and Archives; Eleanor Marsh Frost to William Goodell Frost, December 6, 1910; William Goodell Frost, "Reports 1904, Extension Division Report," BCA RG 03/3.03 24, ser. 6, box 24, folder 13, Frost Papers; Katherine Jackson French Letter Bequeathing the Ballads to Berea College, 1954, BCA RG 4, ser. 1, Katherine Jackson French Ballad Collection; Rice, "A Perfect Wild Flower." In her letter of bequest, Jackson says that she initially collected "15 or 20 good ones [i.e., ballads]" on her first trip and then, when she visited Berea, "found all [she] already had and many others." She must have had thirty "bad" ones, then, because, as we have seen, Mrs. Frost noted that she had over fifty. William A. Bradley quotes her as saying that she originally had sixty ballads, not counting variants. William Aspenwall Bradley, "Song-Ballets and Devil's Ditties," *Harper's* 130 (May 1915): 901–14, 909, http://babel.hathitrust.org/cgi/pt?id=mdp.39015056097432;view=1up;seq=983.

20. The Campbells had already visited Berea and made the acquaintance of the Frosts in 1908. Williams, ed., *Appalachian Travels*, 69–77.

21. William Goodell Frost to Eleanor Marsh Frost, December 10, 1910, RG 3.03, box 10, subgroup William G. Frost, ser. 2—Correspondence 1909–1912, RG Presidents, Berea College Special Collections and Archives.

22. Katherine Jackson to William Goodell Frost, December 13, [1910?], BCA RG 4, ser. l, box 1, folder 1-1, Katherine Jackson French Ballad Collection.

23. Farr, "Appalachian Ballad Collectors," 9, citing Katherine Jackson to William Goodell Frost from Greenwood Lodge, January 15, [1911?], BCA RG 4, ser. l, folder 1-1, item 15, Katherine Jackson French Ballad Collection. Gummere's communal origin theory of balladry dominated the early American ballad landscape. Contention over this idea fueled the early stages of the Ballad Wars. Jackson recognized his authority and knew that an endorsement would be extremely valuable.

24. Frost Diary, March 11, 1911, folder 36-6, BCA RG 3.30, ser. 7, box 33, folder 8, Frost Papers.

25. Note, March 16, 1911, BCA RG 4, ser. 4, box 1, Katherine Jackson French Ballad Collection.

26. Frost Diary, March 11, 1911, folder 36-6, BCA RG 3.30, ser. 7, box 33, folder 8, Frost Papers.

27. J. C. Lewis to William Goodell Frost, May 26, 1911, BCA RG 4, ser. l, folder 1-1, item 7, Katherine Jackson French Ballad Collection.

28. Katherine Jackson French to William Goodell Frost, January 15, [1912?]. According to the Berea College archivist Harry Rice, Edith Fitzgerald James—a folk music authority who was living near Berea at the time—is probably the person being referenced. It could also be James Watt Raine. Harry Rice, interview with the author, January 16, 2015. "H——" remains unknown.

29. Katherine Pettit, "Ballads and Rhymes from Kentucky," ed. G. L. Kittredge, *Journal of American Folklore* 20, no. 79 (October–December 1907): 251–77. Francis Child, of course, was and remains the touchstone of ballad collecting. His *The English and Scottish Popular Ballads* contained 305 ballads and variants. Jackson and many other collectors measured a direct line to British ancestry of the ballads they found by comparing them to Child's collection.

30. Katherine Pettit to Olive Dame Campbell, March 23, 1911, Campbell Papers, quoted in Whisnant, *All That Is Native and Fine,* 103. According to Whisnant, Pettit's letter about Jackson increased Campbell's sense of urgency and propelled her toward publication. As we have seen, Pettit notes in the same letter that Jackson was "speculating on land" in London, which may not have endeared her to either Campbell or Pettit, given that land was often sold to coal companies. In fact, in 1910 Campbell had already tried to get backing from John Glenn at the Russell Sage Foundation to publish the ballads she had so far compiled, but to no avail. See Whisnant, *All That Is Native and Fine,* 111. She continued collecting and in 1915 embarked on a path similar to Jackson's, contacting a powerful man (Cecil Sharp) who was an authority in the field and enlisting his support, a plan that came to fruition in 1917 with *English Folk Songs from the Southern Appalachians.*

31. Hubert G. Shearin, "*That* as a 'Pro-Conjunction,'" *Modern Language Notes* 25, no. 1 (January 1910): 29–30, and "*The Glove* and *The Lions* in Kentucky Folk-Song," *Modern Language Notes* 26, no. 4 (April 1911): 113–14.

32. Hubert G. Shearin and Josiah H. Combs, *A Syllabus of Kentucky Folk-Songs* (Lexington, KY: University of Transylvania, 1911); Josiah H. Combs, Folks songs du Midi des États Unis" (Folk songs of the southern United States) (doctoral thesis, Université de Paris, 1925); *Transylvania University Catalogue, 1911–1912* (Lexington, KY, n.d.).

33. Frost Diary, March 15, 1911, BCA RG 03/3.03, ser. 7, box 36, folder 36-8, Frost Papers.

34. "Studying Folk-Songs," *Louisville Courier-Journal*, March 19, 1911.

35. Bradley, "Song-Ballets and Devil's Ditties."

36. Shearin and Combs, *A Syllabus of Kentucky Folk-Songs*, 1.

37. How many of these ballads likely came from Jackson, and how many definitely could have come from Combs? If we look at Pettit's "Ballads and Rhymes from Kentucky," for which Combs was a main source, we find the following songs that were also in Jackson's collection: "Barbara Allen," "The Brown Girl" ("Lord Thomas and Fair Ellender"), "Jackaro," "Loving Henry," "Pretty Polly," and "The Turkish Lady." Those six can safely be attributed to Combs. If we look at Campbell and Sharp's 1917 *English Folk Songs from the Southern Appalachians* assuming that Combs is the uncredited Hindman source, we can add "Young Beichan" (collected in 1907, when Combs was a student there) to the list. That brings the total number of ballads that definitely came from Combs, not Jackson, up to seven and leaves up to fifteen ballads that were in Jackson's collection and may have come from her. It is, however, quite possible that Combs knew at least some of these as well or that Shearin had other sources.

38. Shearin and Josiah H. Combs, *A Syllabus of Kentucky Folk-Songs*, n.p.

39. Hubert G. Shearin, "Kentucky Folk-Songs," *Modern Language Review* 6, no. 4 (October 1911): 513–17, and "An Eastern Kentucky Word List," *Dialect Notes* 3 (1911): 537–40.

40. Henry D. Shapiro, "How Region Changed Its Meaning and Appalachia Changed Its Standing in the Twentieth Century," in *Bridging Southern Cultures: An Interdisciplinary Approach*, ed. John Lowe (Baton Rouge: Louisiana State University Press, 2011), 265–87.

41. Thomas Percy, *Reliques of Ancient English Poetry* (1756; London and New York: Frederick Warne & Co., 1887); Sir Walter Scott, *Minstrelsy of the Scottish Border: Consisting of Historical and Romantic Ballads, Collected in the Southern Counties of Scotland; With a Few of Modern Date, Founded upon Local Tradition*, 2 vols. (Kelso: printed by James Ballantyne for T. Cadell Jun. and W. Davies, 1802).

42. Samuel Pepys, the English diarist, famously made the first written reference to the song "Barbara Allen" in 1666. He states that he heard the "little Scotch song of 'Barbary Allen'" sung by "my dear Mrs. Knipp" at a party. (One need read only a bit

further to discover just how dear Mrs. Knipp was to him.) At any rate, Pepys's casual reference makes it clear that the song was in circulation by that date. "The Diary of Samuel Pepys," January 2, 1665/66, https://www.pepysdiary.com/diary/1666/01/02.

43. Shearin was not the first one to use the term *song-ballets*. It was used earlier in Frank Sidgwick's *Old Ballads* (London: Cambridge University Press, 1908).

44. Katherine Jackson French to William Goodell Frost, August 8, 1913, BCA RG 4, ser. l, folder 1-1, Katherine Jackson French Ballad Collection; French, Handwritten Autobiography.

45. Bradley, "Song-Ballets and Devil's Ditties," 907.

46. Katherine Jackson French to Mrs. Ewing Marshall, April 16, 1912, BCA RG 67, ser. 14, box 10, folder 10-6, D. L. Thomas Collection in the D. K. Wilgus Collection, Berea College Special Collections and Archives, Berea College.

47. Katherine Jackson to William Goodell Frost, April 23, 1912, BCA RG 4, ser. l, box 1, item 17, Katherine Jackson French Ballad Collection.

48. Mary Katherine (Kay) Tolbert Buckland, interview with the author, November 22, 2014, and telephone interview with the author, March 6, 2014.

49. Katherine Jackson French to William Goodell Frost, February 3, 1913, BCA RG 4, ser. l, box 1, folder 1, Katherine Jackson French Ballad Collection.

50. Katherine Jackson French to William Goodell Frost, August 8, 1913.

51. Katherine Jackson French to William Goodell Frost, February 10, 1914, BCA RG 4, ser. l, box 1, folder 1-1, item 2, Katherine Jackson French Ballad Collection; "Popular Songs of Olden Times," January 22, 1914, BCA RG 4, ser. l, box 1, folder 1-1, Katherine Jackson French Ballad Collection; Francis B. Gummere to William Goodell Frost, May 16, 1914, BCA RG 4, ser. l, box 1, folder 1, item 22, Katherine Jackson French Ballad Collection. After Smith's death, his collection was eventually edited and published by Arthur Kyle Davis as *Traditional Ballads of Virginia*. Jackson owned a copy and, in the table of contents, carefully put tidy check marks by every ballad that she had collected first. She did the same with her copies of John Harrington Cox's *Folk-Songs of the South* (Cambridge, MA: Harvard University Press, 1925) and Loraine Wyman and Harold A. Brockway's *Twenty Kentucky Mountain Songs* (New York: O. Ditson, 1920).

52. Katherine Jackson French to William Goodell Frost, November 3, 1915, BCA RG 4, ser. l, box 1, folder 1, item 18, Katherine Jackson French Ballad Collection.

53. Katherine Jackson French to William Goodell Frost, May 17, 1916, BCA RG 4, ser. l, box 1, folder 1-1, item 24, Katherine Jackson French Ballad Collection; Katherine Jackson French to William Goodell Frost, December 1915, BCA RG 4, ser. l, box 1, folder 1-1, Katherine Jackson French Ballad Collection.

54. Katherine Jackson French Letter Bequeathing the Ballads to Berea College.

55. M. B. McKellar, "Kentucky Mountaineers Still Sing Old Ballads," *New York Post*, December 28, 1921.

56. Katherine Jackson French, "Lizane of Leatherwood," manuscript, n.d., private collection; *Saturday Evening Post* to Katherine Jackson French, undated letter,

private collection; "Demographics, Neighborhood Info, Leatherwood, KY," Movoto, n.d., http://www.movoto.com/leatherwood-ky/41731/demographics; Shelby Lee Adams, "'The Napier's Living Room' (1989)," American Suburb X, 2010, http://www.americansuburbx.com/2010/11/essay-shelby-lee-adams-napiers-living.html. Several pages of the "Lizane of Leatherwood" manuscript were typed or written on the backs of pages of the stationery of the country club to which William (Frank) was a member during his time as president of Bour-Davis. Katherine (Kay) Tolbert Buckland, interview with the author, November 23, 2014. This dates the manuscript to no earlier than the late 1910s or the early 1920s. Also, the rejection letter from the *Saturday Evening Post* lists George Horace Lorimer as editor. Lorimer reigned as editor of the magazine from 1899 until he died in 1936, so it had to have been written before that date. Perhaps Jackson thought that Lorimer's Kentucky background might make him receptive to her story. Ron Pen points out that the plot of the 1919 *Heart of the Hills*, starring Mary Pickford, was very similar. Ron Pen, personal communication, April 2018.

57. Katherine Jackson French Letter Bequeathing the Ballads to Berea College.

58. Mary Katherine (Kay) Tolbert Buckland, telephone interview with the author, March 6, 2014.

59. Farr, "Appalachian Ballad Collectors," 12.

60. Elizabeth Peck to Katherine Jackson French, September 22, 1954, private collection.

61. Elizabeth Peck to Katherine Jackson French, September 22, 1954, private collection.

62. Gladys Jameson to Katherine Jackson French, August 12, 1954, private collection; Gladys Jameson, *Wake and Sing* (New York: Broadcast Music, 1955).

63. Elizabeth Peck to Katherine Jackson French, September 22, 1954.

64. The question then becomes, Which version of Jackson's collection had been gathering dust at Berea for forty-three years? Peck numbered the four extant versions 1–4. Katherine Jackson French to Mrs. Ewing Marshall, April 16, 1912, BCA RG 67, ser. 14, box 10, folder 10-6, D. L. Thomas Collection in the D. K. Wilgus Collection. E. C. Perrow—who was active at the University of Louisville in the 1910s—noted on "The Salt Salt Sea" (on a copy included in French's letter to Marshall) that the collection at Berea did not have tunes. This cannot be accurate in that Jackson specifically ordered Frost to use the version that had melodies, so the version must have been the one Frost had in his possession and kept at Berea. Of the four extant versions, version 2 is, in fact, partially typed on Frank French's Shreveport country club stationery and, thus, could not have been in existence before the Frenches moved there in 1917. Yet it is the one that contains tunes. So there may have been yet another, fifth version that included tunes as Jackson alluded to one such in her correspondence with Frost (the version 2 music manuscripts are very rough, not type ready). I have not been able to determine the order of the versions with any degree of certainty, having only the relative appearance and age of each and the assumption that Peck initially put them in the correct chronological order to go on.

65. Elizabeth Peck to Katherine Jackson French, September 22, 1954.

66. Elizabeth Peck to Katherine Jackson French, September 22, 1954. See also Farr, "Appalachian Ballad Collectors," 13.

67. Jameson also credited Jackson as "having notated the first large collection to be made—in part from the singing of students on the campus." Jameson, *Wake and Sing*, v. Jackson's copy of *Wake and Sing* (held in a private collection) bears this inscription from Jameson: "To Katherine Jackson French, who knows 'the precious things of the lasting hills' (Wilderness Road, p V, p. 11)."

68. Paul Green, *Wilderness Road* Playbill, 1955, private collection.

69. Elizabeth Peck, *Berea's First Century, 1855–1955* (Lexington: University of Kentucky Press, 1955), 199–200. On the title page of Jackson's copy of *Berea's First Century* (now held in a private collection), Peck inscribed: "In grateful appreciation to Katherine Jackson French for her gift of ballad materials to Berea College."

70. "Ballad Changes in Curriculum for Raine, Ballad Course—Proposed," ser. 6, no. 4, box 1, folder 1-25, James Watt Raine Ballad Collection, Berea College Special Collections and Archives; "Raine AR 1920, How to Get More Ballads," ser. 6, no. 4, box 1, folder 1-27, item 15, James Watt Raine Ballad Collection.

71. Katherine Jackson French to William Goodell Frost, August 8, 1913.

72. Josiah Combs, *The Kentucky Highlanders* (Lexington, KY: J. L. Richardson, 1913), and *All That's Kentucky* (Louisville: John P. Morton, 1915).

73. Elizabeth Peck to Katherine Jackson French, September 22, 1954.

74. William A. Bradley, "Hobnobbing with Hillbillies," *Harper's* 132 (December 1915): 91–103; Bradley, "Song-Ballets and Devil's Ditties"; William Aspenwall Bradley, "In Shakespeare's America," *Harper's* 130 (August 1915): 436–45, https://babel.hathitrust.org/cgi/pt?id=uc1.32106011922611&view=1up&seq=488; William A. Bradley Biography, n.d., Harry Ransom Humanities Research Center, University of Texas at Austin, https://norman.hrc.utexas.edu/fasearch/findingAid.cfm?eadid=00300.

75. William A. Bradley, "The Women on Troublesome," *Scribner's* 63 (March 1918): 315–28. See also Whisnant, *All That Is Native and Fine*, 272.

76. *Vient de paraitre* (Just published) publishes scholarly papers for the Sorbonne.

77. Josiah Combs to D. K. Wilgus, May 12, 1960, BCA RG 67, box 8, folder 8-1, Josiah Combs Collection in the D. K. Wilgus Collection. See also Shearin and Combs, *A Syllabus of Kentucky Folk-Songs*. Combs was not happy with Bradley's translation. He complained that Bradley "messed up the original" during the process. William A. Bradley Biography.

78. D. W. Wilgus, "A History of Anglo-American Ballad Scholarship since 1898" (PhD diss., Ohio State University, 1954), 98.

79. Scott B. Spencer, "Ballad Collecting: Impetus and Impact," in *The Ballad Collectors of North America: How Gathering Folksongs Transformed Academic Thought and American Identity*, ed. Scott B. Spencer (Lanham, MD: Scarecrow, 2012), 1–16, 12.

80. Williams, ed., *Appalachian Travels*, 112.

81. Shapiro, "How Region Changed Its Meaning," 69–78, 209.

82. Spencer, "Ballad Collecting," 8.

83. Clyde Kenneth Hyder, *George Lyman Kittredge, Teacher and Scholar* (Lawrence: University of Kansas Press, 1962), 132.

84. Esther Birdsall, "Some Notes on the Role of George Lyman Kittredge in American Folklore Study," in "American Folklore Historiography," special issue, *Journal of the Folklore Institute* 10, nos. 1–2 (June–August 1973): 57–66.

85. G. L. Kittredge, "The Ballad of *The Den of Lions*," *Modern Language Review* 26, no. 6 (June 1911): 167–69.

86. See Hubert G. Shearin, "British Ballads in the Cumberland Mountains," *Sewanee Review* 19, no. 3 (July 1911): 313–27, n. 83.

87. Hubert G. Shearin, "The *Phoenix* and the *Guthlac*," *Modern Language Notes* 22, no. 8 (December 1907): 263.

88. Williams, ed., *Appalachian Travels*, 111–12.

89. Hyder, *George Lyman Kittredge*, 103.

90. Josiah Combs, "Sympathetic Magic in the Kentucky Mountains: Some Curious Folk-Survivals," *Journal of American Folklore* 27, no. 105 (July–September 1914): 328–30.

91. Mary Katherine (Kay) Tolbert Buckland, telephone interview with the author, March 6, 2014.

92. French, "A Fortnight in Ballad Country," 40.

93. Shearin, "British Ballads in the Cumberland Mountains," 323.

94. *Transylvania University Catalogue, 1911–1912*; Mariam K. Chamberlain, *Women in Academe: Progress and Prospects* (New York: Russell Sage Foundation, 1988), 10. For a discussion of "the marginal position of women teaching in institutions of higher learning," see Alison Prentice and Marjorie R. Theobold, "The Historiography of Women Teachers: A Retrospective," in *Women Who Taught: Perspectives on the History of Women and Teaching*, ed. Alison Prentice and Marjorie R. Theobald (Toronto: University of Toronto Press, 1991), 3–33, 22.

95. Bradley, "Song Ballets and Devil's Ditties," 905–6.

96. The Alphonso Smith Federal Bureau of Education bulletin is mentioned in "Popular Songs of Olden Times," January 22, 1914, newspaper clipping, unidentified publication, BCA RG 4, ser. l, box 1, folder 1-1, Katherine Jackson French Ballad Collection. It is also cited in "News and Notes," *English Journal* 3, no. 2 (February 1914): 132. It indicates that the "Bureau of Education has issued a special pamphlet to assist Professor C. Alphonso Smith of the University of Virginia, in his worthy task of collecting and preserving such unpublished folk-ballads as may still be found in this country." Smith, then, had initially set out to collect ballads nationwide. The scope of the collection was later narrowed to Virginia, but not before Katherine Jackson had nagged William Frost to contact Smith to try to secure publication of her collection. See Katherine Jackson French to William Goodell Frost, February 10, 1914.

97. Frost Diary, May 4, 1912, BCA RG 03/3.03, ser. 7, box 36, folder 36-13, Frost Papers.

98. Eleanor Marsh Frost to William Goodell Frost, July 20, 1913, BCA RG 03/3.03, ser. 7, box 34, folder 34-3, Frost Papers.

99. William Goodell Frost, "Life Sketch of Mathilda Hamilton Fee," 1895, ser. 3, box 14, folder 1, BCA RG Frost Papers.

100. Katherine Bowersox to William Goodell Frost, June 18, 1908, and July 4, 1914, BCA RG 03/3.03, ser. 9, box 40, Frost Papers.

101. By today's standards, Frost's views, not only on gender, but also on religion and race, would be considered insular at best. He speaks, e.g., of Appalachians as "reserve forces in the coming battles of America and Protestant Christianity": "Protestant America needs numerical reinforcement. The sense of this need is forced upon us by the great increase of the foreign born and hyphenated population." Frost, "God's Plan for the Southern Mountains," 405, 412. As to the question of race, some historians have wondered whether his dedication to educating white and black students together was for the benefit of the black students or for the development of the moral sense of the white students.

102. Lee Edward Krehbiel, "From Race to Region: Shifting Priorities at Berea under William Goodell Frost, 1892–1912" (PhD diss., Indiana University, 1997), 114.

103. Krehbiel, "From Race to Region." William A. Barton, a Berea graduate and Congregational minister, is also notable for his publication of *Old Plantation Hymns* (Boston: Lamson, Wolffe, 1899).

104. Krehbiel, "From Race to Region," 115.

105. Katherine Jackson French Letter Bequeathing the Ballads to Berea College; Jerome W. Hughes, *Six Berea College Presidents: Traditions and Progress* (Berea, KY: Berea College, 1984), 38.

106. The labor program at Berea has sought from the beginning to foster a sense of the dignity to be found in labor. Frost gradually phased in the program starting in the late 1890s, beginning with "fireside industries" (home crafts like sewing and weaving), and progressing to the bricklaying that built Phelps-Stokes Chapel and many other tasks as well. Today, all Berea students are required to work ten to fifteen hours a week in various jobs around the college. They therefore graduate with a labor record as well as an academic record. See Peck, *Berea's First Century*, 110–25.

107. Hughes, *Six Berea College Presidents*, 38; Eleanor Marsh Frost Journal, October 21, 1918, and October 21–29, 1918, BCA RG 03/3.03, ser. 7, box 34, folder 37-1, Presidents, Berea College Special Collections and Archives.

6. A Comparison of the Ballads of Katherine Jackson and Olive Dame Campbell/Cecil Sharp

1. Jackson actually had more ballads than Sharp—over 60 to his 55—but he had 118 songs overall in his *English Folk Songs from the Southern Appalachians*.

2. Olive Dame Campbell, Maud Karpeles, and Cecil J. Sharp, *English Folk Songs from the Southern Appalachians* (London: Oxford University Press, 1932).

3. Whisnant, *All That Is Native and Fine,* 112. For a complete time line, see app. C.

4. Jean Thomas, *Ballad-Makin' in the Hills of Kentucky* (New York: Henry Holt, 1939).

5. Ann Ostendorf, "Song Catchers, Ballad Makers, and New Social Historians: The Historiography of Appalachian Music," *Tennessee Historical Quarterly* 63, no. 3 (Fall 2004): 192–202, 194.

6. Campbell and Sharp, *English Folk Songs from the Southern Appalachians,* ix, x.

7. Betty Smith, interview with the author, October 14, 2011. Thanks to Betty Smith for pointing this out. She also pointed out the possibility that Karpeles may have been in love with Sharp and that she wanted him to get all the credit for the collection, hence the removal of Campbell's name from the cover.

8. Katherine Jackson French, "English-Scottish Ballads from the Hills of Kentucky" (version 4).

9. Rosaleen Gregory and David Gregory, "Jewels Left in the Dung-Hills: Broadside and Other Vernacular Ballads Rejected by Francis Child," n.d., https://journals.lib.unb.ca/index.php/MC/article/viewFile/21624/25113.

10. Mike Yates, "Cecil Sharp"; Benjamin Filene, *Romancing the Folk: Public Memory and American Roots Music* (Chapel Hill: University of North Carolina Press, 2000), 25, 157. Sharp did publish four collections of piano settings of English dance tunes from 1909 to 1911, three of them through the Novello Press (the fourth publisher is unidentified). However, Sharp did not collect Appalachian dance tunes for *English Folk Songs from the Southern Appalachians.*

11. Campbell and Sharp, *English Folk Songs from the Southern Appalachians,* vii.

12. It should be mentioned, however, that a music manuscript of "Sourwood Mountain" in the James Watt Raine Collection bears the credit "Miss Jackson." In addition, while a copy of a thirteenth-century song, "Summer Is a-Cumin' In," was originally part of one version of her collection, apparently Jackson did not mean to include it among the ballads for publication.

13. Jackson, "English-Scottish Ballads from the Hills of Kentucky" (version 4).

14. Campbell and Sharp, *English Folk Songs from the Southern Appalachians,* ix–x.

15. Jackson, "English-Scottish Ballads from the Hills of Kentucky" (version 4).

16. Polly Stewart, "Wishful Willful Wily Women: Verbal Strategies for Female Success in the Child Ballads," in *Feminist Messages: Coding in Women's Folk Culture,* ed. Joan Newlon Radner (Urbana: University of Illinois Press, 1993), 54–73.

17. ABCB: "Roses are red / violets are blue / sugar is sweet / and so are you."

18. A′ is a phrase similar to the phrase A but not identical.

19. The Ionian mode is the same as the contemporary seven-note major scale. The pentatonic mode is a major scale minus the fourth and seventh steps. It can claim any note as the home tone.

20. A gapped scale is simply a scale that is missing a note. The most common gapped scales in Appalachian music are gapped Ionian/Mixolydian (missing the seventh step), Ionian, and Dorian.

21. Campbell and Sharp, *English Folk Songs from the Southern Appalachians*, xv, xviii, xix. Bertrand Harris Bronson counters Sharp's assumption that the pentatonic scale or gapped scale indicates antiquity, concluding: "There is no dependable evidence, either internal or external, for [the ballad tunes'] ultimate age." Bertrand Harris Bronson, *The Traditional Tunes of the Child Ballads* (Princeton, NJ: Princeton University Press, 1959), xx.

22. William Chappell, ed., *Popular Music of the Olden Time*, 2 vols. (London: Cramer, Beale & Chappell, 1855–1856; reprint, London: Dover, 1965); James Johnson, *Scots Musical Museum*, 6 vols. (Edinburgh: Johnson & Co., 1787–1839), vol. 1, https://digital.nls.uk/special-collections-of-printed-music/archive/87793664; Bronson, *The Traditional Tunes of the Child Ballads*; and John Playford, *The English Dancing Master* (London: Thomas Harper, 1651). Specifically, 85 songs were taken from Chappell, 96 from Johnson, 127 from Bronson, and 60 from Playford.

23. Nor does my thirty-seven years' experience as a classical and folk dance musician.

24. The Ionian was certainly in use in Europe by 1547, when Heinrich Glarean's *Dodecachordon (Basel, 1547) declared it to be one of the most widely used modes, and in England by the early years of the seventeenth century. Gapped scales were used as well, but instances of the pentatonic are rare. For an English translation of the Dodecachordon, see Clement A. Miller, Heinrich Glarean Dodecachordon, Musicological Documents and Studies 6 (n.p.: American Institute of Musicology, 1965). For a succinct synopsis of Glarean's modes, see "Dodecachordon," in A Dictionary of Music and Musicians*, Wikisource, https://en.wikisource.org/wiki/A_Dictionary_of_Music_and_Musicians/Dodecachordon.

25. The other 3.5 percent are split between Mixolydian, Dorian, and Aeolian.

26. Liza DiSavino and A. J. Bodnar, "Mountain to Mountain: A Comparison of Music of the Catskill Mountains with That of Southern Appalachia," Berea College Sound Archives Fellowship Report, June 2012, https://libraryguides.berea.edu/ld.php?content_id=35420813. Whether, and to what extent, Native American music influenced Appalachian ballads remains largely a matter of conjecture and is a subject ripe for exploration. (Irregular phrase length and the use of the pentatonic scale are two examples of traits in Appalachian music possibly picked up from or reinforced by their occurrence in Native music.) Nonetheless, such influence has been denied out of hand. For example, I must disagree with my good friend Deborah Thompson, who states: "Few musical influences on the dominant Appalachian vernacular music, however, seem to stem from Native American cultures." Thompson, "Searching for Silenced Voices in Appalachian Music," 70. Jennifer Howard points out that the music of Native Americans was silenced by the white majority and that "the . . . assimilation [of the Cherokees] pushed them more quickly into American culture, including its music." Jennifer Camille Howard, "Sounds of Silence: How African Americans, Native Americans, and White Women Found Their Voices in Southern Appalachian Music" (MA thesis, North Carolina State University, 2012), 40–56, 77 (quote).

27. Only three of the twenty-two artists at the Bristol Sessions were from Kentucky.

28. Olive Dame Campbell, Maud Karpeles, and Cecil J. Sharp, *English Folk Songs from the Southern Appalachians* (New York: Oxford University Press, 1932). Among Sharp's sources for this edition were three of the same individuals Jackson had used, Ollie Huff, Mrs. James Baker, and Jennie Combs. None of the sources of the 1917 edition had been used by Jackson.

29. Josephine McGill, *Folk-Songs of the Kentucky Mountains* (New York: Boosey & Co., 1917); Loraine Wyman and Howard A. Brockway, *Lonesome Tunes* (New York: H. W. Gray Co., 1916).

30. For a longer list of collectors, see app. C.

31. Smith is also of importance in that he indicated scale steps by number. This seems to make him an early, if not one of the earliest, progenitors of the Nashville Notation system.

32. "Barbara Allen" and "The Daemon Lover," RG 6, ser. l, box 1, folders 1-1 and 1-3, James Watt Raine Ballad Collection. "The Demon Lover" was later published in *Mountain Ballads for Social Singing*, collected and selected by James Watt Raine, music collected by Cecil J. Sharp (Berea, KY: Berea College Press, 1923), RG 5I, ser. 2, box 1, folder 21, James Watt Raine Ballad Collection. The following music manuscripts are all found in the James Watt Raine collection and are credited to Katherine Jackson French: "The House Carpenter," "Sourwood Mountain" (folder 1-17), "The Jew's Daughter" (folder 1-9), "Lord of the Old Country"(1-18), "A Wealthy Young Farmer" (1-18), "A Lady Gay"(folder 1-21), "Lord Bateman" (folder 1-21), and "Lord Thomas and Fair Ellender" (folder 1-21), "A Serving Maid" (folder 1-21). She is also credited with the lyrics to "The Fate of Lovers" (folder 1-21) and "Lord Lovely" (folder 1-21). All are found in found in RG 6, ser. l, box 1, James Watt Raine Ballad Collection.

33. For an example from the Thomas collection, see "The Salt, Salt Sea" (with a letter from Katherine Jackson French to Mrs. Marshall, London, KY, April 16, 1912), folder 10-6, Accession 67, ser. 14, box 10, D. L. Thomas Collection in the D. K. Wilgus Collection. As for the contents of the Jameson collection, it would seem that Gladys Jameson transcribed ballads in the exact same order as they appear in "English-Scottish Ballads from the Hills of Kentucky," version 2. "Barbara Allen's Cruelty," "Lord Randall," "Lord Bateman," "Little Hugh; or, The Jew's Daughter," "Lord Thomas," "Sweet William and Lady Margaret," "Lord of the Old Country," "The Serving Maid," "The House Carpenter," "A Lady and a Lady Gay," "A Wealthy Young Farmer," and "Pretty Polly" all appear in Jameson's manuscript book attributed to Jackson, and a loose manuscript fragment containing "Pretty Polly" appears to be in Jackson's hand. Musical MSS, Notebook, RG 9, ser. l, box 1, folder 4, Jameson Papers.

34. John Jacob Niles, *Impressions of a Negro Camp Meeting* (New York: Carl Fischer, 1925), and *Seven Kentucky Mountain Songs* (New York: G. Schirmer, 1929).

35. Ron Pen, *I Wonder As I Wander: The Life of John Jacob Niles* (Lexington: University Press of Kentucky, 2010), 105–6.

36. These can be found among the gems in the Berea College Sound Archives (part of the Special Collections and Archives): Addie Graham, "We're Stole and Sold from Africa," Sound Recording, RG SAA 92, box 2, BK OR 013 001-004, Barbara Kunkle Traditional Music Collection, https://soundarchives.berea.edu/items/show/7158; Mary Lozier, "Pretty Polly," July 29, 1973, Sound Recording, RG SAA 92, box 2, BK OR 009-001, Barbara Kunkle Traditional Music Collection, https://soundarchives.berea.edu/items/show/717; Frankie Duff, "A Home Just over Yonder," June 20, 1968, William H. Tallmadge Baptist Hymnody Collection, https://soundarchives.berea.edu/items/show/5655.

7. Introduction by Elizabeth DiSavino

1. Robert Jamieson, *Popular Ballads and Songs* (Edinburgh: Archibald Constable & Co., 1806).

8. Introduction by Katherine Jackson French

1. See Child, *The English and Scottish Popular Ballads,* 3:166, 4:266.

Appendix C

1. Lila W. Edmunds, "Songs from the Mountains of North Carolina," *Journal of American Folklore* 7, no. 21 (April–June 1893): 131–34.

2. Louise Pound, *American Ballads and Songs* (New York: Charles Scribner's Sons, 1922).

3. Susannah Wetmore and Marshall Bartholomew, *Mountain Songs of North Carolina* (New York: G. Schirmer, 1926).

4. Bradley Kincaid, *My Favorite Mountain Ballads and Old-Time Songs* (Chicago: Prairie Farmer, 1928).

Bibliography

Archives

Barnard College Archives, New York.
Katherine Tolbert Buckland, Private Collection.
John C. Campbell School, Brasstown, NC.
Centenary College Archives, Shreveport, LA.
Columbia University Archives, New York.
Filson Historical Society, Louisville, KY.
Hindman Settlement School, Hindman, KY.
Berea College Sound Archives, Hutchins Library, Berea, KY.
Berea College Special Collections and Archives, Hutchins Library, Berea, KY:
    Josiah Combs Papers.
    Faculty and Staff Records: Sidney Saylor Farr Papers.
    Faculty and Staff Records: Elisabeth Sinclair Peck Papers.
    Federal Music Project, Eastern Kentucky Folk Song Collection.
    Katherine Jackson French Ballad Collection.
    W. G. Frost Papers.
    Gladys Jameson Papers.
    Bradley Kincaid Collection.
    Katherine Pettit Collection.
    James Watt Raine Ballad Collection.
    John F. Smith Traditional Music Collection.
    D. L. Thomas Collection in the D. K. Wilgus Collection.
    Leonard Ware Roberts Collection, 1949–1983.
    Mary Wheeler Papers.
Laurel County Historical Society, London, KY:
    Jackson Family Folder.
    Jackson Family Notebook.
    Laurel Seminary Folder.
    McKee Family Folder.

Louisiana State University Archives at Shreveport:
  Woman's Department Club Collection.
Ohio Wesleyan University Historical Collection, L. A. Beeghly Library, Ohio Wesleyan University, Delaware.
Harry Ransom Center, University of Texas at Austin.
Science Hill Female Academy Collection, Shelbyville, KY.
Shreveport First Methodist Church of Archives, Shreveport, LA.
Louis Round Wilson Special Collections Library, University of North Carolina at Chapel Hill.
Woman's Department Club of Shreveport, Shreveport, LA.
Yale University Archives, New Haven, CT.

Sound Recordings

"Banjo Music by Kentucky County." Berea College Special Collections and Archives. https://libraryguides.berea.edu/banjomusicbykycounty.

Couch, Jim. "Lord Bateman." 1954. Sound recording. BCA RG no. SAA 57, LROR027, box 50, Leonard Ware Roberts Collection, 1949–1983, Berea College Special Collections and Archives.

Fraley, J. P. Sound Recordings. RG SAA 92, box 2, BK OR 009-001. Barbara Kunkle Traditional Music Collection, Berea College Special Collections and Archives. http://digital.berea.edu/cdm/search/collection/p15131coll4!p272901coll4/searchterm/j.p.%20fraley/order/nosort.

Gage, Jim. "Dog and Gun." 1974. Sound Recording. Berea College Special Collections and Archives. Recorded at the Berea College Celebration of Traditional Music.

Graham, Addie. "We're Stole and Sold from Africa." Sound Recording. RG SAA 92. box 2, BK OR 013 001-0014. Barbara Kunkle Traditional Music Collection, Berea College Special Collections and Archives. http://digital.berea.edu/cdm/singleitem/collection/p15131coll4/id/4338/rec/4.

Graham, Addie, and Opsa Guthrie. Sound Recording. RG SAA 92, box 2, BK OR 013 001-0014, Barbara Kunkle Traditional Music Collection, Berea College Special Collections and Archives.

"Hymns." Sound Recordings. Berea College Special Collections and Archives. http://digital.berea.edu/cdm/search/searchterm/Hymns/order/nosort.

Kincaid, Bradley. "Dog and Gun." Sound Recording. AC 002-02, B20. Berea College Special Collections and Archives.

———. "Fair Ellen." Sound Recording. AC 002-A1, 011. Berea College Special Collections and Archives.

Lozier. Mary. "Mary Lozier: Unaccompanied Singing and Interview." Sound Recording. RG SAA 92 009-001, box 6. Barbara Kunkle Traditional Music Collection, Berea College Special Collections and Archives.

Ritchie, Jean. "House Carpenter." Sound Recording. Berea College Special Collections and Archives. http://digital.berea.edu/cdm/singleitem/collection/p15131coll4/id/419/rec/21.

———. "Lord Thomas and Fair Ellender." 1949. Sound Recording. Alan Lomax Collection, Berea College Special Collections and Archives. http://digital.berea.edu/cdm/search/collection/p16020coll7.

Ritchie, Jean, and Edna Ritchie. "Wars of Germany." 1941. Sound Recording. Berea College Special Collections and Archives. Recorded at the Berea College Celebration of Traditional Music.

Stamper, Hiram. "Indian Nation." Sound Recording. Berea College Special Collections and Archives. http://digital.berea.edu/cdm/singleitem/collection/p15131coll4/id/135/rec/15.

Stepp, William H. "Bonaparte's Retreat." Sound Recording. Berea College Special Collections and Archives. http://digital.berea.edu/cdm/singleitem/collection/p15131coll4/id/1429/rec/3.

Wallin, Chappel. "Lord Bateman." Sound Recording. Berea College Special Collections and Archives. http://digital.berea.edu/cdm/singleitem/collection/p15131coll4/id/4199/rec/1.

Other Primary Sources

AAUW of Louisiana conference booklet. April 2–3, 1948. Private collection.

Adams, Shelby Lee. "'The Napier's Living Room' (1989)." *American Suburb X*, 2010. http://www.americansuburbx.com/2010/11/essay-shelby-lee-adams-napiers-living.html.

Bascom, Louise Rand. "Ballads and Songs of Western North Carolina." *Journal of American Folklore* 22, no. 84 (April–June 1909): 238–50.

Bradley, William Aspenwall. "In Shakespeare's America." *Harper's* 131 (August 1915): 436–45. http://babel.hathitrust.org/cgi/pt?id=ucl.32106011922611;view=1up;seq=493.

———. "Song-Ballets and Devil's Ditties." *Harper's* 130 (May 1915): 901–14. http://babel.hathitrust.org/cgi/pt?id=mdp.39015056097432;view=1up;seq=983.

Bronson, Bertrand Harris. *The Traditional Tunes of the Child Ballads*. Princeton, NJ: Princeton University Press, 1959.

Brockway, Howard A., and Loraine Wyman. *Lonesome Tunes*. New York: H. W. Gray, 1916.

Campbell, Olive Dame. *Appalachian Travels: The Diary of Olive Dame Campbell*, ed. Elizabeth McCutchen Williams. Lexington: University Press of Kentucky, 2012.

———. *The Life and Work of John C. Campbell*. Edited by Elizabeth M. Williams. Lexington: University Press of Kentucky 2017.

Campbell, Olive Dame, Maud Karpeles, and Cecil J. Sharp. *English Folk Songs from the Southern Appalachians*. London: Oxford University Press, 1932.

Campbell, Olive Dame, and Cecil J. Sharp. *English Folk Songs from the Southern Appalachians*. New York and London: G. P. Putman's Sons, 1917.

Chappell, William, ed. *Popular Music of the Olden Time.* 2 vols. London: Cramer, Beale & Chappell, 1855–1856. Reprint, London: Dover, 1965.

Child, Francis James. *The English and Scottish Popular Ballads.* 10 bks. in 5 vols. Boston: Riverside Press/Houghton/Osgood & Co., 1880.

———. *The English and Scottish Popular Ballads.* 10 bks. in 5 vols. New York: Dover, 1882–1898.

Combs, Josiah. *Folk-Songs of the Southern United States.* Austin, TX: American Folklore Society, 1967.

Cox, John Harrington. *Folk-Songs of the South.* Cambridge, MA: Harvard University Press, 1925.

Davis, Arthur Kyle, Jr., ed. *Traditional Ballads of Virginia.* Cambridge, MA: Harvard University Press, 1929.

———. "On the Collecting and Editing of Ballads." *American Speech* 5, no. 6 (August 1930): 452–55.

"Demographics, Neighborhood Info, Leatherwood, KY." Movoto, n.d. http://www.movoto.com/leatherwood-ky/41731/demographics.

Dooley, Isma. "The Social Whirl: Visiting Women." *Atlanta Constitution,* April 9, 1916.

Eberlein, Lou. "Reminiscences of Mrs. Eberlein." Typescript, June 1943. Private collection.

Faris, C. B., John Pitman, and W. T. Moren. *Laurel Seminary: Brief Sketch of Its History.* London, KY: Mountain Echo, 1891. Laurel Seminary Folder, "Schools" File, Laurel County Historical Society, London, KY.

Fifty-Fourth Catalogue of Ohio Wesleyan University, 1898. Delaware: Ohio Wesleyan University, 1898.

Fifty-Sixth Catalogue of Ohio Wesleyan University, 1900. Delaware: Ohio Wesleyan University, 1900.

Fifty-Seventh Catalogue of Ohio Wesleyan University, 1901. Delaware: Ohio Wesleyan University, 1901.

Fifty Years of History of the Ohio Wesleyan University. Cleveland: Cleveland Printing and Publishing Co., 1895.

Folk Songs of Old Kentucky: Two Song Catchers in the Kentucky Mountains, 1914 and 1916, with Arrangements for Appalachian Dulcimer. Selected and arranged by Ralph Lee Smith and Madeline MacNeil. Fenton, MO: Mel Bay, 2003.

French, Katherine Jackson. "A Fortnight in Ballad Country." *Mountain Life and Work* 31, no. 3 (1955): 30–40.

French, Katherine Jackson, and F. H. E. Ross. *The Story of the Years in Mountain Work.* Nashville: Woman's Missionary Council, [1918?].

Frost, William Goodell. "Our Southern Highlanders." *The Independent* 72 (January–June 1912): 708–14.

———. "God's Plan for the Southern Mountains." *Biblical Review,* July 19, 1921, 405, 412.

Gummere, Francis. *Old English Ballads.* Boston: Ginn & Co., 1897.

———. *The Popular Ballad.* New York: Dover, 1907. Reprint. New York: Dover, 1959.
Hopper, Carol, and Daniel Hopper. *1880 Laurel County Census with Vital Statistics.* Lily, KY, 1989.
"In Kentucky's Mountains: The Quaint Customs and Manners of the Highland Population . . . Simple and Honest Folk." *New York Times,* December 12, 1898.
"In Old Kentucky." *New York Times,* August 29, 1893.
Jackson, M. Katherine. *Outlines of the Literary History of Colonial Pennsylvania.* Lancaster, PA: Press of the New Era Publishing Co., 1906. http://books.google.com/books?id=rIcOAAAAMAAJ&printsec=frontcover&dq=inauthor:%22M.+Katherine+Jackson%22&hl=en&sa=X&ei=4ovHUofNH6OdyQGrzoDQCw&ved=0CC8Q6AEwAA#v=onepage&q&f=false.
Jameson, Gladys. *Wake and Sing.* New York: Broadcast Music, 1955.
Jamieson, Robert. *Popular Ballads and Songs.* Edinburgh: Archibald Constable & Co., 1806.
Jean Ritchie's Singing Family of the Cumberlands. New York: Geordie Publishing, 1980.
Johnson, James. *Scots Musical Museum.* 6 vols. Edinburgh: Johnson & Co., 1787–1839. https://digital.nls.uk/special-collections-of-printed-music/archive /87793664.
"List of Post-Graduate Students." In *Yale University Catalogue, 1907–1908,* 622. New Haven, CT: Tuttle, Morehouse, & Taylor Co., 1907.
Lomax, John. *Cowboy Songs and Other Frontier Ballads.* New York: Sturgis & Walton, 1911.
Madsen, Clifford K., and Katia Madsen. "Perception and Cognition in Music: Musically Trained and Untrained Adults Compared to Sixth-Grade and Eighth-Grade Children." *Journal of Research in Music Education* 50, no. 2 (Summer 2002): 111–30.
McGill, Josephine. *Folk-Songs of the Kentucky Mountains.* New York: Boosey & Co., 1917.
Miles, Emma Bell. *The Spirit of the Mountains.* New York: James Pott & Co., 1905.
"Mountain Songs." *Berea Quarterly* 14, no. 3 (October 1910): 25–29.
Mountain Ballads for Social Singing. Collected and selected by James Watt Raine. Music collected by Cecil J. Sharp. Berea, KY: Berea College Press, 1923. RG 5I, ser. 2, box 1, folder 21, James Watt Raine Ballad Collection.
Mutzenberg, Chas. G. *Kentucky's Famous Feuds and Tragedies: Authentic History of the World Renowned Vendettas of the Dark and Bloody Ground.* New York: R. F. Fenno & Co., 1917. https://archive.org/details/kentuckysfamousf00mutzuoft.
"New State President." *The Magnolia* (Louisiana Division of the AAUW), Bulletin no. 15, April 1941, 1.
Percy, Thomas. *Reliques of Ancient English Poetry* (1756), 2 vols. (reprint, London: J. M. Dent & Sons, 1910).
Pettit, Katherine. "Ballads and Rhymes from Kentucky." Edited by G. L. Kittredge. *Journal of American Folklore* 20, no. 79 (October–December 1907): 251–77.
Playford, John. *The English Dancing Master.* London: Thomas Harper, 1651. Tran-

scription by Eric Praetzel available at http://sca.uwaterloo.ca/~praetzel/music/playfd.pdf.

"President's Report." *The Magnolia* (Louisiana Division of the AAUW), Bulletin no. 17, April 1942, 1.

Raine, James Watt. *Land of the Saddlebags.* New York: Council of Women for Home Missions and Missionary Education Movement of the United States and Canada, 1924.

Sandburg, Carl. *An American Songbag.* New York: Harcourt, Brace & Co., 1927.

Scarborough, Dorothy. *A Song Catcher in Southern Mountains.* New York: Columbia University Press, 1937.

Scott, Sir Walter. *Minstrelsy of the Scottish Border: Consisting of Historical and Romantic Ballads, Collected in the Southern Counties of Scotland; With a Few of Modern Date, Founded upon Local Tradition.* 2 vols. Kelso: printed by James Ballantyne for T. Cadell Jun. and W. Davies, 1802.

Shearin, Hubert G. "The *Phoenix* and the *Guthlac*." *Modern Language Notes* 22, no. 8 (December 1907): 263.

———. "British Ballads in the Cumberland Mountains." *Sewanee Review* 19, no. 3 (July 1911): 313–27.

———. "Kentucky Folk-Songs." *Modern Language Review* 6, no. 4 (October 1911): 513–17.

Shearin, Hubert G., and Josiah H. Combs. *A Syllabus of Kentucky Folk-Songs.* Lexington, KY: University of Transylvania, 1911.

Sidgwick, Frank. *Old Ballads.* London: Cambridge University Press, 1908.

Tevis, Julia. *Sixty Years in a School Room.* Cincinnati: Western Methodist Book Concern, 1878.

"Textile Work at Berea College." *Columbia Daily Spectator* 46, no. 65 (January 7, 1903): 3.

Thomas, Jean. *The Traipsin' Woman.* New York: E. P. Dutton, 1933.

———. *Ballad-Makin' in the Hills of Kentucky.* New York: Henry Holt, 1939.

Transylvania University Catalogue, 1911–1912. Lexington, KY, n.d.

Williams, Cratis. "Ballad Collecting in the 1930's." *Appalachian Journal* 7, nos. 1–2 (Autumn–Winter 1979–1980): 33–36.

Williams, Fannie Barrier. "The Club Movement among Colored Women of America." In *The New Woman of Color: The Collected Writings of Fannie Barrier Williams,* ed. Mary Jo Deegan, 13. DeKalb: Northern Illinois University Press, 2002.Reprinted in *Before They Could Vote: American Women's Autobiographical Writing, 1819–1919,* ed. Sidonie Smith and Julia Watson, 283–84. Madison: University of Wisconsin Press, 2006.

Woman's Department Club 25th Anniversary Yearbook, 1919–1944. Shreveport, LA: Woman's Department Club, 1944.

Yoncopin. Shreveport, LA: Centenary College, 1924, 1930, 1931, 1934, 1948.Private collection. Centenary College yearbook.

Dissertations and Theses

Armour, Eugene. "The Melodic and Rhythmic Characteristics of the Music of the Traditional Ballad Variants Found in the Southern Appalachians." PhD diss., University of Michigan, 1961.
Jackson, Katherine. "Outline of the Literary History of Colonial Pennsylvania." PhD diss., New York: Columbia University, 1906.
Krehbiel, Lee Edward. "From Race to Region: Shifting Priorities at Berea under William Goodell Frost, 1892–1912." PhD diss., Indiana University, 1997.
McCormick, Scott. "Scale and Structure in Anglo-American Folk Songs: An Analysis of Child Ballads in the Sharp Collection." Master's thesis, Northwestern University, 1989.
Rumbley, Erica. "From Piano Girl to Professional: The Changing Form of Music Instruction at the Nashville Female Academy, Ward's Seminary for Young Ladies, and the Word-Belmont School, 1816–1920." PhD diss., University of Kentucky, 2014.
Wilgus, D. W. "A History of Anglo-American Ballad Scholarship since 1898." PhD diss., Ohio State University, 1954. Reprint, *A History of Anglo-American Ballad Scholarship since 1898* (New Brunswick, NJ: Rutgers University Press, 1954).

Secondary Sources

"About the NSCDA." n.d. National Society of the Colonial Dames of America. http://nscda.org/about-us/membership-inquiries.
Agnes Scott College. http://georgia.teach-us.org/203-agnes_scott_college.htm.
Alvey, R. Gerald. "Phillips Barry and Anglo-American Folksong Scholarship." In "American Folklore Historiography," special issue, *Journal of the Folklore Institute* 10, nos. 1–2 (June–August 1973): 67–95.
"Another Landmark Removed." *Mountain Echo*, January 6, 1899.
Arendt, Emily J. "'Ladies Going about for Money': Female Voluntary Associations and Civic Consciousness in the American Revolution." *Journal of the Early Republic* 34, no. 2 (Summer 2014): 157–86.
Atkinson, David. "Folk Songs in Print: Text and Tradition." *Folk Music Journal* 8, no. 4 (2004): 456–83.
———. "The Ballad and the Idea of the Past." In *The Ballad and Its Pasts: Literary Histories and the Play of Memory*, 1–30. Martlesham: Boydell & Brewer, 2018.
Baker, Bruce E. Review of *Jane Hicks Gentry: A Singer among Singers*, by Betty N. Smith. *Journal of American Folklore* 113, no. 448 (Spring 2000): 229–30.
Bell, Michael J. "'No Borders to the Ballad Maker's Art': Francis James Child and the Politics of the People." *Western Folklore* 47, no. 4 (October 1988): 285–307.
———. "'The Only True Folk Songs We Have in English': James Russell Lowell and the Politics of the Nation." *Journal of American Folklore* 108, no. 428 (Spring 1995): 131–55.

"Berea College: The Great Commitments." 2017. Berea College. https://www.berea.edu/mc/graphic-style-guide/the-great-commitments.

Birdsall, Esther. "Some Notes on the Role of George Lyman Kittredge in American Folklore Study." In "American Folklore Historiography," special issue, *Journal of the Folklore Institute* 10, nos. 1–2 (June–August 1973): 57–66.

Brandon, Betty. "Women in Southern Politics." In *The New Encyclopedia of Southern Culture,* vol. 10, *Law and Politics,* ed. James W. Ely Jr. and Bradley G. Bond. Chapel Hill: University of North Carolina Press, 2008.

Brewer, Mary Taylor. *Rugged Trail to Appalachia: A History of Leslie County, Kentucky and Its People, Celebrating Its Centennial Year, 1878–1978.* Wooten, KY, 1978.

Burnside, Jacqueline. "Educated and Organized: Women at the Center of Berea College History, 1850s–2000s." April 26, 2018. Hutchins Library, Berea College. http://libraryguides.berea.edu/genderessay.

Chamberlain, Mariam K., ed. *Women in Academe: Progress and Prospects.* New York: Russell Sage Foundation, 1988.

Clarke, Kenneth, and Mary Clarke. *Kentucky Singers.* Lexington: University Press of Kentucky, 1974.

"The Collecting of English Folk-Songs." *Musical Times* 46, no. 746 (April 1, 1905): 258.

Corrales, Barbara Smith. "Parlors, Politics, and Privilege: Clubwomen and the Failure of Woman Suffrage in Lafayette, Louisiana, 1897–1922." *Louisiana History: The Journal of the Louisiana Historical Association* 38, no. 4 (Autumn 1997): 453–71.

Davis, Arthur Kyle, Jr. "Some Problems of Ballad Publication." *Musical Quarterly* 14, no. 2 (April 1928): 283–96.

Doyle, Charles Clay, and Charles Greg Kelley. "Moses Platt and the Regeneration of 'Barbara Allen.'" *Western Folklore* 50, no. 2 (April 1991): 151–69.

"Down upon the Big Sandy." *Milwaukee Journal,* July 14, 1891. http://news.google.com/newspapers?nid=1499&dat=18910714&id=3UMaAAAAIBAJ&sjid=bSAEAAAAIBAJ&pg=1708,959243.

Dyche, Russell. *History of Laurel County.* London, KY: Laurel County Historical Society, 1954.

"Eleanor Marsh Frost." *Register of the Kentucky Historical Society* 94, no. 3 (Summer 1996): 225–47.

"Epworth League." n.d. *Encyclopedia of Cleveland History,* Case Western Reserve University. https://case.edu/ech/articles/e/epworth-league.

Filene, Benjamin. "Our Singing Country: John and Alan Lomax, Leadbelly, and the Construction of an American Past." *American Quarterly* 43, no. 4 (December 1991): 602–24.

———. *Romancing the Folk: Public Memory and American Roots Music.* Chapel Hill: University of North Carolina Press, 2000.

Geiger, Roger. *The History of American Higher Education: Learning and Culture from the Founding to World War II.* Princeton, NJ: Princeton University Press, 2015.

Gibson, Robert A. "The Negro Holocaust: Lynching and Race Riots in the United

States, 1880–1950." n.d. Yale–New Haven Teachers Institute. http://teachersInstitutee.yale.edu/curriculum/units/1979/2/79.02.04.x.html.
Green, Karl Keith. "UK Professor Confronts Appalachian Stereotypes." *Corbin (KY) Times Tribune,* March 5, 2009. http://www.thetimestribune.com/features/x1065251980/UK-professor-confronts-Appalachian-stereotypes.
Grobman, Neil R. "David Hume and the Earliest Scientific Methodology for Collecting Balladry." *Western Folklore* 34, no. 1 (January 1975): 16–31.
Harker, Dave. "Francis James Child and the 'Ballad Consensus.'" *Folk Music Journal* 4, no. 2 (1981): 146–64.
Harris, Leslie M. "The New York City Draft Riots of 1863." Excerpted from Leslie M. Harris, *In the Shadow of Slavery: African Americans in New York City, 1626–1863* (Chicago: University of Chicago Press, 2003), 279–88. http://www.press.uchicago.edu/Misc/Chicago/317749.html.
Harris, Richard. "'Lord Thomas and Fair Ellinor': A Preliminary Study of the Ballad." *Midwest Folklore* 5, no. 2 (Summer 1955): 79–94.
Heart of the City: A History of the Shreveport First United Methodist Church. Shreveport, LA: First United Methodist Church, 1995.
Hughes, Jerome W. *Six Berea College Presidents: Traditions and Progress.* Berea, KY: Berea College, 1984.
Hutson, C. Kirk. "'Whackety Whack, Don't Talk Back': The Glorification of Violence against Females and the Subjugation of Women in Nineteenth-Century Southern Folk Music." *Journal of Women's History* 8, no. 3 (Fall 1996): 114–42.
Hyder, Clyde Kenneth. *George Lyman Kitteredge, Teacher and Scholar.* Lawrence: University of Kansas Press, 1962.
Ikard, Robert W. "The Cultivation of Higher Ideals: The Centennial Club of Nashville." *Tennessee Historical Quarterly* 65, no. 4 (Winter 2006–2007): 342–69.
Johnson, Joan Marie. *Southern Women at the Seven Sister Colleges.* Atlanta: University of Georgia Press, 2008.
Jones, Loyal. *Minstrel of the Appalachians: The Story of Bascom Lamar Lunsford.* Lexington: University Press of Kentucky, 2015.
———. *My Curious and Jocular Heroes: Tales and Tale-Spinners from Appalachia.* Lexington: University Press of Kentucky, 2017.
Leviten, Daniel. *This Is Your Brain on Music.* New York: Penguin, 2006.
"Lynching in America." n.d. American Experience, PBS.org. https://www.pbs.org/wgbh/americanexperience/features/emmett-lynching-america.
"Lynching in America: Confronting the Legacy of Racial Terror." n.d. Equal Justice Initiative. https://eji.org/reports/lynching-in-america.
Montgomery, Rebecca S. *The Politics of Education in the New South: Women and Reform in Georgia, 1890–1930.* Baton Rouge: Louisiana State University Press, 2006.
Montell, William Lynwood. "Obituary: D. K. Wilgus (1918–1989)." *Journal of American Folklore* 104, no. 411 (Winter 1991): 72–73.
Olson, Ted. "Sharp in the Mountains." *Appalachian Heritage* 19, no. 1 (Winter 1991): 20–26.

Orr, Doug, and Fiona Ritchie. *Wayfaring Strangers*. Chapel Hill: University of North Carolina Press, 2014.

Ostendorf, Ann. "Song Catchers, Ballad Makers, and New Social Historians: The Historiography of Appalachian Music." *Tennessee Historical Quarterly* 63, no. 3 (Fall 2004): 192–202.

Palmer, Roy. "'Veritable Dunghills': Professor Child and the Broadside." *Folk Music Journal* 7, no. 2 (1996): 155–66.

Passet, Joanne. *Sex Variant Woman: The Life of Jeannette Howard Foster*. Cambridge, MA: Da Capo, 2008.

Peck, Elizabeth S. *Berea's First 125 Years, 1855–1980*. Lexington: University Press of Kentucky, 1982.

Pen, Ron. *I Wonder as I Wander: The Life of John Jacob Niles*. Lexington: University Press of Kentucky, 2010.

Pollard, Kevin M. "A 'New Diversity': Race and Ethnicity in the Appalachian Region." Washington, DC: Population Reference Bureau, 2004. http://www.prb.org/pdf04/anewdiversityappal.pdf.

Potter, Eugenia K. *Kentucky Women: Two Centuries of Indomitable Spirit and Vision*. Louisville: Big Tree Press, 1977.

Prentice, Alison, and Marjorie R. Theobold. "The Historiography of Women Teachers: A Retrospect." In *Women Who Taught: Perspectives on the History of Women and Teaching*, ed. Alison Prentice and Marjorie R. Theobold, 3–33. Toronto: University of Toronto Press, 1991.

Rice, Harry. "A Perfect Wildflower and the Straightjacket of Lines and Spaces: Berea's Two Spheres of Music." 2014. Hutchins Library, Berea College. http://libraryguides.berea.edu/musicspheresessay.

Rieuwerts, Sigrid. "'The Genuine Ballads of the People': F. J. Child and the Ballad Cause." In "Ballad Redux," special triple issue, *Journal of American Folklore* 31, nos. 1–3 (January–December 1994): 1–34.

Roberts, Sam. "No Longer Majority Black, Harlem Is in Transition." *New York Times*, January 5, 2010.

Roby, Pamela. "Women and American Higher Education." *Annals of the American Academy of Political and Social Science* 404, no. 1 (November 1972): 118–39.

Scott, Anne Firor. *Natural Allies: Women's Associations in American History*. Urbana: University of Illinois Press, 1991.

Shapiro, Henry D. *Appalachia on Our Minds: The Southern Mountains and Mountaineers in the American Consciousness, 1870–1920*. Chapel Hill: University of North Carolina Press, 1978.

———. "How Region Changed Its Meaning and Appalachia Changed Its Standing in the Twentieth Century." In *Bridging Southern Cultures: An Interdsiciplinary Approach*, ed. John Lowe, 244–65. Baton Rouge: Louisiana State University Press, 2011.

Sisson, C. J. Review of *A Bibliography of the Writings of George Lyman Kittredge*, comp. James Thorpe. *Modern Language Review* 44, no. 1 (January 1949): 118–19.

Smith, Betty N. *Jane Hicks Gentry: A Singer among Singers*. Lexington: University Press of Kentucky, 1998.
Smith, Reed. "The Traditional Ballad in the South during 1914." *Journal of American Folklore* 28, no. 108 (April–June 1915): 199–203.
Spencer, Scott B. "Impetus and Impact." In *The Ballad Collectors of North America: How Gathering Folksongs Transformed Academic Thought and American Identity*, ed. Scott B. Spencer, 1–16. Lanham, MD: Scarecrow, 2012.
Mintz, Steven. "Statistics: Education in America, 1860–1950." 2017. History Now, Guilder Lehrman Institute of American History. https://www.gilderlehrman.org/content/statistics-education-america-1860-1950.
Stewart, Polly. "Wishful Willful Wily Women: Verbal Strategies for Female Success in the Child Ballads." In *Feminist Messages: Coding in Women's Folk Culture*, ed. Joan Newlon Radner, 54–73. Urbana: University of Illinois Press, 1993.
Stewart, Susan. "Scandals of the Ballad." *Representations*, no. 32 (Autumn 1990): 134–56.
"Studying Folk-Songs." *Louisville Courier-Journal*, March 19, 1911.
Temin, Peter. "The Post-Bellum Recovery of the South and the Cost of the Civil War." *Journal of Economic History* 36, no. 4 (1976): 487–92.
Thompson, Deborah J. "Searching for Silenced Voices in Appalachian Music." In "Geography and Music," special issue, *GeoJournal* 65, nos. 1–2 (2006): 67–78.
"US Population from 1900." 2001. *Demographia*. http://www.demographia.com/db-uspop1900.htm.
Wade, Stephen. *The Beautiful Music All around Us*. Urbana: University of Illinois Press, 2015.
Wall, Mary Jean. *How Kentucky Became Southern: A Tale of Outlaws, Horse Thieves, Gamblers, and Breeders*. Lexington: University Press of Kentucky, 2010.
Welter, Barbara. "The Cult of True Womanhood: 1820–1860." *American Quarterly* 18, no. 2, pt. 1 (summer 1966): 151–74.
Wilgus, D. K. "Shooting Fish in a Barrel: The Child Ballad in America." *Journal of American Folklore* 71, no. 280 (April–June 1958): 161–64.
Whisnant, David. *All That Is Native and Fine*. Chapel Hill: University of North Carolina Press, 2009.
William A. Bradley Biography. n.d. Harry Ransom Humanities Research Center, University of Texas at Austin. https://norman.hrc.utexas.edu/fasearch/findingAid.cfm?eadid=00300.
Wilson, Shannon. "William Goodell Frost: Race and Religion." December 8, 2017. Hutchins Library, Berea College. http://libraryguides.berea.edu/frostessay.
Winkelman, Donald M. "Musicological Techniques of Ballad Analysis." *Midwest Folklore* 10, no. 4 (Winter 1960–1961): 197–205.
"Women at Columbia." March 2004. Columbia 250, Columbia University. http://c250.columbia.edu/c250_events/symposia/history_women_timeline.html.
Yates, Mike. "Cecil Sharp in America: Collecting in the Appalachians." January 15, 1999. https://www.mustrad.org.uk/articles/sharp.htm.

Tertiary Sources

"Black Milestones in Education: Columbia Lions Edition." April 18, 2008. Twilight and Reason. https://twilightandreason.wordpress.com/tag/columbia-university.

"Callahan" The Fiddler's Companion. https://tunearch.org/wiki/Annotation:Callahan_(1).

Hale, Whitney. "Hatfield and McCoy Events Chronicled in Digitized Newspapers." *UK Now/University of Kentucky News,* May 24, 2012. http://uknow.uky.edu/content/hatfield-and-mccoy-events-chronicled-digitized-newspapers.

"Hillbilly." In *West Virginia Encyclopedia,* 2019. http://www.wvencyclopedia.org/print/Article/376.

"History of Science Hill." 2014. Wakefield-Scearce Galleries. http://www.wakefield-scearce.com/science-hill.

Mountain Echo, 1873–1879: Excerpts from the Mountain Echo. Transcribed by Geri Sutton. London, KY: Laurel County Historical Society, 2001.

Perrow, E. C. "Songs and Rhymes from the South." *Journal of American Folklore* 26, no. 100 (April–June 1913): 123–73.

"Science Hill." In *The Kentucky Encyclopedia,* ed. John E. Kleber. Louisville: University Press of Kentucky, 1992.

"Science Hill Female Academy." In *The Kentucky Encyclopedia,* ed. John E. Kleber. Lexington: University Press of Kentucky, 1992.

"Shelbyville." In *The Encyclopedia of Louisville,* ed. John Kleber. Lexington: University Press of Kentucky, 2001.

"Shelbyville." In *The Kentucky Encyclopedia,* ed. John E. Kleber. Lexington: University Press of Kentucky, 1992.

Index

Page numbers in italics refer to ballad collection entries.

American Association of University Women (AAUW), 38–44
Aberdeenshire, 125
Adams, Shelby Lee, 96
Age of Reason, The (Paine), 22
Ambrose, Nathan, 79, *158, 159*
American Folklore Society, 92–93, 104
American Revolution, 29
Ancient Scottish Ballads (Kinloch), *153*
Anglo-Saxon(s), 59, 61, 63, 141–43
"Annie Laurie" (song), 65, 142
Appalachian(s): ancestry, 60; food, 65; "mountain people" stereotypes, 61, 95; music, 59–204; quilting bees, 65; and William Goodell Frost, 60–61, 73–74, 76, *223*
"Appalachian Ballad Collectors" (Farr), 73
Appalachian women: ballad-singing, 61–72, 115–16; community, 65; food, 65; quilting bees, 65

"Bailiff's Daughter of Islington, The" (song), 67, 87, 90, *182*
Baker, Mrs. James, 79, *154, 164, 176, 186, 189*
Ballad-Makin' in the Hills of Kentucky (Thomas), 113
ballads (Appalachian), 2, 56, 59–204; African American influence upon, 127–28; ballad wars, 81–95, 102–6; "ballets," 66, 84, 101, 108; at Berea, 73–77; bias in collecting, 59–61, 116–18, 125–28; characteristics of ballads, 63; collectors, 1–2, 44–45, 59–215; colloquialisms in, 68; as communal entertainment, 65, 70, 116; gapped scales, 125–26; gender in ballads, 119–20; Katherine Jackson ballad paper, 45; men eschewing ballads, 65; Native American influence upon, 127; North Carolina ballads, 135; refrains in, 66; similarity to older British versions, 63–65, 68–69, 71; styles of singing, 63, 72; women as ballad keepers, 63–72, 114–116; written collections, 66–67, 72
ballads (general history): Anglo-Saxon connections and identity, 58–61, 63, 83, 113, 117–18, 124–28, 135–36, 141; British collectors, 59, 64, 71, 81–86, 90–91, 112, 102–5, 108, 113, 116–17, 125, 135 ; British Isle ballads, 59; characteristics of ballads, 63; Francis Child, 59; communal vs. individual theory, 102, 105; dead vs. living, 24, 68; as a living art, 68; medieval literary balladry, 59; origins, 102; northern collectors, 103; Scottish, 60, 65, 69, 71–73, 82, 85, 91, 94, 96, 99, 115–16, 119, 122, 124–25, 128–30, 135, 137, 140, 141, *201*
"Ballads and Rhymes from Kentucky" (Pettit), 81, 104

Index

Ballads of Peasantry (Bell), *195, 197*
banjo(s): clubs, 17; ignored by Sharp, 116, mountain style of playing, 64, 72; played by men, 115; tunes, 64
Banks, Lucy, 79
"Barbara Allen" (song), 3, 46, 65–66, 69, 83–84, 86, 90–91, 95, 123, 132, 143, *176–81*
Barnard College, 15, 22
Barry, Phillips, 103
Barton, William E., 110
Beckett, Gilbert, *158*
Beckett, St. Thomas, *158*
"Beggar Girl, The" (song), *67, 87, 90, 182*
Begley, Farris, 68
Begley, Hiram, 68
Begley, Justus, 68
Begley, Martha ("Sister Marthy"), 63, 65, *165*
Begley, Mary, 68
Belhaven College, 20
Bell, Robert, *195, 197*
"Ben Bolt" (song), 65, 142
Bennett, Belle, 26–28
Berea College, 1–4, 24, 26, 28, 61–62, 73–83, 90, 94, 96–101, 103–4, 106, 108–11, 128–29, 130, 133, 135–36, 139
Berea Quarterly, 73, 110
Berea's First Century, 98
Bethlehem Houses, 27
"Binorie" (song), *150*
Birdsall, Esther, 104
"Blackest Crow, The" (song), *171*
"Blue Bells of Scotland" (song), 65, 142
Blue Diamond Mine, 95
Bodnar, A. J., 1
"Bonny Barbara Allen" (song). *See* "Barbara Allen"
"Bonny Doon" (tune), *156*
Boston, MA, 103
Bour-Davis, 28
Bowersox, Katherine S., 109–110
Bronson, Bertrand, 125–26

Bradley, William Aspenwall, 79, 89, 90, 92–93, 101–2, 106–8, 133
Brevard College, 28
Bristol Sessions, 129
British Museum, 40, 84, 95
Brockway, Harold and Lorraine Wyman, 129, 135
Brown, Charles, 38
Bryn Mawr College, 15, 20, 24–25, 75, 77–78, 82
Buckland, Kay Tolbert, 39, 46–48, 52–54, 96, 106
Burns, Robert, *156, 171*

"Callahan's Confessions" (song), 64, *201*
Campbell, John C., 79, 81, 103
Campbell, Olive Dame, 1–2, 69, 72, 79, 81, 83, 92–93, 102–3, 105–7, 112–36, 139
Canterbury Tales, The (Chaucer), 38, *185*
Catching, Mamie Jackson, 10, 14
Centenary College, LA, 56, 36–40, 44, 46, 48–51
Chappel, William, 90, 125–26, *174, 179*
Chaucer, Geoffrey, 38, 63, 68, *183*
Chiesman, Professor, 10
Child, Francis, 59, 71, 81–86, 90–91, 102–5, 108, 113, 116–17, 125, 139–40, *146–93, 200*
Chi Omega, 44, 50
Cincinnati Conservatory of Music, 10
Civil War, 9, 14–15, 20–21, 24, 29
Clay County, KY, 68
Collection of Old Ballads, A (Whittington), *167*
Colonial Dames of America, 44
Columbia, SC, 52–53
Columbia University, 1, 20–25, 40–45, 59, 78, 107, 128
Combs, Bettie, 79, *149*
Combs, Jennie, 79, *155*
Combs, Josiah, 59, 82–85, 89–90, 100–102, 105–6, 108, 129
"Come All You Fair and Tender Ladies" (song), 132

"Confession of Edward W. Hawkins" (song), *202*
Corrales, Barbara Smith, 30
Cornett, Jane, *155*
Couch, Jim, 134–35
Council of Missionary Workers of the Women of the Methodist Church, 28
Cox, John Harrington, 113, *201*
"Crossing the Bar" (Tennyson), 52, 53
"Cruel Mother, The" (song), 66–68, 85, 119, 143, *155*
Cruikshank, George, *160*
Cumberland Falls, 26
Cumberland Valley Teachers Association, 94
Cut Shin Creek, KY, 67

"Daemon Lover, The" (song). *See* "House Carpenter, The"
"Den of Lions, The" (song), 104
Davis, Arthur Kyle, 45, 103, 113
Day Law, 111
Decatur Female Seminary, 15
"Declaration of Independence," 7
Dialect Notes, 83
Dizney, Elijah F., 78–79
"Dog and Gun" (song). *See* "Golden Glove, The"
Douglas, Alice K., 76–78
"Douglas Tragedy, The" (song). *See* "Earl Brand"
dulcimer, 66, 71
Dryden, John, 64
Dyche Cemetery, 47, 54

"Earl Brand" (song), 85, *149*. *See also* "Fair Margaret and Sweet William"; "Lord Thomas"; "Young Hunting"
"Eastern Kentucky Word List, An" (Shearin), 83
Eberlein, Lou Jackson, 28, 47
"Edward" (song), 67, 85
Ellerbe, Cecelia, 31, 35, 54, 56
English and Scottish Popular Ballads, The (Child), 59, 71, 85, 140

English Dancing Master, The (Playford), 125–26
English Folk Songs from the Southern Appalachians (Campbell and Sharp), 1–2, 72, 112–35, 139
English–Scottish Ballads from the Hills of Kentucky (French), 73, 85, 91, 94, 96, 99, 115–*204*

"Fair Ellender" (song). *See* "Earl Brand"
"Fair Margaret and Sweet William" (song), 63, 66, 86, 98, 114, *168, 169*. *See also* "Earl Brand"; "Lord Thomas"; "Young Hunting"
Farr, Sidney Saylor, 73, 79, 96
Farrar, Geraldine, 32
Favorite Old-Time Songs: Volume 2 (Kincaid), 131
Federal Bureau of Education, 94
Fee, John G., 109
Fee, Matilda, 109
fiddle tunes, 64, 72, 114
Fitzgerald, F. Scott, 102
Flanders, Helen Hartness, 103
Fletcher, John, *168*
Folk-Songs of the Kentucky Mountains (McGill), 129
Folk Songs of the South (Cox), 113, *201*
"Forked Deer" (tune), 64
"Fortnight in Ballad Country, A" (French, article), 61
"Fortnight of Balladry, A" (French, manuscript), 61, 99, *171, 201*
Franklin, Benjamin, 22
French, Katherine, 44–46, 50
French, Minerva Katherine Jackson: AAUW, 40–44; in Alabama, 18; ballads, 24–25, 45, 59–215; ballad-collecting trip, 59–72; in Ballad Wars, 81–95, 102–6; at Belhaven College, 20; at Bryn Mawr, 2–4, 24, 78; Berea College, 24, 26, 73–101, 109–11; childhood, 9–11; at Centenary College, 36–39, 48–50, 56; class, 10–11, 14, 17–19, 68; comparison

French, Minerva Katherine Jackson (cont.) to Sharp, 112–36; comparison to Shearin, 83–89; dean at Sue Bennett Memorial School, 26–28; death, 53–54; dissertation, 22–23; education at Columbia University, 20–25, 78; education at Ohio Wesleyan, 14–19, 78; education at Science Hill, 11–13; education at Yale, 19, 24–25; "English-Scottish Ballads from the Hills of Kentucky," 145–204; family history, 7–8; financial difficulties, 46; *Harper's*, 89, 92–93; health, 44; Katherine Jackson French collection, 96–99; London home, 20, 25; London Homecoming, 46–47, 50; London summers, 46–48; marriage to William Franklin French, 26; miscarriage, 28; at Mount Holyoke, 24, 78; musical education, 10–11, 16–17; organization affiliation, 44; publishing difficulties, 81–96, 99–111; religious affiliation and activities, 28, 32, 37, 44, 48, 56; retirement, 48–52; Science Hill, 39–40, 78; Scottish roots, 61; Shearin's use of ballads, 81–89; Shreveport, move to, 28; Shreveport Women's Department Club, 29–36, 52, 56; social life, 37, 39; southern identity, 20; in Texas, 14; travel, 46, 91; tutors, 14; writing style, 22

French, William Franklin, 26, 28, 46, 52, 106

Frost, Cleveland, 111

Frost, Eleanor, 75–80, 83, 94, 99, 108–9, 111, 128–29

Frost, William Goodell, 60–62, 73–77, 79–81, 83, 89–94, 99–103, 106, 128

Gage, Jim, 129–30
gapped scales, 125–26
Garrard, Will, 8
Geiger, Roger, 15
gender, 2, 10–17, 20–24, 26, 28–39, 41–46, 52, 54, 56, 59, 65, 69–70, 75–77, 78, 106–110, 113–16, 119–20, 129, 135

Gentry, Jane Hicks, 114
Glenn, John, 105, 107
"*Glove* and *The Lions* in Kentucky Folk-Song, The" (Shearin), 82, 108
"Golden Glove, The" (song), 87, 129–30, *195–97*
"Golden Vanitee, The" (song), 84, 87–88, *189–90*
"goodnight" ballads, 65, 84, 88
Graham, Addie, 136
Green, Margaret, *170*
Green, Margaret Combs, *191*
Green, Margaret Corbin, *193*
Green, Paul, 98
"Green Willow Tree, The" (song). *See* "Golden Vanitee, The"
"Greenwood Side, The" (song). *See* "Cruel Mother, The"
Gummere, Francis B., 80, 92, 94, 99, 100, 102, 105–6

Hackney, Ruth, *183*
Hancock, John, 7
Hancock, Stephen, 7
Harper's Magazine, 79, 89, 92–93, 101–2, 109
Harris, Ellen Agnes, 42–43
Harvard University, 103
Harvard University Press, 103, 105
Haverford College, 80, 92
"Hawk and Chicken" (tune), 64
headless horseman, 65
Herder, Johann Gottfried, *154*
Hicks, S. B., 31
Hindman Settlement School, 81
"Hobnobbing with Hillbillies" (Bradley), 101
"House Carpenter, The" (song), 67–68, 87, 90, 130–31, *186, 187, 188*
Huff, Mrs. Olive, *157*
Huff, Mrs. Ollie, 79, *179*

Hypatia Club, 31

Impressions of a Negro Camp Meeting (Niles), 134
"In Shakespeare's America" (Bradley), 101
Ionian mode, 123, 125–28, 130–31, 135
Irving, Washington, 65
"It Rains a Mist" (song). *See* "Sir Hugh"

"Jacobite airs to Prince Charlie, The" (tunes), 64, 115
"Jackaro" (song). *See* "Merchant's Daughter of Bristow, The"
Jackson, Adelaide, 18
Jackson, Jarvis, 7, 10
Jackson, John (founder of London), 7, 47
Jackson, John (1610), 1
Jackson, Maria Louisa McKee, 8, 10, 13, 17–18, 35
Jackson, Mary Hancock, 7, 47
Jackson, Minerva, 7
Jackson, Stephen, 7
Jackson, William Harvey, 7–10, 11, 13, 18, 26
"James Harris" (song), *186, 187*
Jameson, Gladys, 96–98, 133, 139, *147, 150, 155, 159, 166, 169, 172, 178, 186, 197*
Jameson, Robert, *186*
Jamestown, VA, 7
"Jew's Daughter, The" ("Little Hugh of Lincoln") (song), 68, 82, 84, 86, *183–85*
"John Reilly" (song). *See* "William Hall"
Johnson, James, 125–26
Johnson, Joan Marie, 11, 20
Jones, Loyal, 73, 132
Journal of American Folklore, 81, 104
Joyce, James, 102

Karpeles, Maud, 112–14, 116,
Kentucky educational institutions, 9, 12–13, 15, 24, 26, 28, 39–40, 78–79, 81, 107, 95–96, 101, 129
"Kentucky Folk Songs" (Shearin), 83–88

Kentucky history, 2–10, 18, 26–28, 46–47, 78, 95–96
Kentucky music: ballad collections, 73, 85, 91, 94, 96, 99, 115–*204*; ballad collectors, 1–2, 24–25, 59–*204*; ballad publications about, 61, 99, 79, 89, 92–93, 101–2, 109; ballad scholars, 1–3, 72–73, 79, 80, 83, 88, 92, 94, 96, 99, 100, 102, 103–7, 132–33; ballad singers, 61–63, 65, 69, 76–79, 59, 79, 82–85, 89–90, 96, 100–102, 105–6, 108, 129–30, 132–36; fiddle tunes, 64, 72, 95, 114; instruments, 64, 66, 71–72, 114; Jackson's ballad collecting trip, 62–72; songs, 63–69, 73, 82–84, 90–91, 95, 98, 113, 123, 129–134, 136; writings about, 79, 89, 90, 92–93, 101–2, 106–8, 133
Kidson, Frank, *198*
Kincaid, Bradley, 59, 61
Kinloch, George Ritchie, *153*
Kittredge, George Lyman, 3, 83, 88, 103–7
Knight of the Burning Pestle (Fletcher), *168*

"Lady and a Lady Gay, A" (song). *See* "Wife of Usher's Well, The"
"Lady Isabel and the Elf Knight" ("Pretty Polly") (song), 67, 85, 136, *146–48*
"Lass of Loch Royal, The" (song). *See* "Lovers Farewell"
"Lass of Roch Royal, The" (song). *See* "Lovers Farewell"
Laurel Seminary, 9
Leatherwood, KY, 95–96
Levi Jackson State Park, 46
Lewis, Charles, 78–79
Lewis, J. C., 26, 80
Lily, KY, 9
Lindsey, Judge Ben, 32
"Little Hugh" (song). *See* "Sir Hugh"
"Little Musgrave and Lady Barnard" (song), 67, 84, 67, 84, 86, 120, 123, *173–75*

"Little Willie" (song). See "Two Brothers, The"
"Lizane of Leatherwood" (unpublished play), 95
Lomax, Alan, 68, 130, *201*
Lomax, John, 83, 103
London, KY, 1, 100; Brick Drug Store, 10; history of, 7–8; homecoming, 46–47, 50; London Brass (Cornet) Band, 10; London Opera House, 10
Lonesome Tunes (Brockway & Wyman), 129
"Long Yeared Mule" (tune), 64
"Lord Bateman" (song), 67, 85, 98, 131–32, 134, *158–61*
"Lord Lovel" (song), 66, 86, *170*
"Lord Maxwell's Goodnight" (song), 64, 142, *200, 202*
"Lord of the Old Country" (song). See "Twa Sisters, The"
"Lord Randal" (song), 66
"Lord Thomas" (song), 63, 73, 86, 90, 92, 123, *165, 166, 167*. See also "Earl Brand"; "Fair Margaret and Sweet William"; "Young Hunting"
"Lord Thomas and Fair Annet" (song). See "Lord Thomas"
"Lord Thomas and Fair Ellender" (song). See "Lord Thomas"
"Lovers Farewell" (song), 67, 69
"Loving Henry" (song). See "Young Hunting"
"Loving Nancy" (song). See "Young Hunting"
Lozier, Mary, 136

Madison County, KY, 7
Magneetic Springs, 18
"Maid of Dundee" (song), 65, 142
Maize, Ellen, *153*
Mann, Erika, 41
Marshall, Mrs. Ewing, 91, *188*
"Matty Groves" (song). See "Little Musgrave and Lady Barnard"
"McAfee's Confession" (song), 84, 87, *200, 201*

McGeachy, Mary Craig, 41
McGill, Josephine, 128
"McPherson's Farewell" (song), 64, 142, *200*
melismas, 135
"Merchant's Daughter of Bristow, The" (song), 87, 132–33, *192–94*
Mickle, J., 48
Miller, Henry, 102
"Miller Boy, The" (song), *154*
Minstrelsy of the Scottish Border (Scott), 140, *153, 186, 188*
Modern Language Association, 44
Modern Language Notes, 104
Modern Language Review, 83
Montgomery, Rebecca, 14
Morgan, Lee, 38–39
Mountain Ballads for Social Singing (Raine), 133
Mountain Echo, 10, 14
Mountain Life and Work, 61, 99
Mount Holyoke College, 15, 20, 24, 44, 46
"My Love Is Like a Red, Red Rose" (song), *171*

Napier, Hiram, 68
Napier, Lizane, 61–63, 65, 69, 96, *168, 171*
National Barn Dance, 131
National Society of the Daughters of the Byrons of Runney, 44
New England, 59
New England Conservatory of Music, 12
New York Post, 95
Niles, John Jacob, 134–35
"Nubbin Ridge" (tune), 64

Ohio-Wesleyan University, 14, 15
Ostendorf, Ann, 113
Oxford, 45

Paine, Thomas, 22
Paris, France, 102
Pastorius, Francis Daniel, 22

Pearl Harbor, 40
Peck, Elizabeth, 96–98, 101
Peer, Ralph, 129
Pen, Ron, 3, 59, 134
Penniman, Ira, 110
Pennington, Eloise Jackson, 53
Pentatonic Doctrine, 124–28
pentatonic mode, 122, 124–28, 131, 135
Pepys, Samuel, 83, *176*
Percy, Thomas, 64, 83–84, *158, 183*
Perrow, E. C., 139, *188, 186*
Perry County, KY, 68, 90
Pettit, Katherine, 69, 81, 101, 104, 105–6
Philadelphia Ladies' Association, 29
Phi Theta Kappa, 44
Playford, John, 125–26
Pollard, Annie Jackson, 47–48, 52
Popular Ballads (Jameson), *158*
Popular Music of Olden Times (Chappel), 94, 125–26, *174*
Pound, Louise, 102
Poynter, Clara, 12, 40
Poynter, Wiley Taul, 12, 40
Poynter Sisters, 12
"Pretty Peggy, O" (song). *See* "Trooper and the Maid, The"
"Pretty Polly" (song). *See* "Lady Isabel and the Elf Knight"
Primitive Baptist, 136

Queen Elizabeth, 64

racism, 21, 28, 29, 30, 59, 61, 111, 116, 118
Radcliffe College, 15
Raine, James Watt, 73–74, 76–78, 99–100, 128–29, 133, 139, *150, 166, 172, 185, 186, 190, 197*
Ralph, James, 22
Ramsay, Alan, *176*
Randolph, Vance, *201*
Raymond, C. Rex, 76–77, 83
Reid, Helen Dwight, 43
Reliques of Ancient English Poetry (Percy), 84, *168, 176, 183*

Renaissance music, 125
Rice, Harry, 1, 73
Richmond, KY, 7
Ritchie, Jean, 132–33,
Roby, Pamela, 15
Rodgers, Richard, 40
"Rosin and Bow" (tune), 64
Rumbley, Erica, 10
Russell Sage Foundation, 105, 113
R. Z. (French family servant), 53

"Salt, Salt Sea, The" (song). *See* "House Carpenter, The"
Sassafras, KY, 67
Saturday Evening Post, 95
Scarborough, Dorothy, 68
Science Hill Female Academy, 11–13, 15, 24, 26, 39–40, 78
Scots, 59
Scots Musical Museum, 125–26
Scott, Anne Firor, 30
Scott, Sir Walter, 64, 83, 140, *153, 186, 188*
Scottish Highlands, 124
Scottish Lowlands, 59, 124
Scottish snaps, 12, 130, 135
Seale, Ellis, 76–79, 99
"Serving Maid, The" (song), 87, 133, *199*
Seven Kentucky Mountain Songs (Nile), 134
"Seven King's Daughters" (song). *See* "Lady Isabel and the Elf Knight"
Seven Sisters (women's colleges), 15, 24–26
Shakespeare, William, 38, 45, 49, 63, 101, 108
Shakespearean Society of America, 44
Shapiro, Henry D., 83, 103
Sharp, Cecil, 1–2, 72, 83, 98, 103, 105–7, 112–29, 131–33, 135–36, 139
Shearin, Hubert G., 81–90, 92–93, 100–108
Shelbyville, KY, 11–12, 78
Shreveport, LA, 1, 4, 28, 29–40, 44–46, 48–51

Shreveport Times, 35, 40–41, 47
Shreveport Woman's Department Club, 29–36, 52, 54, 56
"Sir Hugh" (song). *See* "Jew's Daughter, The"
"Sister Marthy" (Begley, Martha), 65
"Six Pretty Fair Maids" (song). *See* "Lady Isabel and the Elf Knight"
Smith, Ada, 69
Smith, Alphonso, 94, 108
Smith, Jane, *156*
Smith, John F., 128–30, 131–32, 135, 136
Smith College, 12, 15
song-ballets, 84
"Song Ballets and Devil's Ditties" (Bradley), 89, 101
Songcatcher (film), 95
Sorbonne, 102
"Sourwood Mountain" (tune), 64, 95, *204*
Southern Fellowship, 20
Speairs, Betty, 38
Spencer, Scott B., 102
"Squire of Tamworth, The" (song), *195*
Stein, Gertrude, 102
Steuben, Baron von, 7
Stockton, Jeff, 113
Stone, May, 101, 129
"Storms Are on the Ocean, The" (song), *171*
Story of the Years in Mountain Work, The (French), 28
Sue Bennett Memorial School, 26–28, 80, 94, 106
"Summer Is a-Cumin In" (song), 87, *203*
"Swapping Song of Jack Straw, The" (tune), 64, 142
"Sweet William and Fair Ellender" (song). *See* "Young Hunting"
"Sweet William and Lady Margaret" (song). *See* "Fair Margaret and Sweet William"
"Sympathetic Magic in the Kentucky Mountains" (Combs), 105

Syllabus of Kentucky Folk-Songs, A (Shearin), 81–88, 100

Tea-Table Miscellany No. 2 (Ramsay), *176*
Temin, Peter, 14–15
Tevis, John, 11
Tevis, Julia Hieronymous, 11–12
This Is Centenary (Centenary College newspaper), 50
Thomas, D. L., 133
Thomas, Jean, 113
Thompson, Harold, 103
"Three Ravens, The" (song), 85, *156*
Tolbert, Carl, 52–53
Traditional Ballads of Virginia (Davis), 45, 113
Transylvania University, 81, 107
Trent, W. P., 22
"Trooper and the Maid, The" (song), 87, *191*
Tunes of the Child Ballads, The, 125–26
"Turkish Lady, The" (song). *See* "Lord Bateman"
"Twa Sisters, The" (song), 67–68, 85, 123, *150–52*
"Two Brothers, The" (song), 67, 85, *157*
"Two Sisters, The" (song). *See* "Twa Sisters, The"

United Daughters of the Confederacy, 30
University of Michigan, 12

Vassar College, 15
Vaughan-Williams, Ralph, *198*
Vient de paraitre, 102
Viper, KY, 67
Virginia, 7, 59

Wake and Sing, 98
Wallin, Chappel, 132
"Wars of Germany" (song). *See* "Merchant's Daughter of Bristow, The"
"Waxford Girl, The" (song), *154*
"Wealthy Merchant of London, The"

(song). *See* "Merchant's Daughter of Bristow, The"
"Wealthy Young Farmer, A" (song). *See* "Golden Glove, The"
"Wealthy Young Squire, A" (song), 67
Wellesley College, 12, 15
Welter, Barbara, 11
"We're Stole and Sold from Africa" (song), 136
Whittington, Richard, *165, 167*
"Wife of Usher's Well, The" (song), 68, 86, *172*
Wilderness Road, 95
Wilgus, D. W., 90, 102, 133, *188*
"William and Ellender" (song). *See* "Young Hunting"
"William Hall" (song), 87, *198. See also* "Bailiff's Daughter of Islington, The"
Williams, Elizabeth McCutcheon, 103
Wilkinson, J. D., 31
WLS (Chicago radio station), 131
women: acceptable gender roles and spaces, 10–13, 14–15, 29–30, 106–10; as ballad keepers, 69–70; community in mountains, 65; in higher education, 14–16, 20, 23–24; preparatory schools, 11; suffrage, 29, 30, 78, 108–10
"Women on Troublesome, The" (Bradley), 102
women's clubs: African American women's clubs, 29; Council of Missionary Workers of the Women of the Methodist Church, 28; history of women's clubs, 29–30; Philadelphia Ladies' Association, 29; Shreveport Woman's Department Club, 29–36; United Daughters of the Confederacy, 30
World War I, 111
World War II, 41–43

Yale University, 19, 24, 25, 104, 107
Yoncopin, 49
"Young Man's Tragedy" (song), *176*
York family, 68
"Young Beichan and Susie Pye" (song). *See* "Lord Bateman"
"Young Hunting" (song), 67, 84, 86, *162–64. See also* "Earl Brand"; "Fair Margaret and Sweet William"; "Lord Thomas"